How to In

MW01194944

Buy, Outfit, and Sail

a Small Vessel Around the World

Living Large—At Sea—on a Micro-Budget

Cap'n Fatty Goodlander

All rights reserved. The entire contents of this book are copyrighted 2011 by Gary M. Goodlander a.k.a. Cap'n Fatty. Except as permitted under the United States Copyright Act of 1976, no part of this material can be reproduced or distributed in any form or by any means, or stored in a data base or retrieval system, without the prior permission of the author.

Contact: Gary Goodlander at Fatty@fattygoodlander.com or visit our website: FattyGoodlander.com

All our books are available in Kindle and other E-book formats. They are also available in soft cover editions at Amazon.com.

Cover photo by Richard West

Books by Cap'n Fatty Goodlander

Seadogs, Clowns, and Gypsies
Kindle edition

Chasing the Horizon
Print and Kindle editions

Collected Fat
Print and Kindle editions

Cruising World Yarns
Print and Kindle editions

All At Sea Yarns
Print and Kindle editions

Red Sea Run: Two Sailors in a Sea of Trouble
Print and Kindle editions

Somali Pirates and Cruising Sailors
Print and Kindle editions

Also by Cap'n Fatty

How to Prepare Your Vessel to Survive a Hurricane
 in the U.S. Virgin Islands
Pamphlet for FEMA

St. John People
Editor and Writer

Celebrating Marie
Editor and Writer, private printing

Dedication

This book is dedicated to three men who spent thousands of hours teaching me how to use my hands and my brain at the same time.

They were my childhood heroes—and still are my heroes.

I vividly remember their gnarled hands. Their hands looked as if they'd stuck them in a meat grinder—all scarred, greasy, bloody, smashed, caked, split, cut, chewed, bruised, calloused, thick-veined, and muscled.

They seldom spoke, and they never boasted—but each mechanical or electrical item that malfunctioned around them was both a challenge and an opportunity.

To quietly assist me in becoming who I am today, they'd nonchalantly toss me a starter motor, or the anchor windlass, or the steering quadrant, and say, "Fix it."

Then they'd just watch—occasionally muttering something like, "Careful!" or "…try hitting it?" or "…maybe some heat?" They knew when to use a clean, soft, lint-free cotton rag and a micrometer—or a battle-scarred sledgehammer, crowbar, and yardstick.

"…use the bench vise, maybe?"

They greatly admired all knowledge if it could be practically applied for immediate benefit to the task at hand. If not, well, "…screw it," as they'd say in curt dismissal. They were strictly results-oriented. If you fixed it, you won. If you didn't fix it, you were beaten. It didn't matter if you didn't have the right parts or the correct tools or the proper test equipment—if you didn't fix it, you failed.

I rapidly learned that, in order to consistently fix mechanical things, I had to fully understand them and the physical work they were intended to accomplish—how all their individual parts moved and why. The mechanical world is a very simple and very beautiful, logical, elegant place. There are, after all, only six basic tools.

I also learned to never offer excuses—just try, try, and try again. And I ultimately aspired to be exactly what they were: handy.

"He can fix anything," is the highest compliment I've ever heard.

Thank you, James "Guru" Goodlander, for not only being my father—but my shipwright as well. And thank you, Jerry "Gyroaster" Kennedy, for teaching me how to fix anything automotive from a dome light to a crankshaft. And, most of all, thank you, Joey Borges, for tirelessly shifting that chewed toothpick in your mouth and saying relentlessly, "…try again!"

Table of Contents

Preface

Our lives, to an amazing degree, are within our control. We have choices. We can, for example, play it safe. We can spend our lives preparing for our eventual retirement—which we may, or may not, be alive for.

No one will criticize you for not living fully. In fact, it is the accepted, most direct, least confusing route to death. The current conventional wisdom is that we are born, grow up, learn to become consumers, consume, and die.

Of course, we can reject this path, and—even more audacious—chart our own course in life.

I did.

At an early age I decided I wanted to be the freest man in the universe. I kid you not. That was my Overall Mission Statement—To Be the Freest Man in the Universe.

I realize that this is an audacious goal—but hey, why not aim high?

So the first thing I did was attempt to define—in a very subjective and personal way—what freedom is to me.

This wasn't easy. But I kept at it, and eventually I decided that freedom is the right to control your own destiny, to empower yourself, to go and do and think and write and say what you want, when you want, how you want. It is also the right to pick and choose cultures and lifestyles and professions. It is the right to say no to almost anyone about almost anything.

It is, first and foremost, the right to refuse the cultural blinders and self-imposed limitations of your fellow man.

It quickly became apparent to me that many things limit us. Our poverty and our wealth, for example, both limit us. Our country limits us. Our religion limits us.

I decided to opt out of my tribal branding—of being a Christian American who eats at McDonalds, watches MTV, and labors daily in the corporate vineyards to pay all the monies demanded by various governments and global conglomerates.

In order to do this in the most fun, convenient way possible, I realized I needed my own private kingdom, my own small country, my own tiny universe.

That's right—I decided to buy a sailboat.

This was an easy choice for me because I grew up aboard the 52-foot John G. Alden-designed schooner *Elizabeth*.

My childhood was one long idyllic Huck Finn and Tom Sawyer adventure—until my father got Parkinson's disease, we moved ashore, and my life became hell-amid-the-dirt-dwellers.

Thus it was only natural that I wanted to escape from the drudgery of shore and experience the freedom of the sea once again.

So I did.

At the age of 15, before I owned a car or could legally drive one, I purchased a cedar-planked William Atkin-designed 22-foot double-ender named *Corina* for $200.

Once word got out that I was King of My Own Kingdom, girls flocked. One of those girls, a lovely Italian lass by the name of Carolyn, came aboard to sew up my curtains. She's been sewing love into my life ever since. We're now on our 41st year of living aboard together.

So far, so good. I was King. I had a Kingdom and a Queen. But I soon realized that there was no personal freedom without economic freedom.

The standard solution to this was to work hard and earn a lot of money—and eventually retire. But I neither wanted to work ashore nor amass money. And ¬besides, it seemed to me that money (and things) had a way of owning their owner. I knew a lot of wealthy people and many of them spent an awful lot of time servicing their money. Yeeck.

After much thought, I came up with a complex, highly sophisticated (if short) literary essay to explain my feeling on this intricate monetary matter.

"Fuck money!" I shouted with a giggle.

But alas, a man has to pay his own way in the world or he is someone's boy. I did not aspire be to anyone's boy.

So I decided to be a writer. I'd live a life of rare adventure—physically, mentally, and socially—and write it down. I'd kiss life full on the lips. I'd grab every day of my life with both hands and shake it. And my faithful readers would shower me with coins—not a lot, perhaps, but enough to get by.

This was around 1968, a magical time in American history.

I also decided that nationalism was just cultural egotism run amok. I needed to see who my fellow human beings were and how they lived. So I decided to make the entire world my classroom. I'd travel to its farthest corners to quench my thirst for knowledge.

Of course, the greatest adventure in life is family. And every kingdom needs a subject. Thus our daughter Roma Orion was born.

We sailed away. We not only sailed away from home and country, we sailed away from All the Rules. We took an entirely fresh look at Life, the Universe, and Everything. And we put it back together in a logical, natural manner that made sense to us: with art and music and literature and friendship and adventure and learning ranking far above material things.

We soon found our watery tribe: the international sea gypsies who are constantly passing through Panama, Tahiti, New Zealand, Thailand, Cape Town, and St. Thomas. They are from France and England and Africa and Asia and Germany and Scandinavia. They don't care one iota where you are from or what you own or who you know—only what is in your heart.

Do you know how to laugh? Smile? Are you honest? Can you be trusted? Are you in the moment? Can you fix an outboard, tie a bowline, and catch a fish? Can you endure without complaint? Do you know how to spin a yarn? Do you know how to give as well as take? Are you a good shipmate?

Respect in the offshore cruising community has nothing to do with money or plastic toys—and everything to do with your true worth as an individual.

Or, as one cruising friend put it, "All the money in the world won't help during an offshore gale."

All my life I'd prayed there were other free-thinking people who'd grabbed the tiller of their own life and were living it to the hilt—and now I was surrounded by them. And they welcomed me with open arms.

We lavished the few pennies we earned on buying experiences, not trinkets. We didn't measure ourselves by the physical stuff surrounding us, but rather the spiritual stuff filling us with joy.

We became unabashed hedonists.

Above all else, we strove for balance: love and lust, work and play, swimming and hiking, travel and learning, earning and spending, eating and exercising, running and meditating, thinking and doing.

I'm now 59 years old. I've lived 51 glorious years afloat. I wouldn't change a thing. For me, the life of a modern sea gypsy is unparalleled in its many diverse freedoms.

I feel I am rich in everything that truly counts: friends, family, and freedom.

The physical key to this freedom is the boat. Without the boat, the rest can't happen. The boat is the magic carpet.

A sailor without a boat is helpless. A sailor with a boat is Master of His Universe.

As I've said, I purchased my first boat at 15 years of age for $200. I also built a 36-foot ketch at 19 years of age—and started her with $600 in my pocket. In 1989, in the aftermath of Hurricane Hugo, I purchased salvage rights to the severely damaged 38-foot fiberglass sloop, *Wild Card*, for $3,000.

Wild Card, a Hughes 38, is a modest boat with much to be modest about. She lacks refrigeration and running water, doesn't have an electric autopilot or watermaker and, with only 10 feet of beam, has little interior room compared to most modern cruising vessels.

Still, we've managed to sail her around the world twice over the course of the last 21 blissful years of ocean wandering. I feel it is fair to say that she has given us good value with an initial purchase price of three cents a mile (initial $3,000 price divided by 100,000 ocean miles).

How did I manage to buy a boat for $3,000 and sail it around the world a couple of times for almost nothing?

The answer lies within these pages. To explain my "sea gypsy" concept (that any working man who is handy and is willing to work hard can inexpensively and safely buy, outfit, and sail a small vessel around the world) is the exact reason I wrote this book.

This book is a step-by-step instruction manual to help you accomplish your dream of going to sea—inexpensively and safely.

…notice I didn't say easily? If all you have is sweat-equity, it takes a lot of sweat to sail around the world.

Parts of this manuscript may strike you as a tad loony. That's fine. I'm a high school drop-out. I'm a rebel. I'm a non-conformist. I don't give a shit what most landlubbers think. And I'm loony. Example: Most authors would not admit to being loony in the first few paragraphs of their how-to book. I can. I do. I just did. And you're still reading, aren't you? The sky didn't fall. Yes, I have a strange and twisted sense of humor—for better and worse. I am proud of being forthright. I like blurting out what other writers would not dare whisper.

Above all, I prize honesty and truth.

I will make sweeping statements in this book which will shock you—hell, they will shock me!

The reason they will shock us both is because the truth is so rarely told. Money isn't everything. In fact, it is almost nothing. Often, it is an impediment to freedom. Piles of stuff mean little.

I did not write this book to show you how to save 10 percent while circumnavigating. I wrote it to help you buy, outfit, and sail a boat around the world for 10 percent of what the guy currently anchored next to me spends—while having twice the fun.

The ideas expressed within, however, are not utopian or pie-in-the-sky. They are practical, tried-and-true techniques that work. I live them every day—and have for over 51 wonderful years.

Is it easy? No.

I won't kid you.

It is easier to vegetate ashore—to drift—and to allow life to pass you by.

But the trick is, according to my friend Bob Taylor who has circumnavigated three times, "to live while you're alive."

That makes sense, doesn't it?

Your friends and relatives won't criticize you for not living—only for attempting to live. Why? Because they are experiencing, as Henry David Thoreau pointed out so many years ago, "lives of quiet desperation."

They have failed to achieve their dreams. Reality got in their way. Their cherished dreams turned to chalk. They have given up. They have their blinders on. And sadly, it pains and threatens them to come across someone who has not.

You'll be shocked at their vehemence, if they think there is the remotest possibility you may escape and break the velvet chains of their video-screened, air-conditioned, Facebooked existence.

Brace yourself!

They will also strongly criticize me for even suggesting you do anything but work/consume, work/consume, work/consume/die.

Of course, ocean sailing is but one way to break free. It is the particular route I have chosen to my personal, private Nirvana. There are many others—in wheat fields, atop mountains, in Siberia, on the equator, at the South Pole.

It isn't important what your dream is—but that you begin right now to accomplish it.

My friend Jim Sublett lived far above the Arctic Circle in the vast, uncharted wilderness of Alaska. He made his living hunting and mining for gold. He couldn't swim a stroke and didn't know how to sail. One evening (it was 40 degrees below outside) he read my story The Sea Gypsy's Guide to Circumnavigating in *"Cruising World"* magazine—and became inspired. He sold this and he sold that—and hopped on a plane to New Zealand. He purchased a 30-foot locally-built steel sailboat, anchored it next to *Wild Card* in Opua, and asked, "Where to next, Cap?"

At first, I thought he might be nuts—until later, I realized he was nuts. But he was a real fun nut, Jim was. We had a wonderful year together cruising to Tonga, Wallis, Samoa, Fiji and numerous other bits of Paradise in the South Pacific.

Jim lived his dream—and discovered the wonders of the Land of the Long White Cloud as well. He is currently mining gold in South Island, New Zealand—in preparation for his next waterborne adventure.

Basically, a penniless sailor with no boat can think one of two things: "I will never get to sea." That's the conventional, shore-hugging wisdom. Anyone who thinks that is absolutely right. They won't. I repeat: A person who sells himself short is always proven correct. Or, to put it another way; can't never did nutt'n!

Or the potential sailor can think: "I, too, can get to sea. Others have—with far fewer advantages than I have. It just takes hard work, focus, and tenacity. Will it be easy? No. Could it be fun—absolutely!"

If you currently have a job, a place to live, and drive a presentable car— basically, if you are a reasonably sane, reasonably intelligent American—you can inexpensively buy, outfit, and sail a small boat around the world safely. I have—and many of my friends have. All it takes is hard, sustained work.

I and my friends are no smarter than you. We're just more effective at accomplishing our dreams.

I will show you, step by step, how to join us.

Wild Card *sailing in the Caribbean*

Introduction

I am neither against money nor the spending of it. The best possible way to get to sea is to buy a new German Frers-designed Hallberg Rassy 48 Mk II, outfit it from the pages of West Marine, and leisurely sail it around the world—with stem-to-stern refits in New Zealand, Thailand, Cape Town, and Trinidad.

There's only one problem with that—most people can't. They can't afford it. They don't have two million plus hanging around.

Money is good for some things and not good for other things. One thing money isn't good for is to use as a lame excuse for not accomplishing your dreams.

In my humble opinion, there is no correlation between money spent and happiness received when it comes to a boat. None. Zero. In fact, the penniless sailor aboard a 20-footer is often happier and less stressed than the rich yachtsman who suffers from too many complex options.

Nor is a big boat safer. My buddy Seiko Nakajima came across the Atlantic in a well-found, well-thought-out powerboat only 21 feet long. It was, in my humble opinion, inherently safer than most power yachts quadruple its size. (Did I mention its sole power source was an off-the-shelf two-horsepower Tohatsu outboard?)

My friend Paddlin' Sue is a 60-year-old endurance athlete who loves the water and the Caribbean in equal measure. She has traversed the entire Lesser Antilles, from the Virgins to Grenada, aboard an extremely modest craft—a 14-foot surfboard. She doesn't even use oars or paddles—she just uses her hands. Sometimes a support boat accompanies her, sometimes not. She carries a tiny bit of food in re-sealable bags, and a bottle of water. "My holding tank is small," she admits shyly.

All kinds of people say Paddlin' Sue is nuts. The case can easily be made that she is. But Paddlin' Sue is doing it. She is living her dream. Her next goal: to circumnavigate Puerto Rico.

I admire Paddlin' Sue.

However, I don't want to be like her.

Ditto, Seiko.

My friend Webb Chiles sailed an open, deckless boat across the Pacific. Numerous times he was swamped, rolled, and thrown in the water alongside his awash craft—in the middle of a storm-tossed night. Most of his food and safety gear were swept away at one point. Twice he didn't have the energy to immediately swim back into his craft—just sort of floated alongside his upturned vessel, suspended between heaven and hell.

I admire Webb Chiles.

However, I don't want to be like him.

I want to sail my wind-borne home around the world. I want to sail around the world in relative comfort with my wonderful, sensuous wife. I am neither an athlete nor adventurer. I admire them, but I am not one.

I'm just an ordinary Joe with a *HUGE* dream—to be the Freest Man in the World.

The key to accomplishing this distant-but-achievable goal is my boat.

The Boat

Which leads us to our first consideration: What is a boat? A sailboat? A sailboat suitable for circumnavigating?

An offshore boat is a container of air that keeps the water out. As long as it does this, everything is fine. A boat that contains air and no water is in a seaworthy state.

What characteristics does it need to contain that air and keep out that water? Well, it has to be strong. It can't shatter like an eggshell when hit by a wave. It also must be sealable so that, no matter how many times it is rolled, it won't allow water to replace the air. In addition, the mast shouldn't slip off its step and impale the hull. The keel should stay attached so that the hull is righted as it pops to the surface.

The boat needs to be well-designed so it sails properly and keeps the mast skyward and the keel down.

So, to sum up, you need a strong, well-designed boat filled with air that has a mast that won't come down and a keel that won't fall off.

That's logical, isn't it? You don't need air conditioning! That's heavy, expensive, and complicated. It will make your dream boat less seaworthy, less fun, and far more costly. So let's eliminate air-conditioning from our list of "must-haves."

Good. We've just saved about $6,000.

Size

How big or small should our boat be?

Small boats can be just as safe as large boats in adverse conditions. Small boats are cheaper. Why not sail around the world in the 20-footer?

You can. People have. I met a very happy young family (father, mother, and two kids) sailing around the world aboard a Cal 25—an extremely modest boat.

We later met Marvelous Mary in Chagos, in the middle of the southern Indian Ocean, circumnavigating on a Lyle Hess 20-footer. She got tired of living in her geodesic dome in Northern California and decided, impishly, to take to the sea. She was 68 when we met her midway through her circumnavigation—and living life to the hilt.

But a small boat has a number of disadvantages: you can't carry much, it is slow, the motion is extreme. It is often difficult to claw off a lee shore in severe conditions with a boat of less than 28 feet.

You have to be far more active to sail a small boat. Or, as my buddy John Foster once told me after a grueling offshore ocean race aboard a 29-footer named *Magnificent 7*, "Small boats beat old men to death!"

For many young single-handers, a small boat is fine. But it is far, far easier to pick up members of the opposite sex with a slightly larger boat. In essence, a pocket cruiser is fine for a one-night stand—but 30-plus- footers work better for long-term love affairs. (This statement isn't directed solely towards men. We know a number of single-handed cruising women who, shall we say, enjoy sampling the delights of the local lads?)

Big boats have disadvantages. They cost more in terms of everything: money, time, material, weight, renewable resources, etc. Yes, they are more comfortable in a blow offshore—but they are no safer. The loads are high. You need to be younger and wealthier to safely sail a 60-footer versus a 40-footer.

Docking a 30-footer isn't difficult at all. Docking a heavy displacement 50-footer in a cross-wind can be a life-threatening event.

Plus, if you aren't wealthy, you usually can't afford to purchase or fix up a 60-footer.

The bottom line: I recommend a vessel between 28 (single person and destitute) and 46 feet (couple, middle-class) to sail around the world.

I have a relatively lightweight (13,000 pound) 38-foot sloop. *Wild Card* puts in good daily runs offshore, is well-mannered in a blow, claws off a lee shore well, is fun to sail, and carries two people and all their worldly possessions with grace.

Ounce for ounce, we feel good about having paid $3,000 for her.

We may retire to a smaller boat after completing our third circum-navigation. I would consider a 32-footer. My wife Carolyn thinks a 42- to 46-footer would be a better retirement craft. (She's never had refrigeration or a watermaker and wants to be spoiled in her old age.)

Mono or Multi?

I have nothing against multihulls. I wouldn't mind owning a Lagoon 50 as a retirement craft, especially if it came with a trust fund. But they aren't cheap to buy, repair, or cruise. They are, literally, double the trouble and expense.

I believe a multihull requires a higher level of expertise to sail offshore in a safe and seaman-like manner.

Don't get me wrong: I think a well-designed, properly sailed multihull can survive anything. But I also believe that a less experienced sailor is ultimately safer on a lead mine (monohull) because the loads are so much lower and there is little possibility of becoming upside-down.

Hull Material

I'd recommend that a rich man buy a brand new steel yacht—and then selling it in five to eight years when too many bleeders begin leaking through the coal-tar epoxy. There's no question steel is strongest. If you want to pound on a reef all night until rescued, steel is the only choice.

But it is relatively heavy and relatively high maintenance. Unless you have welding and metal skills, I would not recommend rehabbing an old steel vessel.

I would not recommend an old wooden boat or a ferro-cement hull either.

I've spent much of my life working on carvel-planked wooden vessels and I will never again attempt to rebuild one—especially if it is far gone. Rot is both contagious and relentless. It never sleeps. I enjoy sleeping. Sure, wooden boats are beautiful. I love them. But my advice is to admire them from afar.

There are a number of very strong, very long-lived, very handsome ferro-cement vessels in the world. I've built, and helped build, a number of them. Perseverance, moored in Scituate, Massachusetts, is 40-plus-years old and still in Bristol condition. But most ferro boats are too heavy, too crude, and too difficult to correctly survey.

I want to relax and sail my yacht—not work on it endlessly.

This leaves aluminum and fiberglass.

Aluminum boats are great if they don't suffer from electrolysis or develop it. This is a complicated, highly technical subject.

Thus I recommend that most people of modest means and modest skills buy a used, mass-produced, fiberglass boat of sound, traditional design to circumnavigate aboard. They are common, cheap, and relatively good at keeping the air in and the water out—if you don't hit a large object. (Puncture resistance is low compared to steel, for example.)

Rigs
Don't worry about what kind of rig. Sloops, cutters, ketches, and yawls are all okay if properly designed and executed. Ditto, schooners over 50 feet.

I do, however, recommend avoiding gaffers. I'm a friend of famed Caribbean designer Paul Johnson and I love his designs—to look at, not to own. In fact, you should avoid all "weird or gaffaroni" rigs. Let someone else spend decades and millions perfecting the aero-rig while you cruise Polynesia. (The Lulu Magras, of St. Barths, term "gaffaroni" refers to gaffers pretending they don't have a gaff aloft and/or Marconi sailors pretending they do.)

Designs
Avoid experimental boats. Avoid ugly boats. My father used to say, "If it looks wrong, it probably is wrong." Stay away from centerboarders for two reasons: small ones are unstable in an ultimate storm, and big ones have enormous loads on the board and are thus harder to maintain on a shoestring budget. (Hauling out on the tide, for instance, isn't a good idea for most large centerboarders.)

Summing Up
If you want to buy a cheap boat to fix up and sail around the world, you want a well-designed, fixed keel, fiberglass production monohull of 28 to 46 feet.

Target Audience
Who is this book written for?

I'd like to think the experienced circumnavigator will get a chuckle or two out of this manuscript—and learn a few things in the process.

Many readers will probably only use one or two sections of the book—most people who buy and outfit a sailboat won't circumnavigate. That's fine.

This book is not written for the boatbuilder. I strongly discourage anyone attempting to build a boat from scratch to get to sea. It is much cheaper, quicker, and safer to follow the directions in this book and buy a derelict hull.

If you must get involved in a boatbuilding project, consider buying a partially completed hull for five cents on the dollar. There are plenty of them around.

The only people to whom I recommend building a boat from the ground up are wanna-be-shipwrights interested in boatbuilding as a profession or lifestyle.

The skills of a boatbuilder and an offshore sailor are vastly different. Only a tiny percentage of amateur boatbuilders stick with their projects to completion and actually cruise the world aboard the boats they built.

The last thing I want to do, of course, is to discourage anyone. If you want to build a boat, go ahead. I did, and I don't regret it. Don't let me stop you. But if you want to go to sea and enjoy a boat quickly and simply, don't build from scratch. Read on.

That said, I need to express how much I admire boatbuilders. I know and love dozens of them. They are the ultimate in "can-do" people.

At 19 years of age, my wife Carolyn and I lofted a Peter Ibold 36-foot ketch and launched it three years later. This was, to put it mildly, a pivotal event in my young life. From that moment on, I knew (if I had the help of Carolyn) that I could accomplish damn near anything.

We helped form a boatbuilding cooperative at B Street and Congress in Boston to accomplish this goal. Six boats were constructed. Our *Carlotta* was the only success for over ten years—until one other vessel (the 52-foot ketch Perseverance, a Cecil Norris C-Breeze design) was launched.

The four other vessels were never launched/sailed by their builders. Fifteen years after the start of their construction, they still were not wet, despite being lavished with money and man-hours all those long, hard years.

This is typical for most amateur boatbuilding projects. Building a boat is complicated, time-consuming, and not-cheap, no matter how you do it.

I repeat: Only build a boat if your ultimate pay-off is building a boat. If you want to get to sea, there are far easier and cheaper ways.

So who is this book directed at? Let's call him Freddy the (former) Farmer. He's 32 years old, married, and has a job. Everything is going pretty well. But he can see the future looming—and he feels that the good life might be passing him by.

He wants to go to sea. Hell, that's not strong enough: He has to go to sea. He has a severe case of Nessomania—a strange affliction which is impossible to shake with logic or common sense. (Nessomania was coined by author James A. Michener. It means "crazy for the sea.")

This Freddy the Former Farmer wants to smell salt air and will work hard to accomplish his goal. He is moderately handy, or at least not a total klutz, when it comes to welding or wielding a hammer, saw, paint brush, wood plane, or grinder. He's sailed a few times, perhaps even chartered in the Virgins. But he's never been able to afford a decent-sized sailboat—neither its initial price nor its upkeep. But he wants to—someday and someway—sail away from reality and live free.

...to Chase the Horizon for as long as it is fun.

In essence, he is full of desire and willing to work hard and long to get to sea, but lacks one important ingredient: money.

This is the person I write for.

I seriously considered writing this manuscript for the more typical, frugal circumnavigator who spends around $100,000 for his boat and has a small stash of money hidden somewhere. That's the bigger market. But that slightly upscale focus would have eliminated much of the truly delicious things I've learned while penny-squeezing down through the salt-stained decades.

So I stuck with poor-but-willing Freddy the Farmer.

Why I Wrote This Book

Writing is what I do for a living as I sail. I'm a fulltime professional writer and have been for almost my entire life. So my primary reason for writing this book is to earn money to keep cruising.

But I'm also motivated by the fact that, strangely, no one has ever written a book like this. Sure, there are dozens of books telling you which boat to buy and which gear to buy to outfit it. But there are none telling you how you can Buy, Outfit, and Sail—even if you only have a pocket full of pennies and some audacious dreams.

I recently read an article entitled, "How To Manage Your Haulout." It chronicled bringing a fancy boat to a pristine yacht yard, and spending $78,000 to have other people work on it.

I don't have a fancy yacht. Nor do I have $78,000. So the article was of no value to me.

I am going to repeat my core premise: You don't need much money to buy a boat, fix it up, and sail around the world—that you can have twice the fun on one-tenth the money of the rich yachtsman who is circumnavigating with a bulging checkbook.

If you don't give up, you will eventually see that I am right.

A Special Note To Women

Many women are sailing around the world with great passion and eagerness. Take Sybille, as an example. She is a skillful sailor who loves the thrill of close-quarter sailing. Thus she helms her family's 46-foot sloop Subeki on the race course, and offshore as well.

Christian, her husband, is ultimately the captain. But she is the sailing master: docking the boat, helming during spinnaker sets, reefing the boat, etc.

"This is how it evolved for us," says Christian. "I quickly realized that I wasn't looking forward to docking—and that she was. And she's better at it than I. So why shouldn't I do the stuff I'm good at and she do the stuff she's good at?"

"It was originally Christian's idea to circumnavigate," admits Sybille. "And, since he has studied the sea so much and has so much experience, he is still the captain. But he isn't interested in changing the oil or docking in a cross wind, so I'm the chief mechanic and helmsperson. This works out just fine for us. Everyone has a job that they are comfortable with and enjoy. Isn't this the whole idea of cruising?"

Sailing requires little body strength. It is a perfect sport and/or lifestyle for a woman.

The only real strength it requires is in the mind.

We met a famous TV personality while cruising Africa. She had been the popular weather woman on CNN for a number of years. She realized the man she'd just fallen in love with was head-over-heels in love with boating as well as with her.

So she immediately took a week off and flew down to Florida for an intensive women only sailing course.

They married.

And, ultimately, they sailed around the world while living happily-ever-after.

Ditto, Erja Vasumaki of Finland. She was living aboard her boat in the Pacific Northwest when she bumped into a long-distance bicycle rider from Canada—and invited Glenn home to her yacht. Almost immediately, she popped the question. "Interested in being a cabin boy?" The rest is history. They now spend most of their time cruising the Indian Ocean, alternating annually between Chagos/Malaysia and Chagos/Africa. Yes, they're still aboard the same boat, a modest Ericson 32 with many, many miles under its keel.

Sailing is a great way to find the perfect spouse—or to avoid them.

More and more single-handers are women. My sister Carole, after her second divorce, retired to the aptly named *Ms Bligh* to avoid further land-bound suitors.

Marvelous Mary was a tad reclusive as well. When I first rowed over and asked her to dinner aboard *Wild Card*, she growled, "I don't have to be nice, do I? Oh—and I don't have to reciprocate, do I?"

"No," I assured her. "You don't have to reciprocate and you can be as mean as you want."

"Oh, good," she said, and flashed a smile. "Then I'll come!"

She did and we had a wonderful evening together and ultimately became good friends. (She gives good relationship value, just no dinner invites!)

Jennifer had an independent streak as well. She'd worked almost a year, slaving away at the varnish aboard a classic wooden boat to earn her Pacific Ocean berth, only to be "let go" from volunteering her services just before the vessel shoved off. (Sigh.)

So Jennifer purchased her own boat and sailed it down to Mexico—where she met a blue-eyed Italian fellow "…with a nice ass," as she put it.

She fell in love.

He and his crew sailed away to Tahiti. She followed, single-handing, on her own boat. Her boat was faster, so she reached the equator first. It seemed sad to cross alone. So she waited for her lover's boat. They sailed "over the hump" in tandem.

They began... er, verbally "doing it" on the VHF. (I assume they didn't use Channel 16).

She'd take nude pictures of herself, print them out, place them in corked wine bottles attached to long poly ropes, and drop them overboard in his path.

He'd retrieve them with a boat hook. Romantic, eh? (Yes, sea-gypsy-love-and-lust is stranger than fiction).

I met her in the loveliest harbor in the world—Fatu Hiva, in the Marquesas. She'd just spent a month at sea alone. "...with only a dog and a cat—neither of which could steer worth a damn," is how she put it.

Shortly thereafter, she met the man of her dreams (who loved her in return) and married him. They now have a wonderful child and leisurely crisscross the Pacific under sail.

We've known a number of marriages that split up when the man wanted to sell the boat. Instead, the woman ditched the man and sailed on.

And I must admit I admired the famous *Wild Heart* lady who single-handed while preying on unsuspecting single-handed men.

She always had the same MO: She'd meet them, raft up alongside, drain their bodily fluids for a week or two—and then cast off when they were too weak to protest.

Oh, she was the prettiest sexual predator I'd ever seen! (Her "victims" clearly enjoyed her attentions while they lasted.)

The point I'm trying to make is that while most women are at sea because of their husband's passion—not all are. Sometimes it is the reverse. And other times, well, the skipper wears a dress.

Women sailors are now so common they barely raise a stir—not like in the 1970s on Jost Van Dyke, when Cap'n Bonnie pulled in after a difficult ocean crossing and Albert the chauvinistic BVI Customs official kept asking her, "What you do wid de mon? You toss 'em over de side? He bad to you? He rough? Huh? What you do, Bonnie, wid de mon? Hit 'em on de head?"

A Special Note To Young Adults

I am now going to reveal to you something you probably already suspect. Since I am an adult, I've secretly promised my fellow adults to lie to you, to tell you what we think you should hear rather than the truth. That's what we adults do and that's why you think of us as hypocrites—because we are.

Thus, I am not at liberty to tell you to buy a boat, drop out of school, and sail away.

And, this is good because I sincerely don't believe most kids should. There will be plenty of time to go cruising after you graduate from college, get a job, get a spouse, have a kid, work forty hours a week for forty years, and retire. (Maybe I should rephrase this to sound a tad more inviting?)

I certainly won't suggest that our society has it ass-backwards. Don't even think about the absurdity of diligently working while you are young and playful. And then later, maybe, attempting to play for a couple of moments as you're dying.

No, don't even think about any of this.

Just follow orders. School. Church. Work. Death.

…just skip the living part.

But, seriously, there are some kids out there who aren't on the fast track to maturity and adult happiness. They aren't in school. They aren't considering the ROTC. They aren't members of the 4H Club. They aren't in church. They are on the mean streets of Chicago, New York, Baltimore, and LA—and they are at extreme risk.

If you're getting high, have seen a street gun, stuck your face in a glue bag, or have ever been arrested—you might consider that you're running the wrong way down a very short street.

Often, modern teenagers don't feel they are living, because they aren't. It is ironic to be told to "think for yourself." But every time you do, people scream at you, "Shut up and stay in school."

In order to learn, you have to make mistakes. There is no better place to make a lot of mistakes than a small boat on a big ocean. Your mistakes will be clear. You will not be able to wiggle out of them. It won't be like a video game. It will be, at times, all too real.

The sea has made men of many boys—and will continue to do so for as long as mankind transverses Mother Ocean.

At 16 years of age, I had three great friends; Butch Anarino, Pinky Weber, and George Zamiar. We were best friends and did everything together. For instance, we partied and… we partied… and, well, we partied!

I had just purchased a 22-foot double-ended sloop. George found that exciting. And together we fixed *Corina* up and went cruising together as teenage yachtsmen. We had a ball—particularly while seducing all the eager city girls in Saugatuck, Michigan, who had been sent there on summer vacation to protect them from the bad boys of Chicago. (Surprise!)

George has since gone on to become a highly successful businessman. The electronics firm he founded is a Microsoft Partner. He has a wonderful wife, Karen, a daughter, Sarah, and a son, Zack.

Butch and Pinky both OD'd on drugs in their early 20s.

They are still dead.

I still love them both and I still miss them. But we all saw it coming from a million miles away. By the time they realized they were on the wrong track, they were in a very scary tunnel and staring at the oncoming train.

Cruising is a perfect way for troubled youths to find themselves. All your decisions will be your own. You will benefit when you make 'em right and suffer when you make 'em wrong.

You will be forced to accept responsibility for your own actions—which is the definition of an adult.

At 16, I took the tiller of my life into my own hands—and pointed my vessel toward a distant horizon.

I was forever changed.

I never came back—not really.

Stay in school if you possibly can. If you can't—and the street calls—consider listening to the call of the sea instead.

I'm astounded that there aren't more teenagers living aboard and cruising. For me, it was the only way to grow up into the man I am today.

But remember: The sea is a harsh mistress, if you don't learn her lessons well—she kills you.

A Special Note To Senior Citizens

I'm 59 years old and have been accused of both sailing when I was too young (at 15) and now when I'm too old.

The conventional wisdom is that older people have far more financial assets than young ones, and so you can afford a nice boat.

I certainly hope that's true in your case.

I certainly wouldn't recommend a that a 70-year-old person buy the burned-out hull of an Irwin 65 and attempt to fix it up in order to sail around the world.

The actualities tables are just too grim, the work just too hard.

However, I do not advise nodding off on a park bench either.

My friend Ted Seymour, the first black man to sail single-handed around the world, spent years knocking around the Caribbean in a Columbia 50 that he'd purchased through clever stock trading. But when the recession hit and retirement arrived, Ted wisely sold that large, complex vessel and moved aboard a very modest 28-foot sloop with an outboard engine.

"It's better for me," he said. "I want to enjoy sailing—not work or worry on my boat. So I've downsized my vessel and maximized my fun. This boat is all I need to knock around the Caribbean. My offshore sailing days are over. Why lug around a massive vessel when a trailer-able one will do?"

We know what keeps people young: intellectual excitement and new challenges. A small boat on a large ocean will give you plenty of both.

Boats are also great devices to assist you in staying active.

The first time we went through the Panama Canal, we met a delightful couple in their late 70s who were heading across the Pacific for the first time. It wasn't that their age was so unusual, but rather the fact that they were greenhorns. We were worried about their transit of the canal, which can be hard physical work. They told us not to worry as they had some young friends flying in for the trip. The following day we met the young friends, 68 and 69 years old respectively!

My 66-year-old buddy Chris on *Harmony* was on his second circumnavigation when his beloved wife died of cancer. Chris was heart-broken and sailed out into a full-fledged hurricane to join her. But, hey, he was too much of a seaman to allow his noble vessel to needlessly founder. So he continued on. And a year or so later, he just happened to pull into a snug little river in Madagascar where a lovely, freckle-faced German girl was….

Life isn't over until it is over. A modest boat can hold large, horizon-to-horizon dreams.

As one old salt-encrusted sailor told me recently, "You are only as old as the woman you feel and the boat you love!"

Our land-centric society, strangely, marginalizes our most experienced, wisest members. Not so in Southeast Asia, where a group of teenagers will approach a senior citizen respectfully, bow, and address him reverently as "Old Man!"

Yes, Asia is a strange place. For years, Indonesia paid the yachts to enter its most prestigious regatta!

Are you a widow or widower? Why not hook up with a new, eager, adventurous first mate on the Internet? We know of at least eight happily married, happily cruising couples who met exactly this cyber-savvy way.

Romance and boats go together hand-in-glove. Why not start again?

Are there more miles left in you? Why not make them sea miles? It will be a lot harder to maneuver you into an old-age home if you are sailing across the Pacific or chasing a Tahitian maiden around a palm tree on Bora Bora.

My friend Bob Griffith of *Awahnee* was a 50-year-old California veterinarian when he was rushed to the hospital and told his heart probably wouldn't pump much longer. He blinked, gulped, sold everything, and went to sea.

I met him 13 years later in Boston. He was working (as a brief lark) as a nav instructor aboard the *Westward*, a large steel sail-training vessel.

"Sailing has given me everything," he told me. "Even life itself!"

"What's next?" I asked him.

"Back to *Awahnee*," he said, "to begin our third circ." (Bob's book "Blue Water" is a delight. He truly had mega-fun on a micro-budget for many years.)

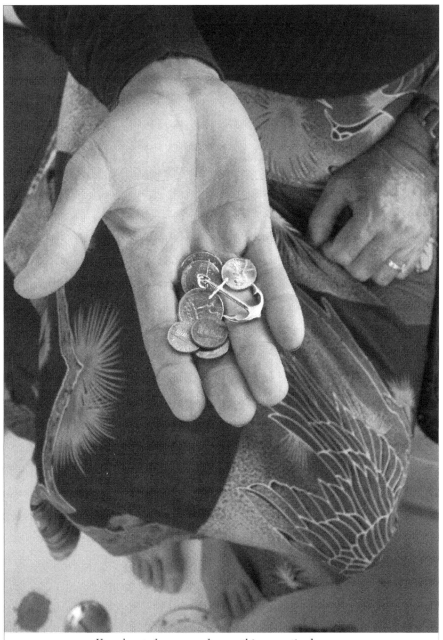

Your boat charm can be anything nautical.

Section I

Buying the Boat

Buying, Outfitting, and Sailing will require a certain amount of organization, some multi-tasking skills, a few grains of intelligence, a bit of risk, some hard work, and much tenacity. The most important of these attributes is tenacity. Tenacity trumps everything else. Intelligence is at the bottom of the list. Tenacity is at the top.

You can't lose if you don't quit.

You are about to set off on a great, exciting, life-altering adventure to Buy, Outfit, and Sail.

Think carefully.

Once you begin, you can't profitably stop until the pay-off: freedom, fun, and mega-adventure.

But there are thousands of steps between buying a boat and completing a circumnavigation. Many of them are enjoyable. But a few are gruesome, too.

I can't tell you if you should take up the challenge. However, I can, and will, guide you every step of the way if you do.

Boat Charm

I want you to find a miniature boat, canoe, or ocean liner that easily fits in your pocket. Remember those old pot-metal Monopoly pieces? Something like that. Or a boat charm that goes on an old-fashioned charm bracelet. It has to be small and it is best if it is cheap. But you have to "think boat" whenever you see it. It can even be the letter "B" or a miniature oar or an anchor—anything clearly marine.

I want you to carry it with you at all times as a concrete symbol of your future. I also want you to pull it out every time you take out your pocket change—to remember that you have a choice on how you spend your money.

Your meager money, from this point on, will be divided into boat money and personal money.

Is it Friday night and you want a beer? Fine, have one. But when you reach into your pocket for that fourth beer, notice the little boat you carry and ask yourself, "What do I really want to do—drink tonight or sail tomorrow?"

Life is filled with choices. If you are a person of modest means, you have to decide what your priorities are. In this case, it is easy. Have a couple of beers and head home to work on your upcoming circumnavigation. Soon you will have far, far more time for sundowners than the drinking buddy who stayed behind.

After you have the toy boat, walk into the cheapest liquor store in town and buy the two cheapest bottles of champagne they have.

Then hide them from your spouse and yourself.

o You Need To Buy a Boat?

, the primary medium of exchange, of course, but there are others. You ... e to be able to decide which boat to buy—and then live with that decision. Your money has to be liquid and available so you can, if needed, act fast. If it is a project boat, you might have to immediately haul it out of the water or move it to… where?

Let's say you want to buy a $5,000 28-footer and the guy you are buying it from will bring it to your backyard and help you take it off his trailer. Fine, the initial cost of that vessel is $5,000.

Let's say you buy a sunken 38-footer for $5,000 and it costs $4,000 for salvers to raise it and transport it to a shipyard. The shipyard will haul it for $500 and only charge $500 per month to keep it in the yard so you can work on it.

Fine perhaps, but this $5,000 boat costs at least $10,000.

Another consideration is any potential liability.

Our S&S-designed Hughes 38's initial purchase price was $3,000. It was holed and sunk on the beach in National Park Service (NPS) waters of St. John, USVI. There was a huge potential liability. I had to remove it without hurting a blade of grass or a lump of coral. I spoke with the NPS prior to purchasing the boat. They were very reasonable. We agreed that I and the Park had the same objective: to remove the vessel without damaging anything. But they also sent out a park ranger to watch the whole time—so they could stop me, arrest me, and/or sue me if need be.

The Park Ranger was nice but firm.

My original plan was to strap pieces of plywood to the temporarily repaired cracked hull and drag it back over the reef it slid in on. I was going to hire a large tugboat to accomplish this. But now this wasn't possible—not with the NPS on the scene. So I hired a floating crane for $4,000 and plucked it off like a Fabergé egg.

So my $3,000 boat cost me $7,000 by any reasonable measure. But it also exposed me to a big potential downside. If I had dropped it, the NPS would have fined me for the damage to the reef and removed the boat at my expense—to the tune of $30,000 or so. Big risk, big gain.

About a month later I had the hole fixed and a $50,000 boat for less than 10Gs.

So knowing the real cost of a boat is important.

In my case, the major added expense was the floating crane. But there might be any number of other expenses related to a purchase; transportation and surveying costs, materials, cost of a cradle, towing fees, etc.

Money

Let us start with money.

If you have enough money to buy a modest boat—then do so.

I do not recommend that a poor person borrow a large sum of money and then pray they can somehow pay it back if... if… they win the Lotto!

As a sea gypsy, I have only one rule: Never get behind the eight ball. By that I mean to never borrow money or get into debt.

But some people do borrow money and sometimes it works out well. I only recommend borrowing for very stable individuals with a long-term, multi-tier plan to buy, outfit and sail.

Most poor sea gypsies focused on a distant horizon should not borrow. How can you pay off a mortgage and fix up the boat and sail around the world?

The word mortgage has death right at its very beginning. Many a sea voyage has been nipped in the bud by too much debt.

But you are going to need some money. Even Kevin Rowlette's BVI-salvaged Beneteau 42 *Fast Buck* (which I raced aboard in Puerto Rico during the Velasco Cup) cost a dollar.

So you have to have a pile of pennies somewhere or you won't be able to quickly take advantage of that Hallberg Rassy 42 for sale for $12,000 because the guy's wife didn't like the blue cove stripe. (Lucky you!)

Let's say, for the sake of argument, Freddy the Farmer has $5,000 tucked away in a sock—far, far from the eyes of the IRS. Good. That's a start.

But it must be added to on a regular basis.

If you want a dream boat tomorrow, you have to begin paying for it today.

I do not recommend borrowing, but I do insist on pre-self-financing.

Only you can pay for your dream—no one else will.

How much can you reasonably put aside right now for your dream vessel? A hundred dollars a week? A thousand dollars a month? Ten dollars a week?

Whatever the amount, start now. If it is only five dollars a week, so be it.

This is, as we already discussed, a big, big, BIG project. In a sense, it isn't as important what you do, as it is that you keep doing it. There will be many times when you will be stumped. I was stumped numerous times while building *Carlotta* and rebuilding *Wild Card*. But I never got stopped. Stumped, yes. Stopped, no. When I couldn't figure out how to fair in the knuckle of the transom, I straightened up my work area and built more sawhorses. When I couldn't figure out where to put or how to align my new engine beds, I oiled all my tools—for two solid days!

When I couldn't go forward—I moved sideways until a door opened.

I would have never found this door if I'd stopped. But I didn't stop. I kept moving—if only sideways.

This whole thing is a giant learning experience. "Change is good," is one of my mantras. "Change is the only constant in our lives!"

If you are going to sail around the world, your spending habits are going to slowly evolve.

The sooner you start, the better.

We currently (after 50 years of living aboard, more than 20 of them on *Wild Card*) spend 25 percent of our money on the boat, 25 percent on food, 25 percent on "other," and 25percent we save.

That's right—we actually save (put money in the bank) as we sail around the world and live like a king and queen in all the trendy spots.

During our second circumnavigation, we left with $5,000 and returned with

$39,000 in the bank.

Yes, of course, we had to work hard to accomplish this. But it is possible. We, and about five thousand other shoestring cruisers worldwide, are living proof.

I have no weekly or monthly bills, and only one annual one: $250 for my Sailmail email account, which allows me to earn my living as we cruise. (In the Med, I have to have $325 worth of liability insurance as well.)

In 1971, when I started to build the 36-foot ketch *Carlotta*, I had $600 in my pocket. Money was, ahem, a factor. So I banded together with my brother-in-law Joey Borges, who also wanted to build a boat. It was immediately apparent to us that we could save a lot of money by buying our hull materials in bulk.

Once that idea jelled in our brains, we put an advertisement in the Boston Phoenix (the local hippie paper) explaining we were going to build some boats and asking if there was anyone else out there interested. There were. Seventy-eight people called us back. We had a pot-luck dinner and more than 30 people showed up.

We immediately formed a boatbuilding commune over beer and hotdogs, and the following day went in search of a place to build six large yachts.

We looked at many locations—too expensive, too small, etc. Finally we found a giant warehouse at B Street and Congress that was going to be torn down in two years, so it didn't matter how badly the building was damaged as we extracted our 20,000-pound vessels. The rental cost of the entire huge building was $125 per month. Split six ways, including electricity, each boatbuilder's initial monthly cost was $25. Eventually, we rented out space to welders and mechanics as well as boatbuilders. And then our monthly cost was less-than-zero (we turned a tiny profit).

That amount of money is just about right for a 19-year-old kid with no job.

One of the few things I did have back in those heady days was a wonderful two-door 1950 Chevy Coupe in mint condition. I sold it for $800 bucks and a Ford panel truck. I also had a dinghy that I sold for $200.

Soon I had a building site and $2,000 in my hand.

Rents in Boston are famously expensive. We pitched a tent (made from two layers of six-mil plastic sheeting) next to our boat inside the warehouse and lived there to save money. (See "*Chasing the Horizon*" for all the gory details.)

Eventually, we were thrown out of the tent and forced to move into the factory washroom. Carolyn made it quite cozy. We knocked down the stall walls and laid them on the three toilets to form a bed. Colorful throw pillows disguised the urinals quite well.

Yes, you have to make serious, significant compromises to build a vessel with empty pockets. We lived aboard and sailed *Carlotta* over 30,000 miles before losing her on September 17, 1989 at 6:23 a.m. during the height of (Category Four) Hurricane Hugo.

Where were we? Ah, yes. Money! There is no getting around the fact that you are going to need some money. So the sooner you begin gathering it together, the better. What can you sell? Is there any way to earn more? How and where can you cut back on expenses?

If, ten years from now, you want to be in the middle of the Pacific Ocean while your friends are still sitting down at the local pub and bitching about how unfair life is—you have to hustle now.

You have choices. Each choice has a cost and a consequence.

Get in the habit of deciding wisely.

No, you don't have to never-ever go out to dinner again or stop snow skiing or sell your cherished porn collection. Just be aware of all your expenditures and how they affect your overall plan to escape to sea.

Look For the Deal, Not the Boat

I have just sailed across the Indian Ocean, come up through the Red Sea, and am now anchored off the delightful Turkish town of Fethiye as I type these words. There is very little chance someone will offer me a great deal on a dog-sled team today.

I'm a sailor, not a landsman. I'm anchored out. I don't know anything about dog-sleds—nor the people who use them. Nobody associates me with dog-sleds. I usually hang out in the tropics, so close to the equator that the TVs showing the snowstorms up north are melting in the hot equatorial sun.

No, there is little chance of me making a clever financial touchdown on a cheap dog-sled today, while anchored along the sweltering south coast of Turkey. So, if I suddenly wanted to buy a dog-sled cheap, I'd have to change my ways—just like Freddy the Farmer would have to if he wanted to buy a cruising boat.

That's logical, isn't it?

But what you really should be looking for, if you only have a pocket full of pennies, is the deal, not the boat.

A friend of mine, just after Hurricane Hugo, decided now was the time for him to buy his dream boat. He wanted a Swan yacht—one of the fastest, best-built ocean greyhounds ever constructed. He found one aground, holed, and stripped in Puerto Rico. He purchased it for $37,000, patched it, refloated it, and brought it to a shipyard. Then he revisited the small village that had stripped the boat and repurchased most of the gear taken from it for ten cents on the dollar.

He now had $50,000 into the project. To make her seaworthy, he spent another $50Gs—for a total cost of $100,000. He then raced her all over the Caribbean for a number of seasons. He did well at Antigua Sailing Week, the Rolex Cup, and the Heineken Regatta. Four years later, he sold her for $250,000 in order to buy a pristine Oyster 46, which he and his wife retired aboard. This worked well for him, but he risked 100Gs, and had to put in a lot of sweat-equity as well.

I was dead broke after losing *Carlotta* and needed an immediate home for my family. Besides, I didn't have $100,000. So I walked the wreck-strewn beaches of St. John in search of a great deal rather than a great boat. "Some of these boats will end up free," I told Carolyn, "and others will go for a pittance.

We just have to be in the right place at the right time and be ready to act, that's all."

The Secret

In order to get a truly great deal, you have to ignore most good boats. Good boats are worth money, remember? And you don't have any money, remember? So finding your dream boat is useless because you can't afford to do anything with your dream boat but dream about it, right?

I repeat: Any boat that is worth something isn't worth considering, if you have nothing.

So forget about specifically buying a Swan 42, or a Pacific Seacraft 36, or a Mason 64. Those are great boats and they don't give them away…

…unless…

…unless…

…they have a major problem and a ticking clock.

That's what you need to look for: a well-designed, fixed keel fiberglass production monohull of between 28 to 46 feet that has a major problem and a ticking clock.

What is a major problem? No engine. No rig. No rudder. Sunk. Holed. Crushed. Burned. Wobbly keel. Loose bulkheads. Shifted keel. Rotten balsa core.

A major problem makes a boat worth very little money.

A ticking clock gives you the chance to buy it right now for even less money.

What is a ticking clock?

Well, death is a common one.

My friend Ken B was one of the coolest sailors ever. We knew him for years as he circumnavigated on his extremely funky 35-foot Cherokee catamaran. He lived life to the max and, at 70 years old, was as wonderful a nutcase as had ever wandered across an ocean. He didn't care what people thought. The fact that (in his own words) people would say, "Oh, no! It's the Beverly Hillbillies," as he anchored nearby didn't matter to him a bit.

A former surgeon, he was handy with his tools but didn't focus on cosmetics.

He single-handed and had many adventures. Many times people thought he'd been lost at sea but he always eventually showed up with a big smile and a half-empty bottle of Scotch.

But one day, he returned home to Canada to take care of some medical insurance paperwork—and, oh the irony—died there.

His boat was in Malaysia. His son flew there and had a giant "boat jumble" from which he netted many of thousands of dollars. (I helped him set this up—to honor his father, Ken B.) That left the odd boat which, basically, had been gutted to house a "Mad Inventor's Sailing Workshop."

The boat was in a small boutique boatyard that was quite pricy. Every month it stayed there, it cost the son $500.

Ken's son, Colin, was a wonderful kid, but busy with his own life. He wisely decided to sell the boat "as is, where is" and did so for $10,000—for less than the brand-new, just installed before he died, Yanmar engine cost.

Everyone was happy, especially the guy who got an ocean-going cat fully ready to cross the Indian Ocean for a few pennies—because it had a ticking clock. (The yard bill was being paid by the young, just-starting-out son).

People die all the time. Many of them have boats. Occasionally, these boats are stuck in exotic places. Because of that, they sell for very little money.

Another common "ticking clock" is imminent divorce. The wife says, "Either that ugly Westsail 32 is gone by Friday—or I am!"

My sister's *Ms Bligh*, a 26-foot Kenner ketch, had been tied to a dock for a dozen years in Fort Lauderdale without moving. All the current owners knew about it was that the rudder was gone. The condo association was demanding it be moved within 14 days or it would be seized. The current owners would be billed for its removable and disposal.

Thus, they had to dump the boat within 14 days or incur substantial charges. This is the best "ticking clock" possible. I visited the boat. The tiller was lying in the cockpit. There was no rudder post sticking up through the rudder tube. I'd expected this, as we'd been told there was no rudder. So I peered down the rudder tube, expecting to see blue water. I did not. It was pitch black. I scratched my head. And rummaged in a cockpit locker and found a long line. I looped it over the transom, lowered it into the water, and walked forward a bit. It hit something. I pulled the line slowly, carefully. And the rudder head emerged from the tube, nice as could be. The boat had a rudder; it had just uncoupled from the tiller head and partially fallen to the bottom. I dove over the side to confirm. The boat was complete. We could sail her away right now.

But it wasn't easy to keep the smiles off our faces as we paid the $600 and motored off with the boat and her signed-over title! (It seldom works like this, but hey, we got lucky. And admittedly, my sister Carole deserved her luck as she'd been hunting for the perfect deal all over South Florida for almost a year.)

The ticking clock can be something as basic as the owner's convenience.

We recently bumped into a guy on a very nice, relatively new Beneteau 38 in the Maldives. The young fellow and his friend were sailing her around the world. She had been a much better deal than our *Wild Card.*

The boat had been purchased new by her (former) rich kid owner who'd sailed her for a year without checking the oil or cooling water. Thus, her engine had seized up. This kid was rich beyond counting. So he ordered a new J/44. Then he spaced out and forgot all about his little Beneteau until his new boat was delivered and he needed his slip, which was convenient to his crash pad. To solve the problem, he put a notice up on the marina bulletin board that read, "48 HOURS ONLY—BEST OFFER ACCEPTED" and a picture of the boat. Our friend saw it and acted immediately. He was in total disbelief that he'd just scored a $100,000 boat (with a blown engine, which would cost under $10,000 to replace) for pocket change. (I'm not sure of the exact figure, but I think it was $5,000!)

Other ticking clocks: foreclosures, yard bills, owner moving, owner in poor health, owner leaving country, owner going to jail, etc.

There is only one reason for Joe Average to buy a boat—because he thinks he will enjoy it. However, there are a million reasons for Joe Average to sell a boat—and, in a few cases, need to sell it quickly.

Repeat

The best way to buy a good boat for almost no money is to find a suitable boat with a major problem and a ticking clock.

   Look for the deal, not the boat.

Needles In the Haystack

How many needles are there in the haystack? You might think that there are only two or three "real cruising boats" in the world that can be had for pennies—or only two or three in the USA.

   You are wrong. If you live in the continental United States, there are dozens in your area, perhaps more.

   Some of them will have ticking clocks. The ticking clock might be, "I have to get rid of her within the year," or, better yet, "I have to get rid of her by Wednesday."

   This is especially good if it is Tuesday afternoon and you are the only guy in the room with a pocket full of pennies.

   These boats exist, believe me. Once you begin hunting, you will discover many more derelict vessels than you ever thought possible. Most, of course, will be awful buys for one reason or another. But it will be immediately apparent to you that there are plenty of "possibles" out there—too many to count—right in your own backyard.

   The trick is to find the one with the ticking clock, and be there at the right time in the right place when the deal goes down. This can be done but it isn't easy. There can be "many a slip between the cup and the lip" as they say.

   I watched a Gallant 52 that was for sale for $150,000 and could be purchased for $120,000 cash. I watched it for years, sitting forlornly in the back of a decrepit shipyard. I found out the owner's name and telephone number and bided my time before calling him. Then, from boatyard gossip, I learned a wonderful thing (at least from my perspective): leaves had blown into the cockpit and stopped up the cockpit scuppers. When the boat cover had blown off years ago, the cockpit had partially filled up and then started draining into the bilge. This had, of course, eventually drowned the engine. Then all the oil flowing out of it had ruined the entire teak-and-holly interior.

   Perfect!

   She was a solid spec-buy at $50,000. My information was that the owner had been informed about all of the above. But alas, he had not been. Maybe someone had been informed, but not him. Thus, he was surprised and outraged at my call, dumbfounded at my news, and horrified at my pitiful offer.

   He hung up while swearing at me.

   I tried a couple of times to reestablish contact and rapport, and failed each time. I wrote him numerous letters with how to contact me, but nothing worked. Later, I heard he'd visited the boat and sadly confirmed all I'd told him.

An acquaintance of mine ended up with the boat—for 42 grand, a most excellent buy.

Win some, lose some.

Communication

In order to "get lucky" and buy a boat for pennies on the dollar, your fellow human beings need to know you are in the market. The more of them who know, the better your chances are of finding that dream boat.

The first thing to do is tell your friends you are interested in buying a boat. Studies have shown that there are only "six degrees of separation" between you and the president of the United States. Or, if you needed to get an important message to him you could give that message to someone who would give it to someone—and six people later, the president would have it.

There's only one president. Lucky for you, there are thousands of very good, very cheap boats for sale. All you have to do is find them.

There are far fewer than six people between you and your dream boat. This is both comforting and frustrating at the same time.

So tell your friends, family, and co-workers that you are interested in buying a "fixer-upper" sailboat. (Don't mention the fact you're going to sail it across the Pacific or they will have you committed to the loony bin.)

Put up notices at the local laundromat even if it is in rural Indiana. (Many a yacht is pining for the sea behind those silos. All you have to do it is find it!)

You have to get the word out. The cheapest way to do that is: 1. Word of mouth. Tell people you are interested in buy a cheap "fixer-upper" sailboat. 2. The Internet. Post to various boat-related blogs in your area. 3. Use the telephone. Call up key people in your area to notify them you are new to the local marine scene and are in the market for a sailboat. 4. Visit shipyards, marinas, and yacht clubs in the area. Again, the more people who know you are in the market for a cheap boat, the more likely you are to find one with a ticking clock.

The First Concrete Step

There is probably some sort of "used boat trader" magazine in your area. Buy a current copy and toss it in your desk drawer. Then find a six-month-old copy and pore over it with a magnifying glass.

These "boat trader" mags are usually a good place to sell outboards and runabouts. Not too many sailboats in your category will be listed. But those that are listed are of particular interest, because the owner isn't using the traditional yacht broker route to sell his vessel. Why? Probably because there's something odd about it or them. Either might be good for you.

Let's say you circle an ad that says, "Westsail 32 sailboat. Diesel engine. GPS. New mainsail. $40,000 firm."

Call up the number and very carefully ask, "Is that Westsail 32 still for sale?" Chances are they will say no. You are SOL (shit out of luck). But don't be too sad. The reason the boat sold is because it was worth something. You don't have anything—or much of anything. So it wasn't really a possibility for you anyway.

If, however, the person says, "Yeah, it sure as hell is—right in the middle of the backyard. But Ralph isn't home right now. He's at the doctor's. He drives for FreightCon and it is hard on his arteries. Anyway, you can try back in a couple of hours."

During the conversation, don't mention any detail you don't have to. Don't mention where you saw the ad, the $40G price tag, etc. Don't give her your number. Tell her you "may" call back later. In essence, don't act too interested.

Now, go to your stack of *"Cruising World"* magazines (yes, I'm the editor-at-large of this fine publication and can say without prejudice it is the best of its type in the world.) and check out any used boat ads for Westsail 32s. Ditto, check out the WWW (World Wide Web) and such sites as www.boats.com (which my buddy John Burnham is involved with).

There are various blogs and websites that are solely focused on the Westsail 32. You will quickly learn it is sometimes called the Wetsnail 32—by certain snotty marine journalists like myself. Regardless, this traditional design is one of the safest and best-constructed boats ever mass produced.

It is easy to learn its design lineage—from Colin Archer to William Atkin to Westsail in California.

Many people think the Westsail 32 to be an ideal boat for a young couple to leisurely circumnavigate aboard. I certainly do.

At the same time, it is fairly useless as a club racer or daysailer—it is intended to survive the North Sea, not dash around the buoys on Wednesday nights. Thus, a lot of people don't want a Westsail 32.

But you do.

Of course, all vessels eventually develop some problems. The sites that cater to Westsail 32 owners will have lots of in-depth discussions about these problems.

Let's return to the Boat Trader ad for a couple of minutes. The price might have been firm six months ago—but it is a safe bet it isn't as firm now as it was then. And we know (or suspect) the wife isn't too pleased with having it take up the backyard and Ralph is a working guy with health problems.

Now if I were going to write that ad, I'd say, "Westsail 32. Hull #123, 1968. Cutter rigged. Perkins 4-107. Monitor vane. Self-tailers. Garmin GPS. Furuno radar. 45# CQR. $40,000, firm."

The ad you saw in the boat trader wasn't (perhaps) written by a knowledgeable sailor. It doesn't read like most of the ads in *"Cruising World"* or on the WWW.

Ralph probably isn't an experienced sailor. He may be a greenhorn. Perhaps he has never sailed the boat. If the engine hasn't run for a couple of years, that makes the whole boat worth a lot less.

Perhaps Ralph had a dream to sail around the world—and that dream was never realized. Perhaps Ralph isn't fully over his dream. Perhaps he now realizes that he will never personally accomplish it, but has not quite relinquished all the emotional baggage associated with his dream. Perhaps he'd like to help someone else accomplish that—even if that someone can't be him.

Maybe that someone is you.

Possible? Yes. Worth checking out? Yes.

Note: We're going to talk about karma a bit later. But we have to take a brief time out and talk a tad about morals.

The best possible way to get to sea—and the quickest—is to have people help you. Ralph is not the enemy, nor should he be ripped off. Your job as a boat buyer isn't to fuck Ralph out of his boat—but rather to find out if Ralph needs to get out from under his boat, and if you can benefit at the same time.

I purchased *Wild Card* for $3,000 from New York Johnny (a.k.a. John Longhi) in 1989. I'm still friends with him in 2011. I regularly send him emails about our travels. He currently lives in Viet Nam with his new wife and young son.

The point I'm trying to make: I feel wonderful about *Wild Card*—and New York Johnny does too. He constantly refers to *Wild Card* in emails as "my boat." That's cool. She was his boat—and still is in his heart.

He could have sold her to someone else—and, for whatever reason—sold her to me.

I appreciate it.

If John had ended up hating me in the process—I wouldn't be nearly as happy and proud of *Wild Card* as I am.

I once sold a business and told the buyer during the closing, "I've failed if you are not happy with this purchase five years from now." Five years later they graciously dropped me a note and reassured me about the wisdom of their decision to purchase.

My friend Steve on the Hans Christian 40 named *Oz* used to own a far more modest boat in the Carolinas. One foggy day, he came across a yacht in distress just outside the inlet. (Its engine had stopped.) He towed the yacht a long way against the wind and admired the heavy displacement double-ender while doing so. Years later, while negotiating for Oz over the telephone, the seller suddenly blurted, "Hey! Are you the guy who towed me in the Carolinas years ago?"

Steve had no idea he was trying to buy the very same boat he'd admired before—from the very same fellow. The owner immediately named his bottom line—and Steve accepted. They became fast friends. The old owner often drops in on Steve as he circumnavigates. It is (and was) a win-win-win for everyone involved.

The point I'm trying to make is—don't allow the buy/sell thing to become adversarial. The guy that can help you most is the guy with the boat. Don't piss him off—befriend him.

Both of you will benefit.

Every month a new Boat Trader magazine comes out. Buy it and toss it into your desk drawer—and then study the six-month-old one with a magnifying glass.

Yacht Brokers

This is what you'll become if you deal with these guys—broker and broker.

Seriously, most boats are worth something and are sold through a yacht broker. The boat that the pocket-full-of-pennies buyer is looking for isn't worth anything because it has a major problem. Brokers avoid such boats.

I don't recommend buying a boat through a broker if you are on extremely short funds. However, I do recommend communicating with them. They can be extremely useful on a number of fronts: helping you determine a good deal, informing you which boats are selling and why, and explaining the local intricacies of proving title, etc.

The very best information they can give you is contact information on the boats they wouldn't touch with a ten-foot-pole—the exact same boats you are trying to find, the ones with major, deal-stopping problems.

Remember: You aren't looking for the perfect cruising boat. Those cost money. You don't have money. Miracles don't take place every day. However, there are boats with major problems that can't be sold "normally" on the open market at list price because of their major problems.

Eventually, nearly every boat with a major problem gets sold or a ticking clock forces it to be sold.

And you're going to be there—waiting, with your pockets filled with pennies.

So cultivate brokers. Chat 'em up at boat shows and at yacht clubs. Most have the gift of gab—or they wouldn't be in the biz. Flatter 'em a bit. They'll go on and on about dream-boats-for-pennies. Don't interrupt. Listen.

Surveyors

Many surveyors are worth their weight in gold. Most surveyors aren't. A few don't know their ass from a hole in the ground.

Good surveyors know, in advance, where to look for problems with various models and manufacturers. It isn't a secret which models of Beneteau and Bavaria spit off their keels in inopportune places (far at sea, for instance). One year all the Valiant 40s were perfect—and in the next year's model, all of them developed horrible, extensive blistering problems. One well-known boat manufacturer mistakenly purchased brass through-hull fittings rather than bronze ones—and their boats started sinking like stones at eight years of age.

Has (such and such a company) ever made a rudder that doesn't leak water into its core? Or have they ever built a keel that doesn't grin (start separating from the hull at its forward edge)? I dunno. Maybe. But I've never seen it, if they have.

Wild Card is a Hughes 38, built in Canada. While many of the boats Hughes built were excellent, a few were constructed so shoddily that company reps once had to be protected by the Canadian Mounties at a boat show so that previous buyers of their product would not do them bodily harm. (Seawater oozed right through some of the early gunited {fiberglass chopper gun} models.)

Many of the Hughes 38s have balsa core problems, especially in the deck.

They all have rotten wood in their chainplate webs and rotten mast steps as well. All of them. That's why you can occasionally buy a Hughes 38 for under $30,000, when a Swan or Hallberg-Rassy of the same size is usually three or four times that.

A good yacht broker or surveyor knows all of this.

One thing a newbie should realize, however, is that there are different types of surveys. There's a seller's survey, which talks up the boat's value; an insurance survey, which has a different focus; and a buyer's survey, which may (or may not) actually take a serious, in-depth look at the condition of the vessel.

So a vessel that has a "recent survey" which says it is in "Lloyds 100A1" condition—probably isn't.

Even if it is, you can get a vehement survey saying it isn't. Just pay the money to certain surveyors and they sing like songbirds to whatever lyrics you provide.

That said, there are many surveyors who honestly work hard for your dollar and will give you full value for it. I'd hesitate to buy a used boat for $100,000 without having Will Howe of Howe Marine Surveys on St. Thomas take a look at it.

However, if I had a chance to snatch an Islander 36 that had been hit by a ferry amidships for $4,000—I'd take a good long look at it myself and leave the surveyor in his air-conditioned office.

Which isn't to say you don't have any use for a yacht surveyor—you do. Find one and buy him or her a drink. Listen, with obvious adulation. They are the perfect people to tell you what boats have a major problem that makes them unsellable—which is exactly the info you are looking for.

Some of those craft are going to develop ticking clocks—which is when you swoop in.

Shipyards

Each year, hundreds of boats are hauled out for major work. The work is begun (which severely lessens the boat's value) and then the money stops flowing and the project stops progressing.

But the bills don't stop. Storage fees still accumulate, now with interest tacked on to boot.

Virtually every shipyard has a few of these boats that have failed to pay their yard bills. They are then legally seized by the yard and sold.

But most yards make their money by hauling and splashing—and so they need the room these "dead" vessels are taking up. It takes a long time to legally seize them and they'd much rather just have the vessel disappear.

Thus, many yards are extremely cooperative about "sneaking you" info on which boats they want out of the yard and why. Some will even give you the owner's contact info.

Others will require a bit more work. You'll have to stroll the yard and bring some donuts/coffee during their break. Or, after work, follow the yard crew to the nearest bar.

Yard workers are poorly paid and often get no respect. Hang on every word. They will love you.

Large Marinas

Many large marinas have annual auctions of derelict vessels—usually small runabouts and small daysailers.

I know one guy who attended one with $3,000 cash in his pocket—in the hopes of buying a fixer-upper. He did, for $800—and then, to his amazement, purchased two other 20-some foot vessels for an additional $1,200. He fixed these two up a bit and resold them and paid for all the luxury gear aboard the $800 one he'd purchased. Within two years, he was cruising in Mexico aboard a well-found, if modest, pocket cruiser in which he had very little money invested.

Used Gear Places

Within driving distance of you is probably at least one "used boat gear" place that sells just that.

Often, these places have an informal "info" board, which is a great place to learn more about the local "fixer-upper" scene.

Once you buy your boat, of course, you'll be coming back here to buy, sell, and trade. You may as well get to know them now.

The guy behind the counter will know almost every amateur boatbuilder within a hundred miles.

Befriend him.

Backyard Boatbuilders

You probably don't realize that there are dozens of boats being built all around you—but there are, if you live in the US or Canada. All you have to do is find one of 'em and that builder will lead you to the rest.

When I was building *Carlotta* I never met another boatbuilder who didn't both teach me something and save me money.

When I started my boat in Boston, there was a guy who'd already been building a lovely steel boat for a number of years. Forty years later, that same fellow is still building that same boat.

I know—because I drop in on him every decade or so.

And, believe me, this fellow knows a hell of a lot more about where and how to buy marine materials in New England than you or I do. He will be happy to stop and tell you. He's in no rush, we know that. In fact, this guy knows pretty much everything—except how to launch!

Hurricane-Damaged Vessels

As I write this, Hurricane Earl is lashing the Virgin Islands. My home harbor of Great Cruz Bay, St. John, USVI, has dozens of craft driven onto the beach.

Some look awful and aren't, others look fairly good and are severely damaged. But all of them are in a much-altered state compared to what they were yesterday—as are their owners. Each vessel now requires a tremendous amount of blood, sweat, and tears to be lavished on it—as well as money.

Not every owner can—or desires to—unexpectedly put so much time into his vessel.

Thus, these vessels are, potentially, extremely good buys.

There will be three waves of opportunity on hurricane-damaged craft. A number of boats will be sold immediately "as is, where is" on the beach. The best deals usually take place during the first horrible week. The second wave of deals take place six weeks to three months later—when the wreck owner realizes that he is paying, paying, and paying, but his boat isn't getting any closer to the water. The final wave is only apparent if you are tracking a number of "possibles." This is when the insurance companies and banks attempt to wash their hands of the whole money-draining mess. These deals aren't usually as dramatic as Fast Buck but this is when the professionals pick up a year-old Little Harbor 57 for 50 grand or so.

There are three types of post-hurricane buyers: the classic asshole, the professional rehabber, and the amateur sea gypsy.

Let's take the asshole first: He rushes down to the islands, laughs at everyone's misfortune, gets punched in the nose and hated, buys a boat, gets hated some more, tries to fix up the boat—but has a rough road of it. Soon he quits, saying, "Gee, those boaters ain't so nice!"

Don't be one of those guys. I've chased a few down the beach while shaking my fist—and, luckily for us both, was unable to catch them.

The professional comes down and usually has a certain type of boat in mind. For instance, some experienced rebuilders like to fix up race boats and others to fix up cruising boats. He watches and waits, while selecting a dozen or two "likely" prospects. Without making waves, he contacts the owners, commiserates, and offers them an immediate, easy way out from under their unexpected, often traumatic, problems.

Nobody minds the professional if they are usually low-key and sensitive.

We sea gypsies show up—and are appalled at the damage. It truly hurts me to see boats smashed, holed, and sunk on the beach. To me it is like looking at a fatal traffic accident—it seems such a stupid waste.

There are people and boats everywhere that need help—the key is to help them. Don't help them necessarily to buy their particular vessel—just help them because they need help lugging stuff and because it will gain you entrée into their world.

While helping the poor shipwrecked sailors who were bloodied during the hurricane, you will begin to notice many vessels which aren't being salvaged and/or repaired. Ask about them. Study them. Contact their owners.

Big risk, big gain. Lotsa work, big gain. Difficult extraction, big gain.

Don't worry about "the deal" too much. Just get the word out gradually that you're in the market and keep slogging through the water humping damp sail bags. If you help out enough people, the deal will find you.

Strange and wonderful things happen after hurricanes. Hundreds of people helped me after Hugo. A flotilla of three vessels (Bounty, Star, and Johanna) loaded with tools, food, and booze immediately left the Virgins once they had heard we'd been shipwrecked in Culebra.

I'll never forget the sight of them sailing around the point. It was one of the happiest moments of my life and I'm still grateful to each and every person aboard.

Sometimes the right thing to do is just as apparent. After Hurricane Marilyn hit St. John, there were hundreds of boats sunk. Most were raised within the next few months, but one was not. It was—or had been—anchored in Cruz Bay. My buddy Eric owned it, but his house and business had been blown away at the same time. His shattered wife was sitting amid the wreckage of their life and couldn't stop crying. Eric didn't have time to deal with his boat.

But he was a good guy.

She was a good woman.

And the boat needed raising—for the good of the boat, the harbor, and the community.

"I'll raise it for you," I said to him. "No strings, no charge."

I did it with the help of about a dozen other yachties whom I corralled to help.

Eric and I are still friends. "Thanks," was all he could say—and all I expected—when he heard the news *Lydia* was floating once again.

Educate Yourself

Sailing around the world is really all about learning—and using our whole planet to do so. Read all the cruising magazines you can. Pore over *"This Old Boat"* and other marine DIY rags. Check books out of the library. Don't know who Eric Hiscock is? Find out. Ditto Joshua Slocum. Robin Knox-Johnson. Lin and Larry Pardey. Beth Leonard.

Put together a file of clipped magazine articles you'll find useful later and/or at sea.

Begin a collection of nautical books, especially how-to ones. Read all the cruising classics from the Venturesome Voyages of Captain Voss to the latest "I-sailed-around-the-world-during-my-lunch-break-while-sexting-on-my-BlackBerry."

Many boat shows have free seminars. Attend every one, at least for a few moments. (Get to mine early. It was standing room only at the Pacific Strictly Sail show in Oakland.)

Pour over the West Marine or Budget Marine catalog—and drool at the gear-porn. (I write the Fat Tips in the Budget Marine catalog—and you'll get a kick out of 'em, I'm sure. Budget Marine gives me total liberty to say whatever I want—and I do. Right next to a product, I'll have a little box telling you, quite forcefully, why not to buy it and/or not to believe the baloney... amazing!)

Haunt the Internet as well.

Other Boats Are Classrooms

Carolyn and I stroll the docks wherever we go. My idea is that every seasoned craft has something to show me—if I look close enough.

This was easier when I did it with my father back in the early 1950s because each boat was then unique. But even in this "cookie cutter" age, there's often still something to be learned from your neighbor's boat.

If you look casually at *Wild Card* as you stroll by, she looks fairly normal in a shabby way. But if you look closely, there are a dozen "Ah, ha!" things to see: my aft boom topping lift whip, for example; my PVC pipe vents; my 20 cent SSB antenna. Etc.

To study rigging and sail-control systems, it is great to view similar-sized vessels to the one you are interested in.

But I don't always look at yachts. I look at indigenous craft in foreign countries and local fishing vessels even more.

Professional sailors and fishermen are a clever bunch who spend most of their lives at sea. They often come up with clever advancements first. And it is only afterward that Harken or Lewmar pick up on how cleverly the problem was solved.

I'm particularly enamored of fishermen. I grew up amongst them. They are a tough-but-giving bunch. Not only are they out at sea in all kinds of weather year after year, but they often have to work through it—with high loads and death at every hand. They know what they're doing because the crew member who didn't—died last month. The most dangerous profession in the world is commercial fishing. So I inspect each inch of every fishing boat I see. I marvel at their cleverness at running gear under load and keeping the water outside.

I'd rather have dinner with a random commercial fisherman than any investment banker in the world.

Another hint: Big boats are expensive. That's only logical. But what might not be so apparent is that medium-sized boats with optimized storage spaces are the cheapest of all. There's nothing better than buying in bulk in the Third World where it is cheap, and consuming that product in the First World where it is expensive. Or, to put it another way, just before leaving Thailand, we stuff plastic bottles full of jasmine rice in every space available.

Wine is dirt cheap in South Africa.

A five-gallon jug of 151-proof rhum in Madagascar will set you back a mere $18 if you bargain hard, ($20 to $25 if you don't).

Monday Nights

Monday night football can be skipped—use it to assess your progress towards purchasing your dream vessel. How many prospects did you call this week? Where did you visit? Who are you supposed to get back to?

Remember—your voyage has already begun. You have a goal (to sail around the world or across the bay) and you are actively taking steps to accomplish it. You can't lose if you don't give up.

You have to do something every day and consider the Big Picture every week if you want to succeed.

I think of this as PEE: Plan, Execute, and Evaluate.

Boat Shows

Attend at least one a year—three is better. Check out every boat and each piece of hardware, etc. Talk to these boating people. For once, they are your captives. There is an equal amount to be learned from those you agree with and those you don't.

I'm not fond of gaff rigs but that doesn't mean my friend, the designer Paul Johnson, can't teach me a million things about boats. He can and does. But I have to listen to learn—not tell him why I think having heavy, swinging clubs held aloft by strings during severe storms isn't such a good idea.

At any good boat show, you will see a lot of new stuff—such as new anchors, blocks, winches, etc. Check out each one carefully. Listen. Think.

Ninety-nine percent of the new anchors don't work worth a shit—but the brochure sounds good, doesn't it? Don't be fooled. Most of the "new improved" stuff that they say you "have

Fatty signing his books at the Oakland Boat Show

to have" isn't actually found on real cruising boats. You don't need it. You don't want it.

But only by allowing tons of misinformation to wash over you, can you ultimately decide which is BS and which isn't.

Auction

I have a friend called the Reverend Captain Tim. He's so cheap, he refuses to pay entrance fees in foreign countries—claiming he's doing the Lord's work. Hardly!

In any event, he skippered a well-known charter boat for many years and had a little nest egg saved up. So he haunted the Internet in search of the perfect yacht. He didn't want just any yacht, but a fine-quality, classy ride. He wanted to circumnavigate in style!

One day he saw a Stevens 47 about to be auctioned off on eBay. It had two major problems—its engine wouldn't start and its interior had been removed for renovation just before its owner died. Basically, it was an empty hull.

Damn! It was perfect for him. Within half an hour, he was out the door to the airport to see it. Once aboard, he learned that the boat had just been released for sale a few days ago—and would have to be moved (towed, at considerable expense) within ten days.

Then he was amazed to learn that there was a whole lot more equipment that came with the boat that wasn't mentioned in the eBay blurb: for instance, the entire undamaged interior with all its electric and mechanical components. So the boat actually had everything. It all was just sitting in a storage shed instead of the boat.

The new owners knew nothing about boats—only that they cost a fortune to maintain regardless of whether they sailed or not.

No one else had looked at the boat—only the Rev/Cap knew the full scoop.

He purchased her on eBay—just like it was a flower pot. Within the first year, it was worth two or three times what he paid for it.

He's now collecting charts for the Pacific and Indian Oceans.

Hands On

If you are serious about sailing, you should sail as much as convenient aboard other people's vessels—within the bounds of frugality.

Cruising people often need and/or desire crew. There are endless possibilities to share charters, both locally and internationally.

But the easiest and cheapest way to get on the water is often your local yacht club. They usually have local, informal, and hotly contested weekly races, and new eager crew members are in great demand.

You might think, "Oh, I can't do that. I know nothing about racing."

Here's how to reassure yourself: Sit down. Can you do that? Good. Fine. That's wonderful. Now, if I told you to get up and move ten feet and sit back down, could you do that too?

OK, you have all the skills required to be a yacht racer. We need rail-beef—slabs of movable flesh on our windward side to hold our boats flatter, which makes them go faster.

All you have to do is be a nice person, show up when you promise, switch sides when asked—and you will be a popular, sought-after sailor at the club.

After the races (not during), you can ask what the hell happened. And the racers will be happy to tell you why the vessel you were on shudda/cudda/wudda won if only blab-blab-blab hadn't happened.

Yacht clubs are great places to learn how to sail and to meet sailors. Most clubs aren't elitist at all. If fact, if you regularly crew, your status will be higher than many of the millionaire owners.

Even better, you will get to sail on a wide variety of craft. These craft, of course, need to be delivered to various race venues. So offshore crewing opportunities will quickly open up to you if you have the time to invest.

Basically, any sailor can waltz into almost any yacht club in America—and immediately be racing aboard a $100,000 yacht.

It doesn't matter if you're black or white or rich or poor—if you can switch sides and grin at the same time—you are in like Flynn!

The US Power Squadron and the USCG Auxiliary

Both organizations have helped a number of people get into boating over the years. Some groups are a tad military. Most, however, are not. They are as welcoming and friendly as can be.

I took a Safe Boating Course back in the 1960s and I'm still using the information gained to this very day.

Turning Down and Losing the Deal of a Lifetime

Most people assume it will take years to find a mega-boat-for-mini-bucks and are astounded to stumble upon a few "perfect" deals early in the game. This is common. Don't fret to pass the first few "super buys" by. No matter how great the deal is, there will be a better one in the future. The only question is how far in the future.

A number of deals will fall through at the last minute. That's understandable. The important thing isn't to act on every good deal that comes your way but rather to buy an acceptable cruising vessel with the paltry sum of money you have.

If you manage to do so, you have succeeded. If you haven't yet, then it is because you haven't tried hard or long enough.

You can't lose if you don't quit.

Longevity and Networking

The longer you network, the more contacts you make and the easier it is to make even more contacts. The first week or two that you begin telling people you are interested in buying a boat—nothing will happen. But six months down the road, hundreds of people (perhaps thousands) will know you want a boat. And a sizable number of them will know where that boat is, or could be.

The trick—before the boat shows up—is to spend all the time you can learning about the boat and deal, so when it appears, you recognize it as such.

Assessing Yourself

Perhaps now is a good time to take a close look at yourself—your abilities or lack thereof.

I have a lot of energy. I am willing to take risks. I am a hard worker. I have a very wide range of technical skills. I can do a little plumbing, wiring, or carpentry if required. Actually, my woodworking and shipwright skills are pretty good—as you'd expect from living aboard two wooden vessels for long periods of time. I'm an okay shade-tree mechanic—but don't enjoy it much. I can't do any overhead welding—but I can lay a fair bead on horizontal steel if required.

I'm impatient—which is good and bad. It is good because I like to work hard, long, fast and get the job done. It is bad because sometimes I get sloppy. My work is always strong, but often looks like an idiot did it (because that is, alas, true)!

I'm a terrible salesman, but a great gabber. I can schmooze people.

I don't have much use for money, but I occasionally want the things it can buy. I want my boat to be functioning and seaworthy at all times. I don't care if she looks like crap compared to the Camper Nic that is anchored alongside if I know in my own heart she is more seaworthy, better equipped, more capable of going to sea in a blow on short notice.

What are your skills? Can you fix cars? Weld? Work with wood? Run wires? Splice rigging?

Are you young, healthy, and foot-loose? Or are you in your 60s and a tad overweight? All this factors into the deal, you see. A boat with a blown engine is nothing to one guy—and a complete puzzlement to another.

"Wait! Wait!" someone is shouting from the back of the classroom. "How come you've never mentioned working with fiberglass?"

Ah! I'm caught, eh? Oh, well. I've put this off for as long as I thought I could. I guess I'll have to plunge in now.

Working With Dried Snot... er, I Mean, Fiberglass!

Working with dried snot—which is often referred to as fiberglass or glass-reinforced plastic (GRP)—is easy to do technically, but difficult to do physically. Fiberglass dust itches horribly. Trust me on this! Various epoxies (which you'll practically bathe in) are so toxic that huge angry welts will explode out of your skin—bigger and bigger, and worse and worse—with every passing day.

But, as miserable as fiberglass is, it is a very forgiving medium. It is easy to work with. All you have to do is suffer, suffer, and suffer some more.

I didn't know a thing about fiberglass when I purchased *Wild Card*. She had a large hole and crushed area just at the boot top (waterline) on the port side. This area was, after I was done grinding it back to clear glass, three feet high and 12 feet long. (When fiberglass has been crushed or shattered, it looks milky instead of clear as glass. You have to grind it back until the entire patch area is clear and clean.)

Basically, the first thing I did to my new boat was to make a very large hole in it—a huge hole—which I didn't know how to fill.

Luckily, I didn't have to. There was a fiberglass repairman in the yard named Mike Sheen. He was a toxically dusted dude who knew everything there was to know about fiberglass work—that he charged around $80 an hour to do.

I went to him and told him I'd just purchased a boat with a large hole in it and that I was a complete idiot.

"Wait," he said. "Did you just say you were a complete idiot?"

"Yes," I admitted. "Anyone who would buy a fiberglass boat with a large hole in it and does not know how to fix it… well, that's pretty idiotic, isn't it?"

"We agree on something," said Mike with a slight smile.

"So I was hoping you could give me a bit of advice."

"Keep on grinding!" he shouted rudely and walked away.

I ground all that day, and the following day, and the day after.

Once, while passing him by during lunch, I whispered, "I'm still grinding," and he said, "I know you are."

Within the week, he was stopping by twice daily to tell me how to dish the repair, use battens to keep the hull shape, and how to tell if I'd ground back far enough into clear glass. He also told me exactly which weight and type of cloth to use, how to mix and apply my resin—basically, everything he'd learned during his 30-plus- years as a dust monkey.

I worked 28 days from sun up to sun down—and a few nights in the dark with spotlights. The finishing touches were amazing. I marked all the highs and lows, and eventually fart-blocked the highs down by manual sanding. (Fart blocks smell like, well, farts, but they sand down only the high spots and are perfect for the final mirror finish.)

When I was done with the fiberglass repair, I-who-didn't-know-nut'n-'bout-glass a month ago—well, I had to smile. The repair was (and still is, 20 years hence) invisible.

"And if you ever have a choice which side to hit something with, hit it with the side of the repair," Mike Sheen advised. "It's a lot stronger than the other side and only marginally heavier by a few pounds. Good job, Fatty! And the secret?"

"Keep on grinding!" I shouted happily.

The fact is that for every difficult job, there is guy with vast experience in that field who would find it very easy to do. You have to find that person and motivate them to help you. I promised Mike a "down payment" of $350 to start coaching me to do a very complex task that he would have correctly charged me tens of thousands of dollars to do himself. Ultimately, the job came out as good (he said) as he would have done. And it was faster, too, since Mike had years worth of work backed up because of Hurricane Hugo.

I tried to give him the $350 and asked how much more he wanted. He refused my money. I had to force him to take $200—which about made up for all the freebie supplies he'd given me along the way.

There's always an expert. Find him. Follow him. Pay him. Hug him. Kiss him. Thank him.

I'm forever in debt to Mike Sheen of the Independent Boatyard of St. Thomas. He is a prince of a man and I greatly appreciate him helping me reincarnate *Wild Card*.

Thanks again, Mike!

Patience Is a Sailor's Virtue

You probably won't be able to buy your dream boat for pennies within a week of reading this book. Perhaps six months is a better estimate. Many cautious folks spend a year or two before they pounce on that perfect once-in-a-lifetime deal.

But at some point, if you don't give up, an amazing boat is going to seek you out and scream, "Buy me, you farmer, buy me right now!"

Don't panic.

Surveying Small Craft

There is no way I can reveal all the tricks and secrets of surveying a modern small craft in a couple of paragraphs. It would take an entire tome to barely scratch the surface. So I am not going to pretend to do so.

But what I am going to advise is that you take a really, really good in-depth look at the vessel. The fact is that every single problem it has—and probably will have in the near future—is revealed, if you but look and think.

That's strong language about a very important concept so I'm going to say it again: All the problems a boat has, or will soon have, are visible to the eye.

Why are those cracks there in the fiberglass, right next to the chainplates? Are they just surface crazing or stress cracks? Why is one of the chainplates three eighths of an inch higher than the others? Why is there an obvious dimple in the starboard topside, just above the water line? Ah, yes, it is right around the bottom of the forward lower shroud!

Is the deck spongy here? Is that milk-white stain on the rail from the saturated balsa core? Is the keel grinning forward? Are there signs (cracks and/or rust streaks) that the rudder is saturated with sea water? Is the prop shaft bent? Are there nicks in the prop blades?

Are the bulkheads rotten? There is rot in the head and under the galley (if the boat's interior is made of plywood and more than 20 years old). If you didn't find it, look again.

Start at the very bow and go over every inch of the boat with a toothbrush, a bright light, and a magnifying glass. Every inch. On deck, outside, and inside. Why is that stain there? Those cracks? Why is the hull underneath the starboard settee freshly painted and the port is not. Was there a patch or problem there?

This takes a long time. Do it.

Later you can invite a dozen of your best friends over to inspect her as well. And it is seldom wrong to hire a knowledgeable surveyor. But the most important thing you can do before you buy a boat is to carefully, repeatedly, look at it in depth.

Bright lights, reading glasses, and a large magnifying lens help.

Making the Move

Our goal, of course, isn't merely to look at boats or find them. It is to buy one and sail away. Thus, at some point you have to poop or get off the pot.

If the boat has a ticking clock or the owner is truly desperate, now is the time to make your move.

Most owners, by this point, are completely discouraged. Time and time again they've thought they were "out from under" the boat—only to have their hopes dashed.

Make sure you avoid knocking and/or criticizing the boat. Don't do it. Do. Not. Do. It.

Instead, smile. Say you like the boat. And then tell the truth. Sadly, you have hardly any money. If you did, you would give the man the amount of money he is asking. You like the boat. Hell, you love it! You think she is worth it. But you can't afford it.

It is impossible.

You have to walk away—despite the fact you want her, like her, love her, want to sail her across an ocean…

…but that is not to be.

Unless…

    …unless…

        …unless…

If it is hopeless, the guy will have already thrown you out at this point. But if he is still listening to you, there's hope because he is not only listening to you, he's listening to the ticking clock as well.

He desperately wants this to be over with. And you are the only game in town. Now is the time you finally get specific. You have $6,800 in cash, the dented Vespa motor scooter you drove up on, a pair of relatively new Crocs, and a Casio Pathfinder waterproof watch worth $200. Will he take it?

He won't. That's fine. Get him talking about why he bought her, his plans, his dreams. And then tell him the truth again—those are your very same dreams, too. And he is the only man in the universe that can make those dreams come true. Him. For you. Right now!

He might say something like, "Just the life raft is worth $2,000!"

"Fine," you say. "You keep it."

He might name a drastically reduced priced—very much lower but still not within your grasp. This is tricky. You are almost there.

Let's say you can only afford $10,000 max, and he is still asking $30,000—a $20, 000 difference.

Tell him you will take him sailing for two weeks every year, a $4,000 value, for five solid years.

Just keep talking. As long as he's talking, he's going to sell it to you. Once he stops, you're in trouble if he's not handing over the title.

If it all falls through, call him up in a week. And then again in three months. And then a year later. Always be nice. A deal isn't sour until the boat is actually gone—and it ain't gone if the vessel is still for sale.

The normal way "asking price" is negotiated is by "deducting" from it. Let's say you are looking at a Swan 42 (you lucky dog!) for $100,000 and you're willing to pay $75,000 for it. You tell the owner you'd be happy to buy if the bottom is stripped of blisters, $15K; the engine has a valve job, $5K; the very tired main is replaced with a fully battened one, $3K; and the windlass changed, $2K. The owner will claim he hasn't the time to oversee such work. So you graciously offer to waste your time instead of his, if he's reasonable and deducts the cost of getting the boat back into Bristol shape.

This often works, as everyone saves face and gets what they want—or almost. But when the price is super low, this method does not work. This is sad but true.

NEVER TELL THE OWNER OF A BOAT THAT HE PAID $100,000 FOR, THAT HIS BOAT IS ONLY WORTH $5,000. It is like calling him a fool. Don't do it. Instead, agree with him: It is a great boat. It is worth more than you can pay. And you'll happily write him a thank you note every single day for the rest of your life if he sells it to you for the pennies in your pocket.

You have to give the seller a reason to sell it to you. He knows about the ticking clock and how he has to sell it and that you are the only game in town. All he needs is a nudge to sigh resignedly and say, "Well, what the hell… okay!"

Make the seller like you at first, and then love you at the end—only then will you have a decent chance.

Seize the Moment

If your offer has been accepted and you want the boat—act immediately. Give him all the money on the spot if you have it—at the very least a dollar bill to seal the deal.

Move heaven and earth to pay him in full and get the clear title ASAP. He can change his mind. And he will, if his buddies ridicule him for being a dummy.

I repeat: Don't waste a second. Complete the deal. Consummate. Or you may regret it for the rest of your life.

Summing Up

Focus on exactly what you are looking for: a modest boat with a major problem and a ticking clock. The easiest way to find one is through a "boat trader" type magazine that is six months old. Call about all the modest production fiberglass sailboats within. (Ignore all wooden and metal craft unless that's your field of expertise.) Most of the vessels you call about, of course, will have been sold. A few will remain. Ignore the boats with high prices and/or that are in good mechanical shape. Instead, zero in on vessels with a major problem (blown engine, missing rig, smashed skeg, holed, previously sunk, etc) and a ticking clock (must be moved by Friday because expiring lease and imminent divorce loom).

Okay. Let's say you find a Tartan 28, Wetsnail 32, Morgan Outhouse 33, Columbia 28, Cal 25, Flicka 20, Alberg 30, Hughes 38, or a 26-foot Folkboat that has been holed and sunk. You take a long hard look at it and, if your luck is good, it is a true mess. Remember, if the boat were worth anything it would have sold. It didn't and it's not. Bingo!

My first boat, an ancient 22-foot Atkins double-ender that I sailed thousands of miles offshore and lived aboard for many years, cost $200 because it lacked a running engine and had no rig. Even better, it had been used repeatedly as a Chicago gang hangout. That's right, gang-slogans were spray-painted belowdecks and someone had actually defecated in her bilge—just perfect!

Tell the seller exactly the truth. You have no money, only passion, only heart. Logic says you shouldn't attempt to sail around the world. But, hey, it is Your Dream and you can't sleep until you try.

If the seller is telling you that you are a fool and you are wasting his time— that's good. He didn't hang up. He's interested. Great!

Warning: Never get into a "what the boat is worth" debate with the owner. Tell him you love the boat, that it is the boat of your dreams. Tell him it is you that is worthless, not the boat. Oh, how deliriously happy you'll be with her varnished tiller in your calloused hand.

People who buy boats are dreamers. You're a dreamer, aren't you? Well, so is the seller. And, even if his dream is in tatters, he still has the ability to assist you in yours. So gently offer him the opportunity, as often as it takes.

Tenacity is the key. You can't (and won't) lose if you don't give up. Your dream boat is out there waiting for you right now, and the only thing standing between you and it, is the hard work required to locate it.

Break Out That First Bottle Of Champagne!

Once you are a boat owner, you are on your way! The boat is the foundation upon which your dream of sailing rests. Up until purchasing the boat, it was all smoke and mirrors, all theoretical. Now, it is not. The boat is proof.

You now have a boat. Never doubt your decision to buy. You did the right thing. And that's that.

Yes, you're a dreamer—and you are going to accomplish your dream. Why? Because you are a "doer" as well as a dreamer.

You bought the boat, didn't you?

Pinch yourself!

You're a yachtsman!

The champagne, no matter how cheap, will taste wonderful.

Carolyn raises a glass on the bow of Wild Card.

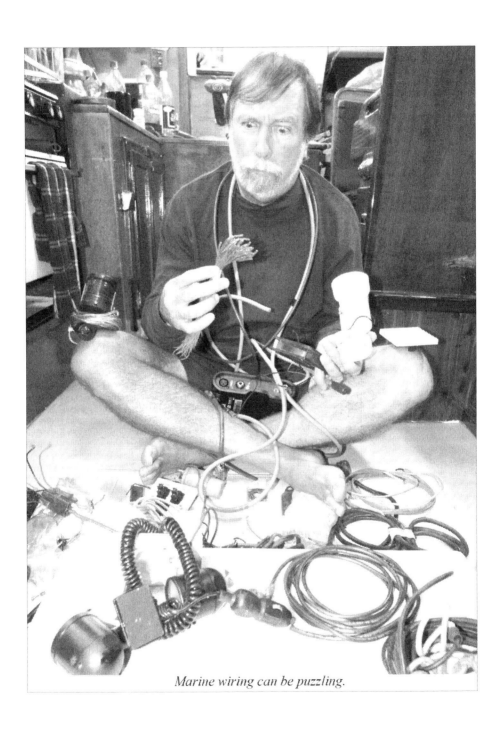

Marine wiring can be puzzling.

Section II

Outfitting

I cannot tell you how to fix the major problem on the boat you just purchased because I do not know what that problem is. But there are people who do. You need to get in touch with them ASAP via phone, email, Skype, letter, video-gram, etc.

Someday, perhaps, I'll write a thick tome called "Yacht-habbing with Food Stamps." Until I do, you'll just have to make do with the dozens of "construct, rebuild, repair, spruce-up-your-yacht" books that are out there.

Almost all fiberglass boats can be repaired. One clever-but-broke fiberglass-sniffer named Dusty in the Caribbean purchased a 41-foot vessel that had just had its bottom/keel/rudder ripped off on a BVI reef. He stashed the almost-new boat in a disused corner of the boatyard, figuring he'd strip it for its gear when he got the time. A few years later, an identical charter boat caught fire and had its deck/cockpit completely destroyed. He also purchased her for peanuts, and then sliced-and-diced them back together into "one boat with two titles," as he put it. Then he sold it for mega-bucks. (A project like this takes major experience. Such a crazy engineering challenge isn't for most of us.)

The key to real-world learning is, simply, to ask someone who really "knows his shit"—a guy like Mike Sheen or Dusty, who snorts polyester resin on a daily basis.

There are numerous sites like the Cruiser's Forum on the web (www.cruisersforum.com) where you can post intricate technical marine questions. The good news is that you will get answers from very knowledgeable people, but alas, also people who don't know what they are talking about.

Phrase your questions carefully. I always answer specific questions that indicate forethought—and skip the dumb ones, "Hey, guys, what kinda sail control systems are best?" If the questioner doesn't have the time to tell me exactly what he wants to control on what size/type boat, then I don't have the time to answer him.

I posted a simple question about prop tip clearance (how close the spinning blades can be to the hull) and immediately received a very clear reply from a marine engineer and a retired yacht designer—both of which were spot-on. (Yes, I got a dozen other responses which varied between poor and worthless, but that is the reality of the web.)

The reality is that no one will work for free—nor should you ask them to. But, that said, people do know a lot of stuff and are often perfectly willing to share their knowledge, if they genuinely like you and think you are diligently putting it to good use.

I help people all the time. But I quickly realize when some people are "posing" questions only to amuse themselves. They really aren't going to do anything to their vessels—just sort of erotically dreaming about what it would be like to do so.

This form of mental masturbation is fine for them. But it is a waste of my valuable time. I've got a very full life to live, and a finite span to do it in. So I let them down once I realize they are dreamers-only, gently at first and then more firmly if need be.

If the boat workers that you are asking for advice know you are using it daily, they will help you. You may have to pay them a few pennies or buy them a couple of after-work drinks. That's fair. Of course, you can't abuse their kindness. You have to be considerate and appreciative. But it is amazing who will help you if you are in a righteous jam, confused, and ask forthrightly.

Early in the building of *Carlotta*, I got stumped in the middle of its lofting. I didn't know what to do, and couldn't puzzle out the answer from the dozen books on lofting at the Boston Public Library.

So I called up one of the most prestigious design firms in the world and asked to speak with John Alden of Alden Design. He was, needless to say, in a meeting. "Tell him it is a call from the crew of the schooner *Elizabeth*."

A few moments later, John Alden was on the line. I knew I only had seconds to make my spiel. I told him I'd grown up on the lovely, very speedy *Elizabeth*, one of his family's Malabar-type series built in 1924. I said that I was 19 years old, eager but dumb, and building a 36-foot 20,000 pound ketch. And then I laid out my lofting query as concisely as possible. He immediately answered without hesitation and then we chatted for a while. Before he hung up he said, "If you get stumped again, Fatty, give me a call. Tell my secretary I said to put you through, that you're the kid building a boat in Southie. I'll help when I can. Good luck."

I only called him twice more. He was always civil and extremely helpful both times I did.

It took a little chutzpah to make that call but it reinforced my opinion that boaters always help boaters if they have a righteous cause and are working hard to achieve it.

The key to fixing the Major Problem is to begin. You will never fix it if you don't begin. Yes, procrastination is the "key to flexibility" as they say. But thinking and being flexible do not get the job done. Only hard work gets the job done. We learn by attempting to do something—and hitting a brick wall. That's the only way a layman can tell where (and what) the brick wall is—by hitting it. Let's say there's a hole in the side of the boat. It seems daunting, but really isn't. First, find someone who knows what they are doing, to expertly guide you. Second, begin grinding day after day to show them (and yourself) that you are going to progress regardless of the difficulty or discomfort of the itchy-bitchy task. Then stop, think, consult, and resume.

I have a friend who is a genius. He is ten times smarter than me. But his life is a complete and utter mess because, while he thinks of wonderful ways of organizing his room, he never actually picks up the soiled laundry on the floor.

Effective people do things. The "doing" part is what gets things done.

It almost doesn't matter where and how you dive in. Once you begin, you start to learn. You realize you are on the wrong track. You start again and this time you're on the right track and you know it.

The key to life is to begin. Don't be a spectator—a person who watches life slip away. Be a doer—a person who makes stuff happen.

Or, as my wife Carolyn puts it, "If you want to get lucky, work hard!"

Common structural problems with boats are: rudders delaminating, keels loosening up, bulkheads coming adrift, rotting mast steps, engine beds, hull or deck core problems, etc.

Many times it is a combo: engines can seize up at the same time rigs fall down.

All of these are major, major problems. I won't deny that or pretend they are not. But all of them can be fixed with a little (borrowed) expertise, a lot of sweat, and a judicious sprinkling of money.

Make sure that you don't initially spend your money on fancy doodads you might use some day. Spend 100 percent of your precious pennies on fixing the major problem and addressing your immediate strength and safety issues.

You can always buy the fancy doodads later.

You will hear me stress the phrase strength and safety often. That's because it is the priority—not new curtains and matching cockpit seats.

The first thing to do is make sure your hull is seaworthy. It must remain watertight in all conditions encountered.

Focus on solving the Major Problem first. Once this is accomplished, you're back where you would be if you'd have had enough money to buy a proper boat.

Once the hull is a hull and the boat is a boat, you can pat yourself on the back. You've come a long way, baby. You used to dream about being a boat owner, a sailor, and a yachtsman and now you is one, dude!

Break out the second bottle of champagne, take a brief bow, and then get back to work.

Prioritize

I'm a big fan of Mick Jagger and the Rolling Stones, who know that "you can't always get what you want…but if you try some time… you might find…you get what you need!"

This is exactly how a poor man outfits a small vessel to sail the world.

Up until now, within these pages, I've often been advising you to accept less—less crap in your life, less boat, less gear, etc.

But our goal this time is as lofty and large as they get: We want your boat to be the safest, strongest, most well-found vessel out there. We can skimp on cosmetics, electrical doodads, exotic sails, wireless-remotes for the auto-pilot—but we cannot (or, more accurately, should not) skimp on structural integrity and offshore safety.

I believe that *Wild Card*, my shoddily constructed, $3,000 boat, is currently more seaworthy and capable than the $600,000 yachts that surround her. Okay, she looks like crap. Okay, she is not nearly as convenient nor as comfortable. Okay, she doesn't have much room. But when push comes to shove during an offshore gale, she does just fine. Why? Because I prepared her (during the rebuild phase) to survive difficult conditions, and I outfitted her to do so as well.

One of the best reasons I recommend not spending too much money on your boat is so you can afford to equip it in a safe and seaman-like manner.

Nothing in these pages that I've already said or will say should be construed as encouraging anyone to go to sea in any craft unprepared for the conditions it will encounter.

My goal is exactly the opposite—to encourage all offshore sailors to hold themselves to a much higher standard than most $600,000 yacht owners do and to realize that everything that happens to their vessel is their fault.

Huh?

What do I mean by that? I mean that if your mast falls down or your engine blows up or your hull comes apart—for any reason—it is your fault, the captain's fault.

This acceptance is key to longevity upon the sea.

There are no excuses at sea. You can't blame the designer because you decided to go to sea in that particular vessel—which might have been intended as a daysailer on a Midwestern lake. You can't blame your builder if your stem cracks, for the very same reason. Diesel engines seldom just "blow up" or stop working. It's because they didn't have their cooling water changed or their exchanger acid-etched... and so are running a tad hot... and then you pick up a semi-floating plastic bag... which allows the engine to get too hot... and the alarm wire is chafed... damn, you were going to fix that... and then the engine seizes up as solid as a brick.

It is your fault, the captain's at fault for everything that goes wrong.

Everything!

Sailors pack their own parachutes, so to speak.

If you are hit by a meteor from outer space, well, as far as I'm concerned, you should have been looking up, pal.

There are no excuses. Everything falls upon the skipper's shoulders. Every. Single. Thing.

So, at the very outset, we need to decide a number of important things.

Intended Use

What are you going to use the boat you just bought for? Day sailing? Sin-or-swim cruises with the local ladies? Coastal work? Marina-to-marina? Offshore? Storm-sailing in the higher lats?

For the sake of this book, we're going to assume that you are intending to slowly and carefully circumnavigate this planet east-to-west during the proper seasons.

That's an audacious goal—but it is achievable.

One of my iron-clad rules: Be in the right ocean at the right time. When I cross the Pacific or the Atlantic or the Indian Ocean, I'm confident my vessel can handle anything Mother Ocean throws at it because I'm transiting in the correct season.

I do not believe that *Wild Card* could necessarily survive an extreme winter gale in the Atlantic, nor would I ever expect her to.

But a leisurely "toddle" downwind across the Pacific, Indian, and Atlantic Oceans is relatively easy. (Just don't go racing with those Kiwi fools on the South Island or join those suicidal Wednesday night racers in Cape Town!)

Level of Luxury Desired

There is a dangerous trend developing: Husbands desiring to circumnavigate with their less-than-enthusiastic wives are telling those wives that they can sail around the world without sacrificing comfort or getting into major storms—that they can have their cake and eat it too.

Bullshit.

First off, boats—no matter how lavish—are uncomfortable at times. The trick isn't to pretend this isn't so but to realize that the ultimate pay-off in freedom, leisure, and enjoyment is so vast that you will gladly suffer though the minor, seldom-occurring inconveniences of shipboard living with ease.

This concept of "never having to go through storms" if you are clever and have the right equipment—is equally wrong.

While it is true that we have much better weather forecasting than we used to, storms still exist and, if you sail long and far enough, you will encounter one. We go through, on average, about four or five gales per year, only one of which is uncomfortable. I've only wondered if I'd see the dawn three times in 50 years of sailing. All three were in severe gales with opposing ocean currents.

That's not too bad, statistically, is it?

I've been closer to death a lot more often in cars than boats.

But we *Wild Carders* know storms are out there and we expect to get in them. In fact, as the storm approaches, we welcome it. We embrace it. We enjoy it.

Gales can be quite enjoyable. What an awesome, immense, awe-inspiring power! What a privilege to see Mother Ocean in a frisky, grand mood!

But I digress.

The point I am trying to make is that you can't have it all offshore and shouldn't expect to—especially if you are on a limited budget.

Carolyn and I started-off as teenagers aboard *Corina*. Our first vessel was a small 22-footer. She had a flathead gasoline engine called a Utility Four which occasionally ran if it wasn't damp—and it was almost always damp. She had one car battery that took forever to charge with the Utility's generator (this was long before alternators). Our running lights were kerosene, as were our cabin lights. We had no VHF, just an RDF (Radio Direction Finder) which received WWV time-ticks that we needed for our trusty family sextant. Our main nav tool was our magnetic compass, which we religiously swung each year to keep our deviation card up-to-date. We had a two- burner alcohol stove—perfect for repeatedly burning off Carolyn's eyebrows. We carried 15 gallons of fresh water, which was manually pumped. We had no dodger, bimini, roller furler, auto-pilot or windvane, outboard, SSB, etc.

But the gimbaled kerosene lamps cast enough romantic light to make love by—and we wandered hither and yon for many years and thousands of miles under those primitive-but-wonderful conditions.

You don't need much to live, love, and smile.

But, of course, your boat can be as complicated or as basic as you desire. Just don't forget: Every decision has a consequence and a cost.

Wild Card has a lot of safety equipment aboard. She is extremely weight sensitive. We both agree we don't need to lug around more weight, to put it mildly. Thus we don't have refrigeration because its weight (not only the unit, but the weight of the additional batteries) and expense.

Carolyn and I have gone our whole adult lives without ever having refrigeration.

We've survived—some would even say we've prospered.

Do you want refrigeration aboard? Fine. You can have it. But it will cost you time, money, aggravation, and weight. I don't need a cold beer that bad. And I'd much rather have the five anchors and seven rodes I carry aboard instead. Not only have I saved my vessel many times because of them—I've saved other people's vessels as well.

Having refrigeration never saved anyone's life.

Refrigeration isn't a "strength and safety" issue. And this is where a poor person has to focus first.

We don't have a watermaker because we don't think they are reliable yet. They will be, hopefully, soon. But right now, our friends spend more time tinkering with (and sending back) their units than we do lugging our water jugs.

We can sail the world for an entire year on what some of our friends have spent on their watermaker during the last year.

Of course, I won't be presumptuous and tell you what level of luxury is right for you. I don't know. I can't say. But I can say that, if you have a limited amount of money, you have to spend that money on strength and safe issues initially. Later, you get such things as flashy captain's hats and matching cocktail napkins with your yacht's name printed upon.

Size Matters

…ask any honest woman.

Oops.

Seriously, large boats cost a lot more to buy, repair, outfit, and sail. There is no getting around this. If you are over 50 years old and have a 40-plus-foot boat, you will need a dependable anchor windlass and 200 feet of galvanized chain. If you are 32 years old and sail aboard a 32-foot boat—you might not.

I sailed around the world the first time without an anchor chain. So can you. But now I'm older—and deeply in love with my toe-operated Maxwell windlass.

Large boats are, comparatively, large headaches.

Plus, there is a lot of cheap gear floating around for a 28-footer—but very little free gear floating around for a 68-footer!

Good News

Because you have a boat, you are now a member in good standing of the marine community. That's all it takes. You might have your project in the backyard, true, but the word will soon get out. That some "nut" down the block is rebuilding a boat similar to the Ark because he thinks the second flood is coming with global warning.

People will start coming around—talking boats. Some of them will be a regular Jack Tarr, with seaweed for hair and a marlinspike on every finger. This is great because these are exactly the people you need to network with to get what you need for your vessel free. (Notice I didn't say want?)

Consider Two-fers

Two-fers, items that serve a double duty, can be vitally important on a small vessel.

Can your boat hook also function as a fish gaff? Your fenders as a swim ladder?

Wouldn't it be easy, while building the navigation table, to incorporate some mounting holes for the steel workshop vise you keep in the bilge?

Example: I stopped in the middle of putting up *Wild Card*'s main bulkhead to mount some emergency rudder gudgeons on my transom. Then I "pre-scribed" all the parts of laminated rudder (even drilling holes for the pintles that ended up tied to the gudgeons with a sack of nails and bolts so they couldn't get lost) into the bulkhead and settee plywood.

So now, if I ever need a spare rudder on *Wild Card* I can just grab my sabre saw, flip on the inverter, follow the heavy pencil lines, slap on some epoxy, pound in some small bronze boat nails which will act as micro-clamps, bolt on the pintles—and get steering fast!

This costs nothing—not even any weight. No, I haven't needed it in more than 20 years and hope I never will. But it is there, already and planned, just waiting to be activated by possible necessity.

Why not carry an extra rudder? Why not carry important wooden parts of your boat disguised as unimportant wooden parts of your boat? Because no one has ever thought of it?

What's the expression: A word to the wise is sufficient?

Make a List

This is the fun part: Make a multi-tiered list of all the stuff you need to launch, sail, coastal cruise, sail offshore, and, ultimately, circumnavigate aboard your boat (see appendix).

My first, off-the-top-of-my-head list went something like this:

Anchors, rodes, windlass
Diesel engine
Sails
Dinghy, oars, lifejackets
Batteries

But it wasn't long before I started adding such items as:

Downwind poles
Storm trysail
Monitor wind vane
Electric autopilot
Dodger
GPS
VHF
Depth meter

And, once we really got serious about circumnavigating:

Paratech sea anchor
Gale-rider
Life raft with survival gear
Jimmy Cornell's World Cruising books
Charts
EPIRB
SSB
Outboard for dinghy
MPS with sock
Anemometer
Spear gun

The reason you need a list—on both paper and in your head—is because you are going to constantly come across one item while looking for another.

You should mark up your Budget Marine catalog (free, in both print and digital versions) extensively—not because you are ever going to buy anything from them or any retail marine supply store—but because you have to know the retail cost of a bronze seacock is $118 in order to snatch one up for $4.

More Crazy, Demented Hints

I do not believe in magic, voodoo, hot-stone treatments, aroma-therapy, or any of that New-Age crap. I mean, really—am I going to run out and pay good money to stick my feet in an aquarium so "doctor fish" can nibble/eat off the skin poisons? Not likely, pal.

Nor do I believe in karma in the mystical sense.

But I do believe in karma as a practical, everyday practice to make this earth a better place and to directly benefit there from.

I've already mentioned Alaska Jim. He sold everything, bolted to New Zealand, purchased a boat, and began cruising Tonga along with us. The only problem was, his engine was only running erratically and thus he had no way to charge his battery to run his lights, radio, and GPS.

I had an extensive collection of solar cells on my boat—including one that I had paid $1,200 for many years before. It still worked perfectly. And it was bolted through my cabin top, just forward of the mast. It wasn't the money that made me hesitate—it was those damn holes. Finally, I couldn't take it any longer.

"Carolyn-honey," I said. "Could you mix me up some epoxy, please?"

Then I grabbed a crowbar, pried that solar cell right off the deck, and carried it over to Jim's boat.

"But," he spurted. "I can't take this!"

I looked him right in the eye and told him the God's honest truth. "Don't be silly, Jim. This is nothing. If I gave you one of these-a-here items once a week for the next year—it won't come close to matching the value of stuff I've been given by other boaters down through the years. Half the stuff on *Wild Card* isn't mine, not really... not fully. I'm just holding it for awhile before I pass it along."

Please don't think I'm a nice guy. I'm not, particularly. But what goes around, comes around.

If you give stuff away, you can, and will, receive stuff in return. Maybe not right away or in the same coin. But for every action, there is a reaction.

If you hug and help people, you are going to get a lot of hugs and help in return.

If you don't, you won't.

It is as plain as the nose on your face.

Perhaps this is why so many wealthy people are so bitter—they've never extended their hand, so they've never had a hand extended to them.

Carolyn is much wiser than me. She summed this up nicely to our young daughter as she was growing up. "In order to get a friend, you have to be a friend."

Exactly.

For a poor man on a limited budget to buy, outfit, and sail a small vessel around this large planet—well, it is going to take a hell of a lot of help from hundreds of people (many of them black and/or Muslim, and surviving on 80 cents a day) for this to happen.

We couldn't have relaxed in the Philippines if all the local fishermen hadn't assured us that they were watching our boat 24/7 and would not allow anything bad to happen to it.

Fishermen are often our protectors. In Sudan, I happened to have some extra cordage and gave it to an elderly fisherman. He promptly stood up, walked over to a local vender, and got him to reduce the price of the veggies we were buying by half.

Ditto Becko, the pearl carver of Polynesia. Before we knew who or what he was, we gave his handsome son a little stuffed toy. To repay the favor, he custom-carved us two giant black pearls!

I sail around the world knowing that people are going to help me almost every step of the way—because, every step of the way, I'm attempting to help them.

Some cruising yachts have a "no locals aboard" rule. I almost have an "only locals aboard" rule.

We reap what we sow.

I don't sail around the world to observe it—but to joyously participate in it. In order to be showered continuously by good luck—we have to deserve it.

This is a tiny little blue-ball-in-space we live on. We have to share. We're all brothers. Ultimately, we'll all succeed or fail as one big family. Greed is both small-time and short-term.

Tomorrow is going to be a beautiful day. Let's enjoy it together.

Fatty with Becko, the pearl carver, and his wife, Janice, on Wild Card in Polynesia

A perfect example of how this "what goes around, comes around" karma works within the cruising community took place just days before we sent this book off to the printer. We were cruising Greece, got hit by a 45-knot meltemi (local gale), and ripped our 12-year-old, 70,000-plus-mile jib to shreds.

We didn't want to order a new jib from Lee Sails of Hong Kong because of the high import duties in Europe. Luckily, we had another (almost-but-not-quite-forgotten-about) headsail stowed under the forepeak—a giant 155 percent genoa given to us by Ronnie and Connie Hobbs on *Old Crow* (whom we'd helped on a number of occasions in the Caribbean after Hurricane Hugo). This allowed us to continue sailing westward. But the genoa was a tad too large to carry to windward in winds over 14 knots.

Luckily, Jimmy and Caroline of *Blue Moon* just happened to be passing by Milos, Greece, and heard of our plight. We'd both helped each other out in a dozen ways while crossing the Indian Ocean together in 2010—especially when they had "fried" their batteries on the way to Aden, Yemen, by charging them at 19 volts for a week (faulty voltage regulator). Anyway, they'd just been given an almost brand new (smaller, thankfully) headsail that was useless to them because it was three feet longer than their forestay. But it fit the loftier *Wild Card* perfectly.

Fatty holds what is left of his torn jib.

The reason we'd stopped in Milos was to visit with our Turkish friends, Selim and Nadire of *Ekip*. They'd wanted to introduce us to the King of Ouzo, a wonderful Greek sailor whom we affectionately dubbed "Papa Gosh" because he was, gosh, so nice!

Papa Gosh had been friends with Selim's deceased father who had told him to "watch out" for Selim—a job he took seriously. We all had a great time cruising the Cyclades together. We'd previously helped Selim with some technical issues concerning the new boat he was having built to circumnavigate aboard. When Papa Gosh heard we needed a new headsail, he immediately dropped off a 130 percent, genoa from a previous boat he'd owned.

Thus, a few days after ripping our jib, we had three almost-new sails (about $6,000 worth) aboard *Wild Card*—a 110 percent, a 130 percent, and a 155 percent genoa! All for free, without a penny being spent. Not only that—

everyone who had donated a sail had done so happily—glad to be able to both help us out and free up some space aboard their vessels. It was a win, win, win for all concerned.

And we were all—Jimmy, Caroline, Ronnie, Connie, Selim, Nadire, Papa Gosh, and us—only doing what we should be doing, which was unselfishly helping out our fellow sailors in their time of need.

In a sense, these three sails were my pay-back for crow-barring off that solar cell for Alaska Jim in Tonga, many years before.

Regardless, we split from Milos ASAP as we'd heard other free sails were headed our way and we didn't want to be any more bow-down than we already were! "Let's get outta here before we drown in jibs!" I quipped to Carolyn as she catted up our anchor.

Odd Items

Once the word is out that you are a righteous dude who "lacks excessive funding," you'll be showered with strange marine gear. Aunt May will lug over a tiny Danforth dinghy anchor—the same week Uncle Lou slides that 75 pound CQR off the bed of his pick-up.

One will be too small for your 38-footer and the other too big. Don't sweat it. Say, "Perfect!" and give them a big hug. Take the freebee knowing that, somewhere at exactly this moment, there's a guy accepting an anchor that doesn't fit his boat but does fit yours.

Some day you are going to bump into each other and exchange anchors—and everyone, and their relatives, will be extremely happy.

One day, a fire truck momentarily pulled into the yard where I was building *Carlotta*, realized its mistake, and roared off to the nearby fire. But one of those firemen was a part-time lobsterman named Joe Hinke who returned and befriended us in a million ways. First off, he was an inventor, so he loved to make strange contraptions to use during various construction phases. Some of them were useless, sure, but most of them were quite useful—and a few were priceless.

Modern fire departments use a lot of high tech rope that has to be inspected every year and discarded if it has the slightest chafe. Much of my running rigging was, initially, courtesy of the BFD. About a year after Joe started hanging around and helping out, the fire department condemned all their spruce wooden ladders and long clear Sitka spruce steadying poles. Half my glowing, varnished interior was made up of ladder parts, as were my early whisker and reaching struts.

Joe's best friend was a chatty and lovable guy named Leo the Telephone Man. He worked as a master electrician (on large jobs like the Federal Building, etc.) with the phone company. Boy, we were drowning in wire, end connectors, junction boxes, etc.

They had access to a flatbed truck. There was a huge once-in-a-century wind-storm in Boston and it knocked down dozens of billboards.

Billboards are made out of exterior grade plywood. Clean up was neither as tough nor as extensive as some had thought it might be. The sign companies quickly had the debris hauled off to the dump. (If you opened up our galley cupboards and peered in behind the soup cans, the Marlboro Man was staring back at you.)

Joe was a part-time lobsterman and he was around commercial fishermen a lot. Often he'd lug back "something to show you, Fatty," that he'd snagged for us.

Joe Hinke was an incredible help to us. I wrote to him for over a decade after we sailed away—right up until he passed on.

I sent him an autographed copy of *"Chasing the Horizon"* which mentioned him and Leo in glowing terms.

Another time, I was working away on *Carlotta* and a pick-up truck loaded with boat gear from a classic 38-foot wooden schooner pulled into the yard. The truck held, like, every single metal piece on a well-found traditional wooden yacht.

The guy got out of the pick-up truck (the woman stayed inside) and didn't waste time. "You can have everything and anything that you can use, but you have to be able to name it and tell me what it is for."

He seemed in a hurry—so I rattled off every single item. Marine nomenclature is a hobby of mine. I got it all, right down to the cranze and gammit irons and the Norman's Cross, too.

He had lost his boat by hitting Matinicus Rock in Maine—and wanted to see someone benefit from his loss. I, of course, assumed the shipwreck had happened a long time ago—until I heard the woman crying in the cab.

"Thursday," the fellow said. "We piled her up on Thursday—and have been salvaging her ever since."

Things like this happen—regularly—when you are engaged in a righteous long-term project like building your own boat.

Let's stop for a second and make sure I'm not mis-communicating here. I never ever stole (or considered stealing) a copper nail or a dab of paint during the construction of *Carlotta* or the rebuild of *Wild Card*.

Never. Ever. I loathe thievery in any and all forms. It is exactly the opposite of everything I believe in.

Clear enough?

But our modern world is filled with waste. "Recycling" stuff before it is carted off to the dump isn't a bad thing.

There was, however, one funny incident concerning stealing during the construction of *Carlotta*. We were having a "business meeting" of our boatbuilding cooperative and someone happened to mention that we needed a small, horizontal-blade portable cement mixer.

We were trying to get through the regular monthly meeting quickly as there was a fellow who'd driven up from Pawtucket, Rhode Island to talk to us.

When we were finished with the meeting, however, he was nowhere to be found.

So we were about to disband, when he came roaring into the yard in his car—with a cement mixer hastily lashed with twine to his rear bumper.

"For you," he said. "Free! They call me the *Pawtucket Pirate* because that is what I am. And I'm here to donate my services to what is, from what I understand, a great bunch of boatbuilding freaks!"

Then he reached into his back seat and extracted a ship's wheel that looked suspiciously like the one that normally lived on the wall of a nearby seafood restaurant.

I marched over to the cement mixer. Its engine was still warm and the cement was still wet. He must have stolen it from a nearby construction site, very nearby!

"Ah, Mister Pawtucket," I said. "We don't mean to be ungrateful for your sterling efforts on our behalf, but we can't accept this stuff. It's stolen. And, besides, aren't you scared of being caught? Somebody might write down your license plate number or something?"

"Ain't my car," said the Pawtucket Pirate, obviously wounded to have his revolutionary offer spurned. "Don't know whose it is, really—don't much care, either."

Oh, the 1960s (well, '72, in this case) was a free-wheeling time in America—and particularly confusing for an LSD-gobbling pirate who was just trying to donate his precious time to a worthy cause. "Well, I ain't taking this shit back," he said stubbornly.

I had to wait until Sunday, when Southie was fairly deserted, to drop the stolen gear back off. I was praying that I didn't get busted and go to jail for being a Good and Goofy Samaritan—in my own straight-arrow, weird, twisted way.

Years later in Cambridge, I was walking through a large parking lot when I happened to spot a familiar face peering into the parked cars.

"Hey, Pawtucket!" I said.

Once he recognized me, he smiled. "You see any of these vehicles with a good sound system, Fatty? I just boosted the latest *Little Feat* tape—and am looking forward to the drive home!"

No, stealing one single dab of paint is far too much on a righteous craft that will sail through God's Own Cathedral—that will pass above King Neptune's disapproving eye.

Free is fine, but there is a thin, tasteful line which must never be crossed. Sure, it is okay to allow people to know that you need stuff. No, it is not okay to ask, expect, demand, beg, or take.

The Golden Rule applies to indigent boatmen most of all.

Good News on Dumpster Marine!

Many of your fellow boaters aren't like you. They have high-paying jobs, have stuck with them, and are, thus, far wealthier. Don't belittle them, especially if you live off the crumbs from their generous table.

They buy a whole new set of sails when their genoa shows a bit of chafe from the bow rail. Ditto, running rigging. New cushions every other year. They like their electronics to match—can't handle some instruments with red lights and others with dim white.

In essence, they are wasteful. This is wonderful for those of us who shop at Dumpster Marine!

Whenever I haul out, I tell the crane operator, "Please put me as close to the dumpster as you can—at least within clear sight of it."

I'm a garbage picker. I know, I know, a lot of people frown at this and think it is beneath their dignity. Why? Recycling ain't bad. And this is recycling at its most elemental and righteous.

I hop right in. I swim around. I weave through the bags.

"Yippee," I scream. "A Skipper bronze head and a broken bronze raw water strainer! A frozen bronze SL555 too! Oh, and a perfectly good stainless steel chock. This one is perfect because it won't match any of the others on the boat, all of which were purchased for BFZ (big frig'n zero) at Dumpster Marine!"

Never throw away or discard anything heavy and bronze. Sell it to the local junkyard for scrap. If you are in a port town, chances are other penny-pinching boaters (recreational and commercial) are doing the same thing. Ask to see the pile of bronze marine gear waiting to be melted down. Who knows? That bronze Luke anchor of your dreams might be waiting there for 50 bucks!

I, personally, don't throw my discarded boat bits into the dumpster—only my garbage bags. I place it all neatly laid out like a "free yard sale" just in front of the dumpster for the benefit of my fellow yachtsmen. Many shipyards and a few marinas are starting to have a "free table" conveniently located near the dumpster, for just such a purpose.

Don't forget, your boat is mobile. During our second circ, our galley top became so rotten that it started to cave in when Carolyn kneaded her bread. (She makes a fresh loaf every other day while we're at sea.)

We were in New Zealand at the time. We went up the river to Whangarei on a rising tide and tied up to some pilings just across the street from the rear doors of a bunch of custom furniture makers.

We did the entire project (and more) using "rescued" lumber from those dumpsters.

Some of the dumpsters were locked to prevent folks from putting stuff in. Once we'd come around a few times and they knew we were looking to take stuff out, and would be neat about it, they'd unlock the dumpsters for us and smile when we swooned in appreciation.

Soon everyone in town knew we were doing a major project with empty pockets. Instead of spurning us, they tipped their hats in respect.

Russ and Shirley were living there aboard their lovely Hallberg Rassy *Wanderer*. They were having some rigging work done. Their Hood furler had spit out its bearings and twisted its foils in the Tasi, so they had bought a new one.

Did we want the old one?

Sure. Two sections of the foils were pretzeled beyond hope. But I cut them away and there was still plenty of length for my shorter staysail stay. Thus, the only thing that would cost me money was the bearings. For $400 or so, we were going to end up with a completely "like new" roller furler. But wait—

Carolyn discovered from the local model steam train rebuilders (weirdly, there were a bunch of them there because of a local museum) that the very same Type 316 (passive) ball bearings that we needed were available by mail order for a pittance in nearby Australia. Thus, our new Hood roller furler cost us less than a hundred dollars, mostly for the new wire.

The cost of the new galley was, of course, far less.

Wholesale/Retail

You should never pay full retail while you are rebuilding or outfitting your boat. Never. Why pay list price when you don't have to?

While I was building *Carlotta* I got a job at Marine Hardware and Supply at 390 Atlantic Avenue on the Boston waterfront. It was established in 1839, and owned by Si Fireman. At the time, it was the largest wholesaler in the area.

I got a job there because I needed a job—and because, as part of my pay package, I was allowed to buy marine gear through them at *their* cost. This was, of course, well below wholesale.

Take marine antifouling paint, for instance. Let's take a quart of International Ultra epoxy that retails for $100. That same can was 50 percent off, or $50, wholesale—and I was paying about $32 for it.

At the conclusion of my first year, they called me into the office and told me I was doing a great job, but asked me how I'd managed to spend more in the store than I'd earned. "Just clever," I told them with a wink. "Oh, and my wife waits tables at Nick's No Name on the Fish Pier!"

"But everyone can't work at a marine wholesaler," you might protest. I'm not sure that's true. You aren't "everyone," are you? But my point is, you don't have to pay list ever if you are located in the same place and working on a boat for more than a year.

Just waltz into a wholesaler and open an account. In many places, this is easy. All you have to do is give them your charge card number and fill out of a form. I tell 'em, truthfully (sort of), that I have a company called Bozo Boat Works, and that our motto is: "We Don't Clown Around."

Some states require a tax number. This can be bothersome. Other wholesalers are very strict to protect their retailers. But many aren't. A wink and smile is all you need.

What do you have to lose by trying? If you succeed, you will have just saved thousands, perhaps tens of thousands of dollars—which you can later use to buy naked French girls shots of rhum at Le Select on St. Barths. (Say hello to Sylvie for me!)

One wholesaler in Florida balked and wouldn't take my credit card for payment. I whipped out $1,000 in cash and pre-paid my bill. Everyone was happy.

Others have a "minimum monthly billing" clause—to weed out guys like me. Almost always, this can be waved at the discretion of the "account executive," which is what the lowly salesman is called nowadays. Remember: wholesalers are in *competition* for your money, same as everyone else. Make it in their best interests to "convince" you to join their team—and then succumb to their sales pitch.

Just because I'm a former hippie with stars in my eyes doesn't mean I'm stupid. I'm not. We live in a capitalist society. It is my duty to get the best price—for the good of global capitalism! (Okay, that's full of crap, but you get the idea. There's nothing wrong with working hard to get the best price. I'm not cheap or stingy, I'm just careful. I don't needlessly waste my pennies on my boat, so I can utilize them while cruising. In essence, I'm in control of my life *and* my purse strings.)

Taxes—you gotta pay 'em but you don't gotta pay 'em when they don't apply. Often, large items purchased over the Internet aren't taxed if they are from another state. Everything I buy and have shipped to a foreign country is marked FOR YACHT *WILD CARD*, YACHT-IN-TRANSIT. This allows me to, in certain countries, not pay import duty on it. In Malaysia, for instance, all marine gear for yachts in transit is completely tax free. (My anchors are tax-free, and so is all my electronic nav equipment, too—that just happens to be a laptop computer!)

Everybody knows about West Marine, but few realize that Port Supply is the same company, operates out of the same warehouses, and has exactly the same products, only the price is 40 percent less.

Do you qualify to buy from them? Why say "no" until you find out the facts? You might save a ton of money.

This isn't cheating. After all, I'm a *professional* sea gypsy—and thus deserve a wholesale price!

I move around a lot—well, continuously—so it is much harder for me to convince a company that I'm an OEM (original equipment manufacturer). But that didn't stop me from waltzing into the BP solar facility in Malaysia and buying my extensive solar array for 38 cents on the dollar.

Do you have a personal computer? Great! That means you have a letterhead and business cards too.

Many small retail marine shops are struggling. A few have wholesalers that will cut them off if their annual sales fall below a certain level. Or, almost as bad, they can reduce their discount and make it even harder for those marginal companies to survive.

If I can't get a wholesale account, I then seek out these marginal companies. I offer them an opportunity to "enlarge their buying power" by allowing me to buy stuff through them at "cost-plus-ten percent."

This can be a win-win. They earn ten percent of what you spend and increase their clout, without lifting a finger. Why would they turn it down?

If you are both convincing and a nice guy, they won't.

In foreign countries, it is a tad harder to do this. But it is possible. Within hours of entering New Zealand, I visited a large marine store to see what I could work out—and was completely rebuffed. The guy's attitude was that I was a visitor and was without any options but to pay full list price. But I never pay full list price and I wasn't about to start.

So I left and went for a stroll around the various shipyards and marinas in the area. I soon came across a boatbuilder named Alan. We got rapping about making sawdust. He had wholesale accounts everywhere. "How about I toss all my business your way and we simply split the discount? If it is paint and you get it at a 50 percent discount, I'll pay you an extra 25 percent and you pocket it for writing up the receipt. Whataya say?"

He said yes. Yippee!

If nothing else, please ask your friendly retailer if there is "10 percent off for yacht club members." Chances are that they will say yes. If you don't need the money personally, email it to me via PayPal.

Note: Please be aware that what you are trying to do is get quality gear as reasonably priced as possible. I'm part of the Budget Marine family (strange to admit or, even weirder, that they allow me to claim such a bizarre thing). They often have very competitive list prices. They are able to do this because of intelligent buying and because they buy in much bigger quantities for their seven stores. Thus, don't get confused by a competitor who offers "15 percent off" a 30 percent higher marked item, or, worse, "unbundles" the antenna and cable from the VHF, so they can sell it to you as a high-priced accessory.

The point I'm trying to make is: look at the real bottom line, and beware of catchy ads that are too good to be true.

We're all looking for the same thing: value. Sometimes, the most expensive item in a marine supply store offers the best value. Back in 1990, when I purchased my Harken roller furler, I thought it was outrageously priced, especially in comparison to the competition. But I believe in the Harken Brothers and purchased it anyway. Now, 20 years and more than 70,000 miles later, I realize it was actually the cheapest one on the market because of its amazing longevity.

Ditto, my Monitor windvane. I sailed around the world and automatically went to rebuild it during a haul-out. Instead, I just dabbed it with metal polish. After 40,000 ocean miles, it didn't have enough slop in the bearings to warrant rebuilding. I sailed it *one and a half times around the world* before I replaced its bearings. WOW!

Other Non-traditional Suppliers

I've already mentioned junk and scrap yards as possible businesses where a salt-stained penny-pincher might profit, but there are others.

Dive companies, for example, often salvage underwater wrecks. Many have a pile of anchors, at the very least.

Fishermen are smart. They don't like to get jacked around. Often the companies that sell direct to them offer many of the same items we sea gypsies need, at greatly reduced prices.

In or Out of the Water?

Where are you going to keep your vessel while repairing it?

If you have a large house or live in the country, your backyard is often a good, cheap option. Your project is right outside your door. No travel time is wasted. You can snatch "a couple of minutes" here and there. These brief forays really add up. Your boat is never out of sight or mind.

But you aren't rubbing shoulders every day with other sailors—a severe disadvantage, in my opinion.

Another common place is a shipyard. Your spouse might like this better. Yes, it will cost you some money, but not as much as you might think, as "long-term" storage fees aren't set in stone. Nothing is. Everything is negotiable. (I often "sell" my liveaboard status as a plus; I'll be their unpaid night watchman, and my presence will cut down on crime. Then I *am*! And I *do*!)

The big advantage here is that you will be quickly embraced by the marine community in a boat yard and might end up saving as much as your yard bill because of it.

But there's transportation time—and out-of-sight, out-of-mind. The last thing a poor working man struggling to make ends meet needs is a yacht he will never launch sucking up his starving kid's milk money.

Many people immediately put their boat in an inexpensive marina to work on it. This marina can be very inconvenient to sail out of and, perhaps, your vessel can even be aground at low tide. None of these matters to you since you won't be using it, you'll be working on it.

Check the marina's policy carefully, however, and talk to the other boaters. Some marinas have a strict "no major work on boats" policy, and aggressively enforce it. That's fine. The people on the boat you share your finger pier with probably don't want to be eating lunch in their cockpit while you "share" your fiberglass dust with them while grinding your cockpit sole.

But most marinas have a "no work" rule in the sense of "don't bother people while you do what you do—which we don't want to know about if no one complains about it." This is fine. All you have to do is be considerate of your neighbors and be low key.

We've done massive interior and mechanical jobs under these conditions—with no one the wiser. All it takes is a little forethought. We chopped up the plywood before we smuggled it down to the boat. (So it fits inside quickly and easily.)

Who really cares if beneath the canvas on the dock cart lurks a rebuilt diesel engine, which you'll noiselessly swing aboard with the main halyard?

Yes, we do this at night or at dawn. Yes, we make sure the security guards are on our side before we make a move. No, we never make a mess, make noise, or pollute in any way.

If anyone complains—oops! Stop. Say you are sorry. Start your boat's engine. Move to another marina across the river and attempt not to wear out your welcome there.

Carolyn and I don't do any of the above because we can't afford a backyard, shipyard, or marina for our vessel—or, hell, even a house for ourselves. So, once our vessel is legal and mobile, we anchor it out for free and/or put it on a mooring for cheap—and live on it while we work on it.

This can be horribly rough on a marriage. I don't recommend it unless you are young and foolish. But that's what we have done—and what we currently do.

I built *Carlotta's* entire deck, cabin, and interior at anchor in the Saugus River (Revere, Massachusetts) with mostly hand tools. (Occasionally I'd borrow a portable gen-set to run a saw or grinder.)

We lived on *Wild Card* on the hard at Independent Boatyard on St. Thomas as we did our Major Repair (fixed the hole in the hull), and, yes, it was grim.

I remember our daughter Roma Orion coming to me with her dark eyes shooting sparks and hissing, "Dad, there's fiberglass dust in my undies *again*!"

Of course, places to anchor out or tie up for free are becoming scarce in the US. But they are still there—you just don't see them.

When we first pulled into Fort Lauderdale, we thought we couldn't stay. There were too many strict regulations and everything was far, far too expensive.

"What are we going to do?" asked Carolyn. "This place is, like—for rich movie stars!"

"Come on," I told her. "Let's hop in the Zodiac and see if we can find the Cruds!"

Growing up on the *Elizabeth*, the "Cruds" are what my sisters used to call the "bad boys" of any town we visited—the boys who drank and smoked and fought and raced around in fast cars.

We Goodlanders have always been more comfortable around misfits than regular people. We find people who are, well, "too fixated on abiding by the law" to be rather dull.

Anyway, the "Cruds" are always there, everywhere you go. Call 'em homeless if you want—or drunks. Or (temporarily) shore-bound sea-gypsies. It doesn't matter. They won't mind.

It took us about two hours and a dozen stops to find Indian Haulover—a bunch of shoddy boats tied up in the outtake canal of the nuclear power plant. (How convenient to have the water glow at night!) They'd been "going to" form a sort of low-rent utopian Mystic Seaport South—but a cloud of ganja smoke got in the way.

We immediately returned in *Carlotta*, but they said it was silly, as they'd all have to leave in a week or two. No one ever asked us for dockage. Six months later, we *did* have to leave. But by that time, we'd discovered another nest of sea gypsies up the Dania Cut-off Canal…

In the heart of the most regulated, most expensive city in South Florida, we lived for free for almost a year. Then we found a perfect dock on the 14th Street Canal, just outside a very noisy prostitute's window, for a mere pittance, if we could handle all the erotic screaming, whip sounds, etc. We could. We did. It was grand!

Of course, living on your boat while you work on it isn't easy. But it can be done. And it is cheap. And you work faster in hopes of escaping the misery.

Don't get me wrong. I'm not advocating doing this. I'm just pointing out that it is an option—for the truly masochistic.

Think Out of the Box

The Chicago River runs right through the center of the city. It is so polluted that it never freezes. I kept *Corina* behind a factory, just south of the North Avenue Bridge, for a couple of years. What factory? I don't know. I never asked. They didn't use the dock and had built a large fence around their compound. Maybe they didn't even realize it *was* their dock. Or, maybe it wasn't. I don't know. I didn't care. Everything was very nice. I was quiet as a church mouse. I never made a mess or drew attention to myself in any way.

It worked well. Not only didn't I pay dockage as I rebuilt my boat in the water, I didn't have to haul her in the winter either. And the river was so polluted that neither barnacles nor worms were a problem. Paradise, sort of.

Alas, I had to have the mast down to get under the fixed bridges. If I wanted to go sailing, I'd have to stop under a city bridge, tie my boat up well, and order my first mate George (with a rope) to climb the bridge and hoist the tabernacled spar up.

Ah, to be 15 and a yachtsman once again! Tom Sawyer had nothing on us.

Some people suggested this might be illegal. I didn't know. I couldn't afford to hire a lawyer. I never asked. Thus, my ignorance is still my bliss.

I never pay to have a mast pulled. Why should I, when mast-pulling stations (well, landlubbers call them bridges because we sailors generously allow the funding taxpayers to drive over them) have been constructed everywhere for, I assume, the convenience of the passing yachtie.

One of the few disadvantages of living in the Virgin Islands and the Lesser Antilles is the lack of bridges. So, when I needed to pull my stick on *Wild Card*, I just powered around Hurricane Hole (very calm, with no wakes) until I spotted two huge sailboats rafted together. Thatcher, a friend, was skippering the 72-foot *Tala* and Teddy was on the 65-foot *Skeets*.

"Mind if I wiggle in, boys?" I asked.

Soon *Wild Card* was sandwiched between them and I was climbing through all three rigs like a monkey. When everything was all set, I strolled aft where they were enjoying happy hour between charters and said, "Muscles?"

Everyone put down their cocktails and strolled up to their respective mast bases. And we lifted my light and low mast from their lofty spars with great care and coordination. They had to hoist at the same time and rate to keep the mast centered. It could have been a Fabergé egg. Never was my mast pulled so delicately.

Or so cheaply.

"It will take me about three weeks to re-rig," I told them with a smile. "Any chance for an encore in a month or so?"

"Fatty, you are incorrigible!" grinned Thatcher.

"Sure," said Teddy. "Anything for a sailor who squeezes a penny so hard that Abe Lincoln weeps."

Underwater

In the Boston and Chicago areas, the harbor water is dirty. But in the islands, mon, it is crystal clear. It is only marginally harder to work underwater. After all, watersports in the Caribbean are half the fun.

Need to rebuild your rudder? Yes, hauling your vessel, blocking it in an elevated position, and digging a hole in the dirt is the accepted way of doing it. But that costs money.

If it is a spade rudder that has a tiller and pokes up through a rudder post (which runs from outside the boat to inside the cockpit), why not just drop it down (with a line attached) and pull it out of the rudder tube from underwater? Then it will cost you nothing. And you'll have more time to allow it to dry and to rebuild it. (Yes, make double-sure that no water will enter the vessel during this process.)

What's a little tropical swim between friends, eh? If your prop shaft needs straightening at a machine shop, you don't have to haul your boat unless you want to. Just be ready with plugs at both ends of your propeller tube. (Carolyn hates doing this—being alone inside the boat while being fire-hosed with seawater and trying to stuff a plug into the inboard end.)

You may or may not have to remove your prop or move your rudder before extracting the shaft. Obviously, the engine coupling has to be removed and smoothed in order for the shaft to pull aft. Suggestion: After replacing your straightened shaft, put a spare zinc about six inches forward of your stuffing box. This not only allows you to always know where it is, it prevents the shaft from slipping out should your coupling pin ever work loose. My, aren't we improving the old tub as we go, eh?

Can you sink your boat this way? Absolutely! Can this be done without sinking your boat if you have a couple of brain cells left over from your teenage years? Absolutely!

Come to think of it—forget the machinist. Just elevate your bare prop shaft above a table on two pieces of notched wood and then rotate it with a borrowed dial gauge clamped so it barely touches the shaft in the center. If your shaft is corkscrewed with a compound curve, then either bring it to a machinist or buy a new one from Frank and Jimmy's in Fort Lauderdale. But that's rare. Normally, your slightly-out-of-line shaft just has a gentle bow it in. Measure how big that bow is and then put the bow on top (and add a small mark to aim at). Hit it with a large, heavy rubber hammer (or a large piece of soft wood). Measure. Repeat. After three or five whacks—and before it bows the other way—stop. You are done.

This is exactly how your machinist does it—for $120 an hour.

Now dive back over the side and toss it back in. How much did you save? $500? $750? $1,000? Enough to live aboard in Thailand for six months or so?

Is it possible to install a transducer in the water? Yeah, but it is more complicated. You can't drill the shaft hole with a 110-volt drill because you'll electrocute yourself when you break through and the seawater fire-hoses in. So use a WD-40-soaked hand drill or battery drill at the very end. Oh, and don't allow saltwater to enter the unit end of the transducer cable. Seal it repeatedly with silicone and plastic bags (which can, of course, fit through the hole that is now leaking gallons of water per second while you dick around). Yes, pre-paint everything that will be exposed with antifouling. You sure won't be able to do that underwater. Yes, you'll have to pre-goop (bedding compound or modern marine sealant) the appropriate areas of the transducer and hull. Be careful not to make a mess!

This isn't a task for the faint-of-heart. Can be it done? Sure... we put a man on the moon, didn't we?

It is probably not a good idea to assemble a Max prop underwater. Too many small parts to lose. If you do (and I suggest you don't), make sure you sling an underwater tarp under your project so that any dropped parts are easily found. I sling this underwater catch-all every year when I re-grease my beloved Max prop while in the water—scared I'll lose those tiny Allen-keyed set-screws forever!

Can you drop your keel while in the water to check your keel bolts? I dunno. And I ain't finding out!

There are limits, even for a cheapskate like me.

Note: We'll discuss careening and hauling on the tide later.

Buy? Don't Buy?

This subject could take up an entire book itself. The good news is that most cruising boats sailing around the world have about $20,000 worth of stuff aboard that I don't think they need.

This, of course, depends entirely on how much money you have. If you've got it, spend it. How nice for you!

But if you don't, don't despair.

You need a strong boat with the water outside, the mast up, the keel down— and not much else.

What Not To Buy, At Least Initially

Don't buy a fancy autopilot, chartplotter, etc. Basically, buy your electronics at the very end, or as you go, or not at all.

The only pieces of permanently mounted electronics you have to have aboard are a GPS and a depth sounder. (Your VHF can be hand-held, as many minimalists' have.)

Do not buy any electronic charts or paper charts; do collect large-scale free ones.

Do not buy any exotic sails or high-tech cordage. Standard nylon lines (docklines, anchor rodes) and standard Dacron polyester (running rigging) are just fine.

Do not buy any MPS sails. Hell, don't buy any new or custom-made sails at all. Buy 'em late in the game and used.

Ignore bow-thrusters, etc.

If you need refrigeration, fine. It's your funeral. Just realize you have to have the batteries, solar cells, and wind generator to back it up. And you just might have to do a compression dive to see your boot top after taking all that heavy gear aboard.

Forget a watermaker and concentrate on being able to afford a sturdy jug or two. (You meet the finest folks while lugging water. We have friends who, once they got their watermaker, said, "We miss the Big Fun with the Jugs, Fatty!")

Forget all wind instruments. Some tell-tales in the jib and a piece of string will do just fine.

Don't buy too many anchors. Once you go to the Caribbean, you can dive for them after hurricanes. They're a dime-a-dozen if you have good eyes and snorkel. (I'm talking about months after a storm, not the following day.)

Don't buy a radar until later.

Don't buy outdoor, weather-proof cockpit speakers for the sides of your cockpit. They will explode their plastic cones if you're pooped and allow massive amounts of water below. Aren't you glad I warned you?

Skip buying signal flags, as fun as they may be. They can get you into serious trouble.

I happened to be at the Bermuda Yacht Club when a very angry commodore came striding down the dock and demanded that the crew of *Desperado* strike its flags immediately. "And," he said, barely controlling himself, "I'd like to see your captain in my office as well."

Quick as wink, I (and everyone else within earshot) dashed below and grabbed my code flag chart. The flags spelled out "Desperate Men will Fuck Anything!" Oops.

Dock Carts

One time I happened to stumble upon my wife walking down the street and she wasn't carrying anything. Of course, I didn't recognize her. Cruising wives are *always* carrying something!

A small folding dock cart makes lugging stuff long distances a lot easier. It would be swell to have one of those gorgeous blue-and-aluminum big-wheelers that West sells, but we just use the cheap and rusty household one we paid eight dollars for, ten years ago. It can handle a 20-pound tank of propane, a six-pack of beer, and a bag of groceries without problem. (I'd love to get one big enough that I could ride in, but Carolyn isn't turned on by this idea.)

Buy or Keep Your Eyes Peeled For

The best way to "buy" peace of mind is to spend all your money, at least initially, on strength and safety issues.

In a perfect world, where everyone is rich and well fed, it would be nice to have a good self-steering gear *and* an oversized, dependable electric autopilot as well. However, if you can only have one, I recommend you don't buy an electric autopilot first.

Most electric autopilots on most small sailboats are crap. They are too small and too weakly mounted. In addition, they suck up massive amounts of 12-volt energy. Many do a fine job upwind in moderate conditions, but aren't "fast" enough in heavy airs while sailing dead downwind. They also tend to fail at about 300 hours. This is fine if you daysail out of Santa Cruz. You might go two or three seasons without a problem. But if you are headed for the Marquesas, 300 hours won't even get you half way.

Compare this with a Monitor windvane, which is almost indestructible if you don't whack it. It draws no energy. And it will work for a solid year, continuously, in a salt-water environment and steer you in 6 to 50 knots of wind without ever tiring. In fact, the harder the wind blows, the better it works.

I repeat: I recommend you get a Monitor or a used Aries before purchasing an electric autopilot.

"Boo hoo!" you might scream. "Steering while sailing is fun, but steering while powering isn't. You've got it backwards, Fatty."

For daysailing, I do. But not for ocean passage-making.

Here's a bold statement: **The single-most important "non-strength and safety" item aboard a small sailboat on a big ocean with only two people aboard is their windvane.**

Some people think the purpose of the windvane is to allow you to not steer. It is not. It is to allow you to do all the other stuff we collectively call *seamanship.* If you have to steer 24/7, you aren't able to be as good a ship's husband as you should be. The windvane frees you up, not just for sex and naps, but for navigation, food prep, engine maintenance, chafe protection, lookout, etc.

I can't stress this enough. All of our ocean passages have been a delight because our windvane did not fail. If it had, our delightful, blissful passages would have immediately become ordeals of drudgery.

No, I'm not a wuss. I hand-steered during my whole childhood on *Elizabeth.* Ditto *Corina.* And it was ten years before I managed to afford an Aries on *Carlotta.* But once I sailed offshore with a windvane, 95 percent of the work was gone and 95 percent of the physical stress as well.

I have a tiller and, thus, my Monitor begins working at about two knots of boat speed. It works fine at 50 knots of wind too, but the boat begins to show signs of wanting to round up. (Whether this is the Monitor's fault or the rudder's I do not know.)

During extreme conditions, it is important to make logical, non-panicky, decisions. Thus, just before we sail into a major blow, Carolyn almost *orders* me into bed while bustling around the galley.

Thus, because of our self-steering, I am always rested, well fed, dry, and properly attired when the gale hits—not frazzled.

This is because we have a Monitor windvane.

Just before my fellow Virgin Islanders aboard *Ursa Minor* shoved off on their circumnavigation, Brian and Judy came to me for advice. They had an extremely dependable autopilot and a cockpit/transom, which made mounting a Monitor windvane extremely difficult.

"Do you think," said Judy, "it would be okay if we just… went with the autopilot?"

"No," I said. "I do not. Mount a Monitor, no matter how much trouble it is."

This is not what they wanted to hear. But they did it.

They've been kicking around the Pacific for five or six years now. About once a year they send me an email, thanking me profusely for convincing them to buy their much beloved/appreciated/admired Monitor.

Do I recommend any of those wedge-shaped self-steerers with their own separate aluminum rudder? Surely, a "safety first" guy like me would see the advantages of having a spare rudder, right?

Yes, a spare rudder would be a nice thing to have. During the famous 1979 Fastnet, as many boats lost their rudders as dismasted. But there's a problem. These types of units only need a tiny rudder under normal conditions, but a large one in a gale. Thus, they work less and less well as the wind increases.

I do think this type of vane has its place on light-displacement racing boats and, perhaps, multihulls. They can effectively do their job some of the time on certain boats, but I would not recommend them for most heavy displacement cruising vessels. Plus, they are *way, way* less dependable. They have many different metals (including aluminum) underwater. If left submerged in the water for any length of time, they don't work.

The Monitor or the Aries almost always work—and work better as the wind increases.

They are the best, most affordable choice.

"What about powering," you ask.

My Monitor steers quite well, if I'm powering into a chop dead upwind. (I crudely adjust most of the slaloming out of it by using different size vanes, and just clothes-pinning various bits to it.) But, of course, a wind vane can't get its proper input with no wind. So I just slip a tiny Autohelm tiller pilot, suitable for an 18-foot dinghy, between my stern rail and the modified stub of the vane and turn it on.

This tiny electric tiller pilot cost me $250 fifteen years and two circumnavigations ago. Since it only has to push the vane with the slightest of force, it draws almost nothing. (The force to steer comes from the Monitor rudder moving through the water *not* the autopilot.)

Thus I have the best of both worlds for only slightly more than the price of one.

Are there disadvantages to this system? Sure, it takes awhile and is a pain in the ass to set up each time: Carolyn has to steer perfectly on course as I drop the auto pilot rod on the vane at just the right moment. This isn't easy at 3 a.m. or when both of us are tired, or when it is raining cats and dogs. (Note: We have a "raincoat" cover that Carolyn specially made for our tiller autopilot. Our previously mentioned friend Thatcher uses the same concept, but his unit is dry under his cockpit locker, with only an elegant Morse cable connecting it to the Monitor. Clever guy, Thatch is!)

The bottom line: If you circumnavigate with a Monitor, you will love both the Monitor and the trip. If you circumnavigate without one, chances are you will regret it.

So keep an eye out for used Monitor or Aires—and rob your blind mother's purse if you have to.

White Floppy Things

Buying new sails is like buying a new car—wonderful if you can afford it. But both cars and sails lose a massive amount of their value upon first use. The best bet is to buy your sails used from Bacon or a similar "pre-owned" sail loft. I buy new sails from Lee Sails of Hong Kong. They are not the best, but they offer solid value.

The US of A makes the *fastest,* most *hi-tech* sails in the world. There is no question about this. I'm very proud of this. However, they charge accordingly.

And, alas, they don't make the best sails. The best cheap cruising sails are made in New Zealand, Australia, and Cape Town. They last considerably longer than their Stateside counterparts. My friend, working at a South African loft that manufactures thousands of the sails that are sold through American lofts under a Major Label, said he was horrified how shoddy the sails he was making were. He said that the Stateside masters wouldn't allow them to take the time to make the sail properly—that the sole emphasis was on initial set, not longevity.

Whingeing About Winches

Many "free boats" salvaged from a beach lack winches because they have been stolen under the pretext of salvage. Most experienced sailors consider three winches—two jib and one main halyard—a bare minimum. But it is nice to have more than three. *Wild Card* has ten.

Thus, if you have empty pockets, don't even consider ordering winches from West Marine.

Buy them used, and buy only non-self-tailers.

I often race on the finest yachts in the world. I love self-tailers. But I don't have a single one on my boat. Nor do I miss them.

If I'm short-tacking up a tight channel, I just tie a figure-eight knot in the bitter end of my slightly longer jib sheets and toss 'em over the side. Instant self-tailers! And affordable, too. The only downside is all my fellow boaters coming alongside and yelling, "Hey, skipper! You're trailing a line overboard!" (Don't forget to haul 'em in before cranking up the diesel.)

Special Offshore Equipment

A vessel intended for circumnavigating or storm-strutting will have certain equipment a coastal daysailer lacks.

Your jack-lines (lines or webbing to clip your safety harness to, so you don't fall overboard) should be extremely strong. And there should be sufficient pad eyes on your vessel so that you can conveniently and comfortably do any deck job without worrying about being swept overboard. (I tell my offshore guests that falling overboard isn't an option. "Picture the side of this vessel as a 10,000-foot cliff. If you fall overboard you're dead before you hit the water," I say. "And if you're stupid enough to fall over, I certainly ain't going back for you!")

Watch the Washboards

The simplest thing that 98 per cent of all cruising boats can do to drastically increase their chances of surviving a severe offshore gale is to secure their companionway washboards to the vessel. These boards should *never* be unattached from the vessel while sailing. Many, many people have drowned needlessly when their washboards were swept overboard and *then* the boat rolled. Hence, without the washboards, their vessel filled with water, sank, and they drowned.

This is so simple, so cheap, and so important. I repeat: Your companionway washboards should *always* be attached to the boat. This means while they are stowed, while they are in place, and while they are in transit between the two.

In addition, they should be able to be locked in place (with a barrel bolt, usually) so they can't fall out while in use should gravity reverse as your vessel rolls 360 degrees.

Lee cloths (pieces of fabric designed to keep you from being tossed out of bed in a blow) should be fitted. If they can be designed to be easy to get in and out of while in place, all the better. (I didn't mind crawling over them at 15 years of age, but am less enamored of doing so at 59.)

On the plumbing side, your **marine head** (toilet) will have to have a holding tank in order to enter many countries (many of which have no realistic way of dealing with the resulting stored sewage). The problem is that marine sanitation laws vary greatly. In New Zealand, for example, overboard discharge is allowed three miles out, not so other places.

Thus we have a passive, gravity-operated **holding tank** (mounted on the head bulkhead higher than the waterline) which can be emptied via a deck fitting or discharged overboard. If I'm in a country that prohibits all overboard discharge, I can close a valve and subtract one piece of hose and be completely legal.

The problem is that my gravity-fed holding tank is small and is only truly useful for four careful days before requiring emptying.

But the law is the law, and we're legal everywhere we sail with the holding tank plumbed this way.

I am currently exploring marine composting toilets and have heard good reports about them. If they truly don't stink and can handle two people 365 days a year, I'll certainly buy one.

Another plumbing consideration is **catching water**. We have various awnings and other devices that catch rainwater and divert it into our main freshwater tanks. In addition, we have an entirely separate "deck water" system (including sink faucet) which comes straight off the deck. This is very effective at trapping water, but, of course, the water isn't drinkable, especially if we've just pulled a muddy anchor.

We also have a saltwater faucet for offshore use as well.

But Carolyn finds using the "semi-clean" deck water much preferable to using the saltwater sink pump because the saltwater stinks, splashes salt, and corrodes the very pots it is supposed to be cleaning.

Carolyn absolutely loves our "deck water" system. Since she is Queen of the

Galley, I make sure every facet of her domain runs smoothly and cleanly. (I use the saltwater faucet all the time—each to his own, I guess.)

Obviously, **self-steering gears**, **MOM** units (Man Overboard Modules), and **life rafts** all have their separate design/mount criteria.

Our storm **trysail** is always on the mast, ready to be hoisted. Ditto, our roller furling storm staysail, which can be unrolled in the blink of an eye.

Each of our three main "storm toys" has its own rode and related equipment; our **Gale Rider** drogue slows us down and keeps our stern to the approaching breakers. Our Paratech sea anchor has 400 feet of dedicated rode, and is potentially the most dangerous thing on the boat (during retrieval). But once deployed, it is marvelous. It keeps our bow pointing into the largest seas without a problem (well, until retrieval). Our **Jordon Series Drogue** is 250 feet long. It doesn't surge (spike-load) the boat nearly as bad as the **Paratech** and is easier to safely deploy and retrieve. However, it does not keep our head into the seas, only our transom. This means we get pooped often, which is a tad stressful.

In one famous case off Bermuda, one of the most expensive mass-produced mid-cockpit 65-foot ketches ever built in the state of Maine was fully pooped and held the multi-ton load for a second… and then the weight of the water cracked the full cockpit clean away from the deck… whereupon it dropped inside the vessel… and dumped its sloshing, chilly contents all over the interior… like a tilted, berserk Jacuzzi of Death! It was a miracle everyone aboard survived.

My advice is to stay away from boats built solely for the super-rich and none-too-bright.

How Do You Pay With No Money?

Good question. The easiest way is to trade. I traded an old too-heavy-for-*Wild Card* manual anchor windlass for the pair of beloved Barlow 28s I use as genoa sheet winches. I have no idea how old they are—they've been on numerous boats before mine. But they've given me perfect service for more than 20 years.

I didn't like my flimsy wheel-steering system when I first started sailing *Wild Card* because, basically, *Wild Card* was designed to be a day-sailer, not an ocean greyhound. Besides, I knew my Monitor would steer much better in light airs with a tiller rather than a wheel.

So I unbolted my steering pedestal and, with the wheel attached, traded it (at Lighthouse Marine, St. Thomas) for a bunch of odd, mismatched winches to use on my mast.

This type of trading is fairly straight-forward.

But "trading" is a concept only limited by your imagination. Just before my first circumnavigation, I thought it would be really cool if I had a set of custom-made sails for the boat. I had a radio show at the time, on which the advertising department of WVWI Radio One hadn't sold all the 30-second commercial spots. So I went to Butch at "The Sail Loft" in Red Hook, St.

Thomas and explained the situation. Butch and I had worked together as volunteers (see the karma?) at KATS, the Kids and the Sea program that teaches local kids to sail. Anyway, Butch said, "Sure!"

He wrote me up an invoice for a lovely main and a very strong jib (I still use the jib daily and it has more than 70,000 miles on it) and I played his radio spots for almost two years.

…so my new set of sails cost zero pennies.

Ditto, Tom at "Parts and Power of Tortola." He needed someone to straighten out his advertising and write some copy—both easy tasks for me. Thus the new M30 Perkins diesel I purchased through him cost me less than a good rebuild.

Ditto, Robbie at "Budget Marine." He does "dis for me and I do dat" for him. We send each other invoices, etc, and at the end of the year we're usually pretty even. (It is nice having an entire marine supply team that will instantly ship you anything to anyplace in the world without question.)

I'm a writer and a media person—so that is what I trade. But the point is, we all have something to trade. Are you a house painter or a welder? Gardener? Professional transvestite? (I know a live-aboard cruiser who professionally dresses like a woman and regularly performs in gay theaters. It is rather odd to hear him say, "It is so hard to keep my gowns nice in the hanging locker!")

Bartering is an ancient art. It existed long before greenbacks.

If you are poor and without employment—look at the bright side. You have plenty of time to barter whatever talents you have.

If life hands you lemons, make lemonade.

If statements like the above strike you as stupid—why? Could it be that you are setting yourself up to lose? Why not set yourself up to win?

Sure, it is easier to make excuses about why you failed rather than to work hard to succeed—but is that what you want, failure?

I once wanted to buy a Whitby 42 but I didn't have any money. Worse, the seller and I didn't seem to be on the same wavelength. But he loved Stinkpot Steve in the BVI. But Steve didn't have any money either. So Stinkpot Steve offered what I thought was the dumbest idea ever. He told the guy he'd take his yacht off his hands (for zero dollars) and fix it up to Bristol condition—and then allow the former owner to charter it for a month for seven years—when it would become Stinkpot Steve's completely.

I laughed in Stinkpot Steve's face. "You are offering him nothing," I said. "Just… *smoke!*"

But the seller guy knew his boat was deteriorating faster than he could fix it. He didn't care too much about the money, but didn't want to charter because he preferred the mental concept of "owning" his own boat. But upkeep was a hassle—and expensive too.

The seller bit. Stinkpot Steve did exactly as promised. Everyone was happy. Very happy. Steve had his own liveaboard yacht for all those seven years, just 11 months at a time. Once the deal was completed, he lived aboard and cruised her for another seven years—before selling her to an uncle of mine (with my strong recommendation) for $100,000.

Who says you can't trade *smoke* for a nice yacht?

Profitable Painting

Marine supply stores are filled with paint, paint, and more paint. I personally think that International and Petit paints work pretty well. I also think that many "industrial" epoxy paints work just as well—for a third of the money.

I recently purchased three gallons of International anti-fouling paint in Malaysia at $300 per gallon—that was crap. (Hell, so much stuff grew on my boat's bottom that it might have been mislabeled fertilizer.)

The problem is identifying which local epoxy is truly good. I do so by visiting a local shipyard and asking the fume-addled fellow spraying topsides which epoxy he uses on his own boat. They'll usually say something like, "Well, I prefer to shoot Awlgrip and it stands up well in the tropics. But when I shot my father-in-law's bass boat, I used Horny Harry's Hardcoat and it came out okay."

There's your answer.

Obviously, all these marine paint companies sell thinners, catalysts, and brush cleaners for top dollar. Fine. Read the label with a magnifying glass. You'll be amazed how much you can save if you buy generic versus brand name. (Yes, of course, you need to have the correct thinner for any given paint. I'm not advising you to be sloppy, merely careful and frugal.)

Sandpaper, masking tape, and other paint-related items are found in any discount hardware store and are seldom cheaper at a marine supply store.

One Final Note To Shake You Up

Often, I've purchased my anti-fouling paint months in advance of my haul-out to save money. Sometimes, the shipyard will have a powerful mechanical paint-shaker on the premises. This used to be common when everyone did their own yard work, but is less so now. So, occasionally I want to have some paint shaken but don't have anywhere to turn. In this case, I wait until I'm about to buy something major at a marine supply store (for myself or, more likely for someone else). And then just before ringing out, I ask them to "shake the cans of paint I won at a raffle." They usually will sigh, grimace, and do so. If they balk, I walk.

Outfitting In 3 Stages and 3 Continents Over 5 Years

This isn't as crazy as it sounds. If you are going to circumnavigate, you have to have all your strength and safety issues taken care of before you leave. If you don't, you might not arrive. But there are many projects, probably, that you'd like to do but can't afford to do.

Example: I wanted to add an inner forestay to *Wild Card* and have a storm staysail on a roller furler, so I wouldn't have to leave the cockpit after triple-reefing the mainsail. The trouble was that I didn't have the parts or the money to buy them. Should I delay my trip around the world?

Example #2: When I initially rebuilt *Wild Card*, I knew the galley needed work. Hell, that's an understatement: I knew the galley countertop was rotten and needed to be replaced. But it wasn't a strength and safety issue. So should I let it go or should I wait another year before shoving off for Tahiti while replacing my entire galley?

Example #3: *Wild Card*'s original cockpit was fine for daysailing with a crowd and wonderful while racing. (It was great to be far aft, away from all the hustle, as my crew pulled the strings and I just stared at my jib tell-tales in splendid isolation.) But Carolyn wanted a cockpit table, I wanted twin tillers, and we both wanted better, forward-facing seating while sailing. I was sure this "cruising couple cockpit" concept would be a vast improvement over the configuration we had. Should we wait another year before shoving off to rebuild the cockpit?

Please bear in mind, our boat was already safe and strong. All three of the projects above were just improvements we wanted to make, not things that our lives might depend on.

Should we wait three more years? Isn't three years a long time? Could one of us get sick—or even die in any three-year span?

I decided that I was a sailor, not merely a yacht-rehabber. I decided that I wanted to "live life while I was alive" not wait until I was dead to find out if all those religious fanatics were right.

I decided to go.

This turned out to be the correct choice. All the stuff for the roller-furling staysail was given to me by Russ and Shirley, as mentioned, in New Zealand. And we did the work at the Whangarei Town Basin, which is perhaps the friendliest, most understanding marina in the world.

Then we blasted north for a year in Tonga, Fiji, and Vanuatu before heading back down to the Land of the Long White Cloud to rebuild the galley with nearby dumpster diving.

The following year we sailed to Asia—where we did the cockpit project when the monsoon turned against us in Langkawi, Malaysia. (Our future retirement island, we hope.)

The point I'm trying to make here is that not everything has to be 100-percent perfect before you shove off across the Pacific—just all the strength and safety issues. If you are not in Bill Gates' tax bracket, it will take you years to work/circumnavigate yourself around the world. Why not wisely save some projects for the future?

Don't procrastinate *if* you have the strength and safety issues taken care of. These need to be taken care of *now*. But don't foolishly keep saying "one more season and we cast off" again and again until a doctor informs you that you're a lot closer to chemo than Tahiti.

Life is to be lived. Kiss it full on the lips. Go!

*I do my metal work, such as this tiller fitting, with hacksaw and drill.
This can be crude and ugly, but effective.*

Lists: Item by Item

Okay. Let's go through a modern cruising boat stem-to-stern.

The most important skill a cruising sailor on a tight budget can have is the ability to anchor safely in difficult conditions. Thus, a sailor with empty pockets has to have more and better anchor tackle than a wealthy fellow in a yachting cap who sits in a marina-with-a-breakwater.

The minimum number of **anchors** to carry is four. Each requires its own rode. If possible, it is nice to carry a "big gun" disassembled in the bilge. A heavy Luke anchor that you can take apart and stow in the bilge is the preferred choice.

Does that seem excessive? Perhaps. But it is *not* excessive. And there have been times when every single anchor on my boat was salvaged for free—a gift from a kind and caring King Neptune.

The reason *Wild Card* is safer than most $600,000 yachts is because she has better gear and a crew more experienced at deploying that equipment under the stress of heavy weather. **I repeat: Don't think "cheap" means weak or dangerous. It does not.** Time and time again, I see two boats leave the harbor: a sparkling fancy one with little safety gear aboard and a shabby one with lots of safety gear aboard and a crew with the experience to correctly deploy it. Which vessel do you think is ultimately safer?

Let the trendy couple aboard their new 58-foot Oyster agonize over their fabric choices. We're going to focus on the real priorities.

The amount of money a boat costs seldom relates directly to its offshore safety.

"Doesn't a more expensive boat generally mean a better boat?" you might ask. The answer isn't a simple "yes."

Boat manufacturers—just like any other manufacturers—tend to spend money on what makes their products sell. I recently skippered (briefly, thank gosh) a 50-foot cattlemaran with five heads, four showers, two refrigerators, one gen-set, and a freezer. In addition, it had three different places to dine—but not one shoebox for tools. The boat drew 30 amps at rest and had no solar panels or wind generator. Thus the noisy gen-set whined eternally. The sales brochure went on-and-on about how the fabric on the cushions and the curtains matched throughout, yet never mentioned the fact that the main boom was so high you could barely touch it, let alone reef the massive mainsail. The boat was three months old and already showing signs of severe wear. Its chintzy headliner and contact-cemented-together interior was already starting to droop, sag, and delaminate. It required about eight hours of maintenance a *day* (not a week or a month—a *day*!) to keep gluing back on the crap that was falling off.

To top it all off, this vessel, which was advertised as "perfect for a family of four to circumnavigate aboard" had four large "windows" in the sides of the hull to enhance a feeling of spaciousness below. If you rolled a fender down the topsides in a gentle docking, each of these Lexan windows would pop right off the hull and immediately sink out of sight. This would leave a two-square-foot-plus hole in the hull through which much air could leave and much water enter.

Carolyn summed it up perfectly, using traditional sailor's language. "Thank gosh we don't own this piece of shhii... crap," she said. "*Wild Card* has never looked so good!"

The boat had just cost some poor sap over one million dollars.

Oops, I did it again.

I got sidetracked. But I can't help myself because I believe that offshore safety is extremely, vitally important and yet it can't just be purchased like a quart of milk. It isn't for sale. Sure, a wealthy sailor can buy two Paratech sea anchors to supposedly double his safety in the Ultimate Storm. But if he attaches that sea anchor to a weak foredeck cleat without a strong backing plate, well, all the money he spent is for naught. Not only will his Paratech sea anchors be worthless, there now might be a hole in the deck as well. And he might even lose his bow rail (or, gosh forbid, his forestay) in the process.

Back to anchors: We carry a 44 pound Bruce on 200 feet of five-sixteenth-inch chain as our primary hook. Also in the forward anchor locker, ready to go at a moment's notice, is a Danforth 12H on 250 feet of braided nylon. We also have a 44 pound Delta that is particularly good in weed. Aft, strapped onto the stern rail, we carry a slightly larger and lighter Danforth-style Fortress anchor. In the bilge, disassembled, is a huge Fortress that we only lug up for severe blows.

This inventory is down from the seven anchors I carried during my first circ. I'm tapering off my anchor addiction gradually.

Minimum scope with chain: five-to-one; with nylon line it should be seven-to-one. If you use less scope, you will drag. (Please slowly read the prior sentence again. If everyone did, boats wouldn't be drifting around every harbor in the world and smashing into boats that *aren't* drifting around because they have the correct amount of scope out.)

A long anchor rode won't save your boat if it is in the anchor locker—only if it is deployed.

As previously stated, Carolyn and I sailed 15 years and more than 50,000 miles without a windlass. But, damn, did I get eye strain watching that woman yo-yo up all that heavy gear. Finally, at age 55, we succumbed and purchased our Maxwell 1700 **anchor windlass**.

It has changed our life. We now anchor more often for shorter time spans because it isn't a hassle to retrieve our gear. If a boat anchors too close or plays loud music too late, we just smile and slip over to the other side of the harbor.

We have **foot switches** in the cockpit as well as the foredeck so I can precisely place the anchor *exactly* where I want it without hassling Carolyn. (We even have a chain counter!)

The key to a successful anchor windlass installation is the electrical cable. The wire size varies, depending on the windlass amperage and the distance it is away from the battery. A too-small electrical cable results in added heat and shortened motor life. Get the proper cable and the windlass will last as long as you do.

I do recommend a top-quality **roller-furler** (Harken, Pro-Furl, or Furlex) for the jib. But I do not recommend refitting your vessel with a Stow-A-Way spar or furling boom. These are very expensive. If the boat you have already has one of these, fine. Rebuild it carefully and go. But don't convert unless you have the key to Fort Knox.

Of course, your ability to reef quickly in all conditions is vital.

The main difference between the inexperienced coastal cruiser and the experienced offshore sailor is that the offshore sailor reefs often and well. He always has the correct amount of sail on his boat, while the greenhorn is intimidated about reefing his mainsail and thus waits too long.

"The first moment you think about reefing, do so," my father used to tell me.

I'm even more harsh. If you suddenly think, "Gee, maybe I should tuck in a reef?" Then you're already too late!

I almost never go 24 hours without reefing and unreefing. One particularly crazy day, I did so 12 times in 18 hours.

I use **slab reefing**, set up so I can easily reef from either side of the boom.

It is much easier to reef from the high (windward) side. If I slip, I'm safely thrown into the sail, not away from it. And besides, the boom cheek blocks don't bind nearly as much if the line pulling them in is being blown away from the boom rather than being crushed into it.

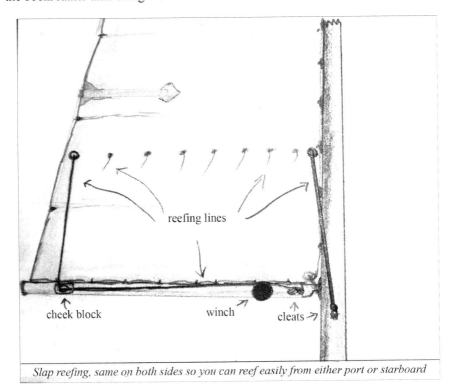

reefing lines

cheek block   winch   cleats

Slap reefing, same on both sides so you can reef easily from either port or starboard

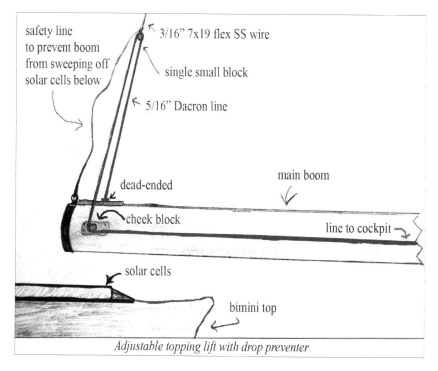

Adjustable topping lift with drop preventer

I can't express how important it is to be able to quickly and easily reef in heavy conditions. It is the bedrock skill of a storm strutter. (Yes, many such crazy, daredevil sailors exist on the South Island of NZ and Cape Town.)

I don't think any cheek blocks or boom winches match in my reefing system, but it works like a charm at three in the morning with 50 knots of breeze.

I like things simple and light. I don't have a rigid boom vang. They are expensive, heavy, and (if misused) can break booms. I just have two permanently-rigged **preventers** made from old chafed halyards that run to the cockpit—lighter, cheaper, and less complicated.

Since I don't have a boom vang or kicker, I have to have a **topping lift**. Mine is permanently mounted. So even if the mainsail halyard breaks, it won't allow the boom to drop to the deck (and/or wipe my solar cells off the bimini top). Yes, I can adjust it from the cockpit because there is a block between the boom end and the dead-ended topping lift cable. However even if this is cast off, the boom can't drop far as there is also a slightly longer line always attached at a fixed length between the boom end and lift. **Travelers** are nice but not necessary if you're not racing. I can place my boom exactly where I want it with my mainsheet and two preventers. So I seldom touch the traveler unless I'm on the racecourse.

My compass used to be one of the most important items on the boat. I hate to

Cap'n Fatty circumnavigated with this auto compass.

admit this because people will howl. But the truth is, I sailed around the world with only a tiny unlit automotive suction-cup-to-windshield automotive compass that cost $2.

Alaska Jim eventually gave me a nice steering compass (perhaps to even us up a tad for the solar cell I gave him) that I use now. But the advent of the cheap $35 GPS (I have seven aboard) has greatly reduced the need for an expensive steering compass. (Oh, I can hear my traditional sextant-worshipping friends howling in outraged protest… such blasphemy!)

I sailed, and extensively cruised, on *Corina* for a year without an **inboard diesel engine**—ditto *Carlotta* for three months, and *Wild Card for five years*. It can be done, especially in the Caribbean. However, I *do* recommend having a dependable diesel aboard. It will greatly add to your fun, safety, and peace of mind.

Don't waste a lot of money on controls such as fancy shifting levers and expensive Morse cables. On both *Corina* and *Carlotta*, I just used some string in a copper tube with a spring for the throttle, and some heavier line with a block as a shifter.

How's that work? Simple: You pull one line and the engine engages in forward. You pull the other one slightly, and it disengages and slips into neutral. Pull it a bit more, and your boat goes backwards. Tie different end knots, say a blood knot and a figure eight, if you get confused.

Can you spend over $1,000 to accomplish the same thing? Sure. Should you? That's up to you. But I don't. I just pull my beloved strings and spend that money elsewhere—on strength and safety issues. Plus, string throttles have the added advantage that you can operate them anywhere—for example at the end of your bowsprit, while you and your partner rhythmically jump up and down (while revving the diesel in reverse) to "walk her off" a sandbar.

See how much fun we have? Isn't being poor and inventive better than always seeing money as the sole solution to every technical problem?

Since I've written for *"Power News"* (the Perkins publication), I must admit I believe in buying quality internal engine parts. A piston made by Perkins is a far, far better piston than a no-name one because Perkins makes dependability such a high priority and knows they'll go out of business if they don't. Not so the no-namer, who is just trying to hustle the piston and has no vested interest in having it perform well over time.

But I'm not so sure this extends to such items as fuel and lube filters. There are a lot of reputable companies out there who make quality filters that many engine companies buy, slap their name on, and jack up the price.

I buy **filters** directly from reputable filter manufacturers.

Your average engine dealer will tell you he "doesn't know" the conversion numbers. But that's because it is profitable for him not to. I just bring an old filter with me to a truck or automotive store and save mega-bucks.

Propellers are expensive. It is often far cheaper to recondition and balance an old prop than to buy a new one. But the prop on your engine must be exactly the correct size in diameter, pitch, and bore. This usually means you have to buy one new. But you should search the used market up until then.

Running lights have bedeviled me my entire life. I'd gladly pay mega-bucks for a set that works and keeps working, especially if it is an LED unit.

Alas, I buy the cheapest, crappiest running lights around. They often fail—but so do their more expensive counterparts.

Let's face it, my forward bicolor actually is underwater at times. Even when it is not, it is being fire-hosed by spray. So I have three systems, my deck system, my shroud system, and my masthead tricolor—and repair/replace the deck system constantly.

This isn't a good solution, I know. But I'm just being honest. The problem is still, at this point, beyond me.

I live in the tropics almost all the time, so ventilation is highly important to me. It used to be, back in the day aboard the *Elizabeth*, boats had bronze deck ventilators, which were expensive and heavy. Some brave person switched to PVC to save money and weight. And then, somebody else a tad *more* clever painted the PVC red on the inside, shaped it a tad, and raised the price accordingly.

I'm not going to spend $200 or more for a PVC ventilator! I use standard PVC plumbing elbows. Of course, some yachties snicker. (Usually these snickerers average about 80 miles a year under sail—slightly less than my 8,000-mile average.) Most people don't even notice. *Wild Card* looks pretty salty, pretty sexy. You can tell she's been around the block a few times. She's been on the cover of a number of fancy magazines—that, ironically, solely exist to sell boats that are absolutely nothing like her.

Oh, the irony!

Fatty made his ventilators from PVC pipe.

If I had a boat with a strong *pedestal steering* system, I wouldn't change it. However, on a well-balanced boat less than 50 feet that I intend to steer with a wind vane 99 percent of the time, I certainly wouldn't buy one either.

When my wheel steering failed on *Wild Card*, I happened to be racing my arch-rival (and dear friend) Thatcher Lord. I was ahead and never considered dropping out just because I couldn't steer in one direction. (I could steer to leeward.) So I over-trimmed the main and kept going while warning the other vessels around me in the Coral Bay Thanksgiving Regatta that I had a steering problem—none of whom believed me!

Anyway, I finished ahead of Thatcher (who is a far better sailor than I and normally far ahead), gloated a bit, and then headed off to the marine supply store to price a new Edson system.

I nearly keeled over when they told me the price. I was so shocked I had to sit down. It was a hot day. The door to the store was jammed opened with a long piece of wood.

I knew I'd never be able to afford a new Edson system. I also knew *Wild Card* would be better off without that weight in the cockpit.

"How much for that piece of wood holding the door open," I asked the sales clerk.

"Oh, that stick? You can *have* that stick for free," he said.

"That's not a stick," I corrected him as I grabbed it and left. "That's a tiller!"

Alternative, Renewable Energy

I never run my engine to charge my battery—well, not for two or three years at a stretch. On a normal day, my **solar cells** have my batteries all recharged before noon. If I'm somewhere where it is cloudy, I just move to somewhere it is sunny. I'm a sun worshipper as much as an ecologist.

Occasionally, of course, I have high energy demands. My boat is my office and occasionally we have three computers and a printer running. If there's only weak sun, I switch on my KISS **wind generator**. If the wind is between 12 and 22 knots, I have far more energy than I can use, even if I turn on everything in the boat! (Note: Energy is seldom an issue on *Wild Card* because we don't have 12-volt refrigeration.)

You can't make your own solar cells, but don't despair. They last almost forever. The units I purchased over 30 years ago are still functioning today. Used panels often come on the market because boats end up with mismatched units and/or want the latest and greatest.

Many people attempt to make their own wind generator. Some people, like Paul on *Elenoa*, have had great fun with this over the years. But I've never seen an elegant, effective homebuilt unit, even though I've seen dozens of them.

The best bet is to buy a used one. They are often on the market cheap because of frozen bearings.

Trust me—buy a wind generator only after your vessel is maxed out on solar and never the other way around!

Fenders

There is little need to buy fenders—unless you are anal-retentive and demand they match.

Good karma will deliver dozens of free ones to you, if you keep your eyes open and boat hook handy.

The moment you get a fender, mark it with your vessel's name in waterproof ink.

If you are in a marina and find a labeled fender, toss it on the deck of the boat that lost it for a nice deposit in your karma account.

If, however, it has no vessel name or is found at sea—well, finders keepers, losers weepers!

Not only am I normally supplied all my fenders by King Neptune—I regularly give away giant ones too large for my vessel. (More karma points.)

Human beings are, basically, sloppy. Many don't want to take the time to label their fenders nor learn how to tie a knot that holds. Like the Dylan song says, "Their loss shall be your gain."

Docklines

The chief enemy of docklines is chafe. This is easily prevented with only a tiny bit of forethought. If you are tying up in a particularly active place where your boat will be in almost constant motion, it is a good idea to use a loop of chain ashore shackled via a thimble to your rope. This eliminates any friction against the cordage, and is a particularly good idea in areas of high surge.

The heavy shock-loads that a surge puts on docklines are often underestimated.

Many well-heeled boaters, bless their hearts, toss out their docklines at the slightest hint of chafe. *Yahoo!* I scoop 'em out of the dumpster, cut away the offending area of chafe, tie them back together stylishly with a double-carrick, and use them proudly. (Anchor lines and running rigging regularly have to pass through blocks and such—but not docklines. Why not recycle them for the good of the planet and your wallet? Because it ain't *yachty*? Puh-leese!)

I suppose it is just class prejudice on my part—but I often think of these prissy, finicky blue-blazered "let's rinse off the boat every ten minutes with freshwater" yachtsmen as folks who want to *appear* to be sailors, and sea gypsies as the ones who actually are. Or, from an entirely different viewpoint—which is saltier: the pristine store-brought, pre-sliced dockline from West Marine, or the tattered, hand-spliced, hand-whipped, double-carricked one?

Anchor light 24/7

There is never a time when *Wild Card* isn't properly lit with an anchor light off my backstay. Modern LED lights draw almost nothing, and protect our floating home if we are unexpectedly stranded ashore with the dirt-dwellers. Thus we leave them on both day and night. We spend most of our cruising time, of course, anchored off some nearly deserted island—far, far from civilization. We know of many boats that have dragged their anchors (or had them inadvertently yanked out of the bottom) in broad daylight at high noon—and were thus "on walkabout" over the horizon when their owners returned at dusk. One vessel in particular (*Forever Young*) was recovered far offshore only because of a dimly lit (and mistakenly left-on) red-glowing cockpit instrument!

Thus *Wild Card* is always lit 24/7.

In addition, we often turn on our masthead LED anchor light as well. This allows other vessels twice the opportunity to spot our vessel. And it also allows us and others to get a sense of her orientation in relationship to the wind via only her lights.

Thus if I'm at a party on a moonless night aboard another vessel and somebody runs into *Wild Card*, I can immediately see her deflection in the dark. (Or more likely, if she starts dragging, for instance.)

The point is, modern marine LED lighting is so stingy on energy that it is silly to lose your $100,000 boat because you didn't flip on a 30-cent LED before heading ashore. (Many skippers are leaving their AIS transponders on 24/7 as well. There's never a problem finding her then!)

Making Your Home Homey

I once was aboard a Nonsuch 30 in St. Croix that appeared, after five years of having someone living aboard, as if it had just come off the factory floor. "I've never changed her in any way, so as not to hurt her resale value," her owner told me proudly. "We've never put a picture up or drilled a hole in her—nothing!"

The boat was completely devoid of personality—just like her owner.

How sad—to allow greed to prevent you from making your home... well, your home.

Carolyn and I have almost exactly the opposite policy. We nail, screw, paste, epoxy, tape, bolt, wedge, cram, pound, and jam goofy things onto our boat all the time. *Wild Card* might not be much, but she is, undeniably, us.

A boat is very small space. The cozy, lived-in, "old shoe" feeling it gives you—and your guests—is very important.

Because we're poor, we have lots more guests than our wealthier counterparts. Why? Well, we don't have to worry that people are after our money, for one. And we often want to repay personal mega-favors. A good, inexpensive way to do this is by having people aboard for dinner or drinks or tea—or even a guitar hootenanny. Plus, we need to frequently interact with the locals to find out where the free water is ashore, the cheapest food, the least expensive diesel fuel, etc. Perhaps the most important factor is—we're just people-oriented. We don't want to "beat them" or "win" over them or "gain" from them—we just want to enjoy them because they are, well, enjoyable. We humans are gregarious, so why shouldn't we invite anyone who passes by in a dinghy aboard for some tea and sympathy? (This "invite 'em all" policy has, so far, never backfired. Yes, we occasionally get a dud {an uninteresting person} but we've never had a guest aboard *Wild Card* that we regretted inviting.)

Usually, a shabby boat's crew will have many times the number of local friends ashore than the pristine yacht does. In part, this is selfish. We really do "...need a little help from our friends!" as the Beatles sang. And this mutual need—this practical "everyday brotherhood" of survival—can be a powerful common bond among highly diverse, fun, interesting people.

So the interior of our boat is a big, messy, crowded, chaotic reflection of our lives—and people pick up on that immediately. Dozens of times I've been lounging around a mega-yacht and had its blue-blazered owner say hopefully, "Let's go back to *Wild Card*, shall we?"

I always grin as I say, "Absolutely!"

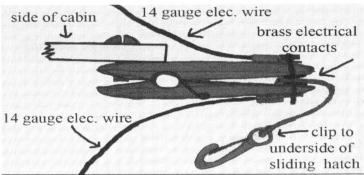

This replaces expensive marine alarms.

Bungling Around With Burglar Alarms

Usually, if we find ourselves somewhere where we're scared of getting ripped off, we sail to somewhere we are not. But that's not always possible. And, don't forget, we spend most of our lives in the Third World—Africa, Asia, the Mideast, etc.

Anyway, we have both a burglar alarm and a stick aboard *Wild Card*. Both cost nothing and give us great piece of mind.

The burglar alarm consists of a modified clothes-pin (with metal contacts) that acts as a switch. When we leave the boat, we attach a strip of nylon webbing to the underside of the companionway hatch and place it between the jaws of the pin/switch. If the hatch is opened more than enough to get your hand in (to disarm it), the webbing pulls out of the clothes-pin, and the metal pins make contact, which causes a loud car siren to wail and sets off our mega-bright outside strobe light.

You'd have to have nerves of steel to continue ripping off the blaring, light-blazing boat.

The stick is just a simple, passive device to prevent the companionway hatch from sliding forward and open (and thus setting off the alarm). Of course, each vessel's hatch design varies. But I've managed on all my boats, to figure out a way to jam a nearly invisible (and/or non-suspect) stick between the inside of the hatch and the cabin top, so that when it is in place, you can't slide the hatch open regardless of how much pressure is applied.

In addition to all of this, we have a hasp and a normal padlock for show (and so we don't encourage people to think our vessel isn't locked).

We also have a "panic button" down below that is wired into the siren and strobe. This means that, if my vessel is boarded while I'm in my bunk in the forepeak, I have a chance to immediately discourage and warn away any intruders. This might gain me precious seconds to organize my defense.

There is no need to spend a thousand dollars on a marine burglar alarm and an additional thousand dollars welding up stainless steel washboards for your companionway when a free clothes-pin and a discarded stick will accomplish the same goals.

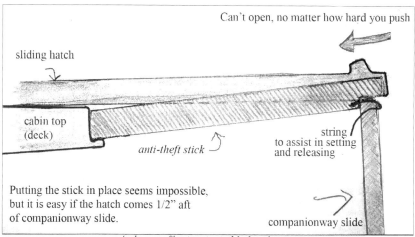

Can't open, no matter how hard you push

sliding hatch

cabin top
(deck)

anti-theft stick

string
to assist in setting
and releasing

Putting the stick in place seems impossible,
but it is easy if the hatch comes 1/2" aft
of companionway slide.

companionway slide

A cheap, effective, invisible hatch jam

If you're on a tight budget, you *really* can't afford to be ripped off. Lock your outboard to your dinghy and your dinghy to the dock while ashore. My dinghy has a prominently visible plaque fastened to it that has all my ownership and contact details. No one can claim they didn't know who owned it or how to get in touch. I always (weirdly, with mystic symbols in the Caribbean) spray-paint my outboard as well.

Don't leave expensive stuff on deck, as a quiet fisherman can "fish" it off without making a sound. Don't dress flashily ashore. Never keep anything important in a backpack or fanny pack. Use a belt with a secret money compartment at all times. If attending Carnival in Brazil, wear some baggy shorts over your real shorts and only carry a little money in an outside pocket—that's what the locals do.

Don't carry what you don't have to. I normally carry a photocopy of my passport info page, not my passport. My wife and I carry only one or two debit cards each, from different banks.

Grates

The good news is that 99 percent of the people we come across while circumnavigating are wonderful people.

I was born in Chicago. I've lived there. I've been shot at there. I've had my nose broken there. I've been stomped into unconsciousness there.

Luckily, we seldom cruise to places as violent as Chicago as we wander (unarmed) through Madagascar, Sudan, Egypt, Yemen—or even Asia and South America.

But sometimes, prudence is preferable to idealism. We take precautions. If my internal alarm bell rings even once with, "Gee, maybe not everyone in this village loves me," then we take defensive measures—especially when we sleep.

A number of our friends have been awakened in the middle of the night to discover a dripping, machete-armed man aboard—only to be sliced and diced before they could react effectively in self-defense.

I don't want to needlessly nor sensationally alarm you. I feel that I am, generally, very safe aboard—far safer than most people in their homes ashore.

However, that doesn't mean *perfectly* safe.

The possibility exists of being murdered in your bed in New York City, rural Montana, or, hell, the White House—as well as a yacht in (false) paradise.

Nowhere is perfectly safe. To be alive is to experience risk, whether we acknowledge it or not.

While living aboard might, generally, make you safer than your shore counterpart, it does not make you impervious. Thus it behooves us world cruisers to understand what happened to the very few, very rare, very unlucky victims of onboard violent crime—to prevent it from happening to us. Please bear in the mind the yacht-related incidents below cover our entire planet over the course of decades—so you're a dozen times more likely to be struck by lightning than experience a similar situation afloat.

Example: Malcolm of *Mister Bean* was (while anchored off a small deserted island on the Thai/Malaysian border) struck in the head with a hammer while he slept in his forepeak. The three young Burmese guys thought they'd killed him and snuck aft to deal with his wife, Linda. Malcolm, however, awoke from his injury with a vengeance and rushed aft to protect her. They killed him in the main cabin and threw his body overboard. Luckily, the killers didn't know anything about boats, got in the dinghy, and stalled the outboard a few feet aft of the vessel. Linda cranked up the boat's engine, ignored the short-scoped anchor, and roared away toward the coast of mainland Thailand. She soon came upon a group of fishermen who were so freaked out by her terrified babbling, they attempted to escape from her. To prevent them from getting away, she rammed one boat and then leapt aboard crying.

Malcolm's body was never recovered.

Under Thai law, if there's no body, there's no murder. Thus, the three boys couldn't be tried for murder despite being caught shortly thereafter in the dinghy and the boat being awash in blood. (Sigh.)

The boaters don't always lose these violent encounters.

A young couple anchored in the southern part of the Caribbean (big area, eh?) were awakened by a nighttime intruder. The husband managed to run aft and switch on the main cabin light, which momentarily blinded the intruder. They grappled. The husband was horrified to see the intruder had grabbed a kitchen knife from the galley and was now trying to stab him. The naked wife was, by this point, hovering near the mast. The intruder was on top of the husband, attempting to stab him with the knife. The woman rushed past them and grabbed a larger butcher knife from the galley. She hesitated, undecided. The intruder slightly stabbed the husband in the shoulder. The husband cried out and lost his grip on the arm with the knife. As the intruder raised his knife high into the air to finish off the husband, the wife buried her large kitchen knife into his back—all the way up to the hilt. This allowed the husband time to knock the knife out of the intruder's hand. Now they were both trying to retrieve it. When the wife returned from her second trip to the galley, she stabbed the guy in the back with a different knife! This injured the intruder enough to enable the husband to seize the discarded knife and bury it deep into the intruder's chest.

Game over—at least for the intruder.

But the survivors were in a very dangerous country that was notorious worldwide for its government corruption. They didn't have much money and had heard horror stories of the local jails.

And here was a local dead guy on the floor literally *bristling* with knives.

They had planned on leaving at dawn. They were cleared out. Their dinghy was already on deck.

What to do?

They left at first light. At noon, they were far enough offshore to drag the guy topsides, wrap him with chains, and deep-six him.

The rest of the voyage was spent trying to mop up the blood and scrub away the DNA.

It wasn't exactly their most joyous passage.

But that was the end of it, thank God.

Was this the right thing to do? I certainly don't know, and I'm not going to second-guess the victims on the scene. In this case, it all worked out okay in the end. But, of course, if they'd have been caught escaping with a dead body aboard...

But I digress. Again.

To prevent being "surprised" by such a rude guest in a dangerous country, we have X-grates made out of aluminum over our two hatches and our companionway so that no one can enter quickly.

Sure, the bad guys can always ultimately get in. But it will take time and make noise.

These grates don't cut down on our precious ventilation but will delay the noisy robbers long enough for me to locate my spear gun, flare gun, and laser (to ruin their night vision and/or fry their retinas).

In cold climes, we've heard of at least two situations with "baddies" on deck and the yachties trapped below. This requires quick action. You have to scare away the would-be intruders before they pour your dinghy gas down a ventilator and flick their Bic. (One guy cranked the engine, hoisted the anchor, and got the boat underway from below, which luckily caused the attackers to flee. (He couldn't steer but they didn't know that. Once the boat started moving, they fled.)

Don't worry about any of this at the beginning. By the time you get to where you'll need grates, you'll be plenty motivated to make 'em!

The problem with many of these "pirate" encounters is that you don't know they are pirates until it is too late.

Some friends of ours were anchored off a remote island in Panama and watched a woman and her teenage sons zoom into the deserted island anchorage for a picnic. It was a getting dark, but it was such a fine, fine evening that my very relaxed friends lingered in the cockpit.

The wife said, "Did you hear something?"

Just then the 62-year-old husband saw a rifle barrel come into his view over his shoulder. Without thinking, he grabbed it and twisted. A young kid came tumbling into the cockpit with the gun. The older man was surprisingly strong. He managed to break off the rifle barrel and start beating the kid over the head with it.

Suddenly, there was a bright light and the middle-aged woman was aboard too. She was yelling at the kid. The husband thought rescue was at hand. However, when he joined in yelling at the kid, the middle-aged woman squinted at him, sized him up, and—with her razor-sharp machete—cut him from his head to his shoulder to his hand and all the way down his right leg.

The three teenage boys took the wife forward—and we'll sadly close the curtain there. (She kept shouting aft to the husband, "I'm okay! I'm okay!")

The good news is that they lived. The wife recovered. But every single thing on the boat was taken—and her sense of bodily security, too.

These incidents aren't typical. I believe that you're more likely to get hit by a meteor than attacked by a pirate. But it does occasionally happen. And it is our job as world cruisers to be as prepared as possible—while not allowing a couple of bad apples per million square miles of ocean to ruin our cruising experience.

The Tender Trap

Dock queens (boats that stay in the marina and never go anywhere) don't need a good tender (dinghy) as much as we sea gypsies do.

My dinghy is my car. It is what I use to zip around in while in port. It is my lifeline to shore. A good dinghy can save you money by allowing you to conveniently seek out bargains ashore. If you are going to live aboard inexpensively, then you are going to spend a lot of time at anchor and riding in your dinghy.

The problem is (you knew there was going to be a complex problem, didn't you?) that a dinghy is a compromise, just like the larger vessel. So it is best to address this "dinghy issue" during the outfitting stage instead of putting it off until the last (expensive) moment.

The problem is: pick-up truck or sub-compact?

A large, fast dinghy of decent capacity is perfect if you are living aboard while you fix up your boat at anchor. This allows you to carry heavy supplies back and forth and quickly dash ashore to the hardware store at will.

While replacing *Wild Card's* mast step and entire interior in lovely Hurricane Hole, St. John, Virgin Islands, I used my six-foot wide, 12-foot long tunnel-hull plywood dinghy to zoom between the boat and Coral Bay, and then over to Jost Van Dyke when I needed to cadge a drink from Foxy. As we were not cruising, I never had to hoist the dinghy or its heavy engine aboard *Wild Card*. I used it to attend all the local regattas, too. It was a great pick-up truck of a dinghy.

Alas, this is not the dinghy you want to take with you while ocean sailing. You want a small, light, easily stowed, easily driven dinghy that can be pushed with a light-weight 2-hp outboard.

Many yacht-habbers (as in rehab) whittle up a **pram-type rowing/sailing tender** from stray bits of plywood lying around the shipyard. If you don't want to mess with the complexities of a centerboard trunk, use leeboards. But it is extremely nice to have a sailing dinghy in such exotic places as Chagos, where the nearest fuel dock is a thousand miles away. Gasoline becomes a precious commodity in such locales. Sailing is slow but it is also sure. Usually, you're sailing at the perfect speed for trolling. Some of our "sailing survivalist" friends think of their sailing tenders as the mini-fishing boats that keep them alive.

But there's no denying a sailing tender has a lot of bits: rudder, tiller, centerboard, boom, mast, sail, strings, etc. Clearly, sailing tenders make more sense on 48-foot boats rather than 28-foot ones.

Most sailors forgo the rigs, and power their tenders with outboard or muscles.

I recommend rowing for young single-handers. You not only save the weight and expense of an outboard, you omit the potential danger of storing gasoline as well. Plus, it will keep you in shape. This is important, considering how much booze you'll have been sucking down. (Yeah, I know what you've been doing, you *dog!*)

But rowing long distances in a heavy chop against a strong wind isn't easy, especially when it is cold.

With two people in the dinghy, it can cross the line from "adventure" and migrate to the "ordeal" side of the equation.

Another factor is your spouse. If they don't like to row or can't row and are going to be using the dinghy half the time, oars aren't the solution. Don't get into the "tender trap" of making dinghy trips ashore a trauma. They shouldn't be. They should be fun.

Enter the lowly, lovely two-horsepower, 2-cycle outboard made by Tohatsu and distributed by Yamaha, Mariner, and others. These are amazing. Once you get used to whipping out the spark plug and draining the carburetor, they will run practically forever.

Just ask my buddy Seiko. He voyaged across the Atlantic and up the eastern seaboard using one as his only means of propulsion.

Just follow the manual and remember to replace the lower-unit grease every year or two. (Buy shear pins by the dozen and be on the dumpster-look-out for a spare prop. If you need an emergency shear pin in a remote location, use a hacksawed stainless steel cotter pin as a temporary fix.)

Of course, the very best yacht tender is an inflatable RIB. I got my $2,400 Apex Nine for $1,200 and it has now lasted for more than 11 years of very hard use. Our secret? We've always kept a custom-made sun cover on it. We've gone through three covers—each completely destroyed by the sun while protecting the dinghy underneath. Our Apex dinghy is very light—only 72 pounds. (Perhaps a bit too light, as it has flipped over numerous times in gusts over 40 knots.) Normally, it lives upside down on the foredeck when we're offshore, which allows us to (almost) have two life rafts.

Yes, $1,200 is a lot of money and it took me awhile to save it up. But that only figures out to $10 a month or (in our case) two cents a mile. Not too bad. And it sure is nice not to have to worry about fenders or nicking someone's pristine topsides.

If you buy an inflatable boat, it must be made out of Hypalon. Do not buy a PVC beach toy and frown when it morphs into a "deflatable" within the first year. Zodiac, Avon, Caribe, and Apex all make good products.

Many people waste money by not being careful with their inflatable dinghy's foot pump. Never keep it in the dinghy. Never allow it to get wet. Always bail your dinghy dry before bringing the pump aboard. If the pump gets even the faintest splash, wipe it down with fresh water, and dry it carefully.

One more hint on inflatable foot pumps: They cost a fortune from some manufacturers but are quite reasonable from others. Often, changing the end fitting is easy. Your dinghy certainly won't mind being pumped up by a different, cheaper model. (Many used gear places have "previously owned" foot pumps for sale.)

If you have to do a major inflatable repair, make sure you do it on the driest day with the lowest humidity possible. (Inflatable dinghy repair shops have massive dehumidifiers, which is one reason their repairs are so successful.)

Summing up: Once you're heading out on your circumnavigation, it is great if you can afford an inflatable. But plywood works, too. And you can often pick up a heavily damaged fiberglass dinghy to patch up for mini-bucks.

Hint: We seldom tow our dinghy. Since it slows us down so much, it is

This is the third cover on our 12-year-old dinghy.

always faster to hoist it aboard. Carolyn has it exactly right when she says, "Never tow a dinghy you can't afford to lose."

Note: To learn what to do when you drown your outboard engine (you will, eventually), see the sailing section.

Plan Now, Pay Later

It would be great if we always had the money to do what we wanted to do, exactly when we wanted to do it! But there are numerous times during the rebuilding and outfitting of an ocean-going yacht when we sea gypsies just don't have the money to buy the stuff (self-steering gear, wind generator, and/or solar cells) we'll eventually want on the boat.

The trick here is to *advance plan* for it. Thus, you can run your heavy ten-gauge wires for your solar cells and wind generator when you rewire your boat, and save a lot of time, trouble, and money in the long haul.

If your mast is down, why not install the sail track for the storm trysail and the upper tang for the staysail? It will be a lot easier, faster, and cheaper now, rather than later.

Just because I can't afford an outboard doesn't mean that I can't afford to build an outboard bracket on my stern rail from that scrap of wood from my galley project.

If you've got the whole boat torn up while doing electrical and plumbing work, why not run the heavy electric cable for your anchor windlass and the hoses for your deck/anchor wash-down pump as well? This will make the installation a snap when Jah "magically delivers" those two items to you unexpectedly.

I do this "pre-plan" drill often. I could only afford one water system in the galley at first, but I put in two matching faucets knowing that one day I'd have another pump and an additional tank for my deck water catchment system. (I should have installed three, as I now have a saltwater faucet as well.)

I know a frugal sea gypsy who really used this idea imaginatively when he constructed an Airex double-ended gaffer on a shoestring budget. He's an artist as well as a builder. So he *painted pictures* of his future portholes around the clear fiberglass areas where he intended them to eventually go. Over the years, he replaced those pictures with the real thing as money permitted.

If nothing else, don't waste money putting stuff where other gear will eventually go. Or, to put it another way, don't buy a transom swim ladder if you plan on having a Monitor or Aries in the same spot!

Life Rafts

Oh, here is a subject fraught with danger!

I will do my best to give you my honest, heart-felt opinion, without the interference of any PC considerations, while bearing in mind this book's focus is on "sailing cheap," not sailing best.

I once read a book called "The Proper Yacht." It was a fine, fine read but had little to do with my daily life as a sea gypsy because I couldn't afford any of the lavish gear so lovingly described in the book. Hell, I had to check the book out of the library because I couldn't afford it. (And it did not stop me from circumnavigating as all the armchair sailors wagged a disapproving finger and said, "It isn't safe to go to sea without a lot of shiny, expensive crap!")

Where were we? Ah, yes. Life rafts.

Some experienced sailors don't carry a life raft. Lin and Larry Pardey pop to mind. Larry once told me, "We don't carry a life raft because our *boat* is the life raft."

I understand this point of view. Certainly, if you need your life raft—then you have screwed up horribly.

Never, ever get into a life raft until a portion of the yacht's rail is beneath the surface. Then, stay clipped alongside (if weather permits) until your vessel sinks out of sight. I repeat: **Never, ever leave your vessel until it is completely under the water.** Or, as my father impressed upon me at an early age, "Only step into a life raft from the spreaders!"

Many half-sunk, abandoned boats have been found sans crew and raft. Don't stupidly commit suicide by choosing a flimsy fabric life raft over a still-floating vessel, no matter how "badly floating" your vessel may be.

I've personally been talking with still-wet "survivors" who "saw her go down" as their still-floating boat was towed through the breakwater—much to their utter astonishment. (Ah, yes, it was a rather embarrassing moment for all of us.)

Certainly my life raft (yes, my lovely Viking raft was another radio ad trade. Thank you, Inflatable Frank) is heavy and takes up a lot of space with all its related safety gear.

The basic question is this: Is a life raft worth carrying if you are on a tight budget?

It is, of course, a judgment call. But I think so. I carry one.

This isn't to say I think Lin and Larry are wrong. I do not. But they are both highly experienced sailors on one of the most well-found wooden boats in the world. What works for them might not work for the 68-year-old on a "converted to a schooner" salvaged ski boat.

Life rafts give you a final chance. And I'm sure there are times when people need a final chance. I haven't ever needed a life raft and pray I never do. But I've always carried one and will continue to do so.

But, damn, they are very expensive! My life raft retails for more than the $3,000 I paid for *Wild Card.*

Here's more bad news: If you get into a life raft in mid-ocean without any water or food or supplies—you are dead anyway.

While many marine life rafts are extremely sturdy and will survive for a long time, many will not. Commercial aircraft rafts are intended to last for days and hours in calm conditions, not for months at sea in brisk tradewinds and large waves.

Boy, I'm just full of depressing news, ain't I?

Can we save any money anywhere in relation to life rafts? Yes, we can, and I have already, saved more than $10,000 on life rafts over the years. Here's how.

First off, if we were rich, we'd buy the most expensive raft possible, mount it in the best possible place for it to be released without getting fouled, attach to it lots of safety goodies, and sail across the ocean.

That's what most wealthy people do today. This is a good way to do it—once. For a crossing. Not as a life-style. This is why 99 percent of all rafts are thrown away or "not able to be re-certified" within a few short years—because they get damaged by salt water incursion—because they are kept outside.

Let's back up. A good life raft costs a lot of money because it is expensive to build. A crappy life raft isn't a good investment because it won't help you in a real emergency; it is really just a placebo for landlubbing worry-warts.

But a life raft is supposed to be recertified every year. This process, if correctly done, costs a lot.

Does a life raft need to be recertified each year? If it is left exposed on your transom and is getting continuously doused with salt water, I believe it does.

If not? Maybe not.

We keep our inflatable dinghy inflated upside down on our foredeck and our Viking life raft inside our vessel, just to port of the companionway, on the quarter berth. Thus, our decade-old raft, after almost two trips around the world, looks almost exactly like a new one because it has never been taken out of its original packaging.

It is still "factory fresh."

I have it recertified every five years, not every year. I'm not saying that recertifying it annually is a bad idea or a waste of money—only that I can't afford it.

There is something I can do, however, to greatly increase my chances of survival over the wealthy guy who has his raft recertified annually and then forgets about it.

I have an extensive amount of carefully packaged life raft supplies that have a high likelihood of accompanying the raft. These are all ready to be deployed along with it.

I have water and a small "squeeze" watermaker. Ditto, a passive, floating solar watermaker (sometimes referred to as a Sea Still). I have various passive (winking CD disks on a waterproof kite tail) and active signaling devices, including a lightweight strobe capable of being deployed on the lifting kite as well. (You can't miss the winking or blinking kite for miles.)

I have fishhooks, line, spears, gaffs, and knives—all stowed in the safest (careful of the life raft fabric), most compact manner possible.

Sure, I have a week's worth of food but, more importantly, I have the fishing and survival equipment capable of securing a *year's* worth of food.

Yes, I have sealed electronics, too. A GPS and a hand-held VHF (powered by rechargeable batteries via the waterproof solar charger they are stowed with) are just two of the units that might come in handy. (I'll include a hand-held AIS transponder as soon as they are manufactured.)

The point I'm trying to make is this: My boat and my life raft are very similar. I hardly paid anything for either. But both are, in many ways, safer and more capable of survival than their more expensive cousins.

All this takes is hard work and careful thought—two things I'm more than happy to spend in large quantities.

Can cheap sailors be safer sailors? You're darn toot'n!

How long will life rafts work without maintenance? It is hard to say. But I once was cleaning out an old marine supply warehouse in South Florida and came across about 20 life rafts, dating back to WWII. I popped each one, just for fun. *All of them* filled with air. Two collapsed immediately with blown seams and four were hissing pretty loudly with obvious leaks. But the remaining 14 seemed serviceable—at least initially.

Not bad. I was impressed.

Where should you keep your life raft? Inside? Outside? I can't tell you. But I will tell you the truth: I keep mine inside. I just can't afford to have it continuously doused with saltwater. It has to last me the rest of my life. If I had mounted it topside 12 years ago, it would be completely worthless today.

Yes, Carolyn and I regularly rehearse our carefully considered *abandon ship* procedures—the gritty details of which are too complex to go into within these pages. But we each have our specific jobs, and our pre-printed three-tier checklist (depending on how much time we have to deploy).

Is this "stowed below" always a perfect solution? No. If my vessel catches fire or explodes, I might not be able to get to the raft inside. Then I will have to rely on my inflatable dinghy, a much grimmer choice.

But I've talked to numerous sailors whose boats have rolled, and lost their "perfectly secured" raft in the process. So everything in life has its pros and cons.

I've made my choice. And I sincerely hope I never have to live or die by it.

Swim Ladders

When in cruise mode, you'll probably always have your dinghy in the water when you're swimming. So not having an expensive swim ladder isn't a problem if you're healthy enough to clamber over an inflatable pontoon.

In an emergency, two or three fenders tied parallel in ladder-fashion works adequately.

Special Gear for Special Places

If you're going to get lost for a decade or two in the Med (which is easy to do) then you might consider mounting a gang-plank pivot device on your transom, and also having a long spool of anchor-rode-webbing on a large reel aft to run ashore.

Once you get there, you can build a quick and dirty gangplank from an aluminum ladder and some discarded plywood, *if* you have the boat-and-end fittings.

If you plan on spending a lot of time in Australia or other areas with extreme tidal range, then you might want to consider folding wheels for your inflatable.

In parts of Canada and England where "mud berthed" boats daily dry out on the tides, some relatively large vessels (up to 50 feet) use "tide poles" to keep themselves upright. I'm not familiar with the specifics of this. It would seem to work only with certain designs, not a fin-keel like my vessel has. But it might be worth looking into a "mud berth" if you could save 5,000 pounds sterling over a summer.

In the Caribbean you don't need anything special: just a Bible, a bottle of rhum, and some virgins to sacrifice during hurricane season.

Velcro and webbing chafe guard

Canvas Stuff

I don't think your average cruisers should attempt to make their own sails unless they get off on such a complex adventure. ("This job keeps me in stitches," laughed one canvas maker to me.)

However, if you like to sew, there are a million little projects to tackle on a cruising boat.

Carolyn sewed up our bimini and dodger, while I bent the stainless steel tubing for the frames. She also made all our cushions, curtains, and sail covers—ditto, our wind scoops (carry three depending on conditions, big, small, and multi-directional) and our fender covers, etc.

If you are not sewing sails, you probably don't need a machine with a walking foot. We searched various bilges for 20 years before finding our Pfaff sewing machine. Thank you Lovely Liz and Wacky Wally aboard the Valiant 40 *Blue Tango*.

If you are making a dodger, use the expensive Strato-glass in the windows as it will last for more than 15 years without cracking or fading. (Most of the plastic windows look crappy after three or four years.) Also make sure to polish them with Pledge spray furniture polish (or generic equivalent) to keep them pliant. But first rinse them with fresh water to make sure you are not rubbing in any salt crystals.

Oh, don't forget to make poly-webbing-and-Velcro into way-cool chafe guards for all your boating friends for Christmas. These are a cheap and appreciated gift—perfect for us grateful sea gypsies.

Tools

Speaking of tools, the less money you have, the more tools you should bring (if you're handy and know how to use them).

Tom Lemm has a full metal lathe aboard his steel pinky *Papillion*, as well as a welding and brazing shop. He not only does all his own work as he circumnavigates, he operates an under-the-table floating machine shop as well. And, in between, he makes beautiful jewelry.

Of course, weight is an issue. You can't carry a welding machine with you on a 30-foot sloop. But the fact remains that a well-financed cruiser can either rent the tool they need and/or someone to operate it, while the less-fixed sea gypsy cannot.

If you're going to be "I'm the guy who has to fix it because I've got empty pockets," you'd best have some tools stashed in the bilge.

Deck Leaks and Other Sad Tales

One thing to consider: If you ocean sail, every bit of your interior will have approximately a bucketfull of saltwater thrown at it once a decade—except for the area around the companionway, which will be hosed with saltwater once a year or every 8,000 miles.

In addition, areas that don't leak while coastal sailing can develop leaks offshore. There is no such thing as a watertight boat in a mature storm. Yes, you may occasionally have dusty bilges if your vessel is steel or aluminum, but not in a gale.

No boat does.

None.

Ever.

Thus, before you mount any item or do anything to your vessel, a little balloon should form over your head with the caption, "Leak?" in it.

"Never, ever, drill a vertical hole in your deck," my father drilled (sic) into me, "especially above a bunk or electronics."

It is difficult to understand how perverse and evil water can be. That's right—I said evil. There's no other way to explain why water flows so determinedly uphill, through sealant, and under gaskets *if there is the slightest chance to drip, drip, drip on your pillow.*

There are at least seven different types of leaks:

1. Rain leaks are from falling droplets and are easy to fix.

2. Sailing leaks develop because areas which aren't normally wet are wet when you sail. Since these (often hull-to-deck joint leaks) are intermittent, they are more difficult to fix. Lessening your angle of heel (reefing) can help.

3. Immersion leaks take a while to get going, and continue longer. These are caused by water pooling in areas where it normally doesn't collect, slowly immersing the area, and then leaking with increasing flow.

4. Wind/spray leaks get worse as the breeze increases. Picture your bow plunging into a solid wall of water during a 50 knot gust. The resulting spray is driven, at 50 knots, under hatches and up/over their carlins with great force.

5. Wave action is the worst, of course. Occasionally my entire bow is momentarily underwater. This is why an on-deck windlass doesn't last as long as a belowdecks one, and why fore hatches are notoriously sadistic.

6. Angle of heel plays a part. Most boatbuilders think of leaks as water flowing *down*, and they're right. But "down" on a boat at anchor and "down" on a boat heeled 45 degrees are vastly different. For example, I've constructed carlins that worked perfectly at rest and collected vast amounts of water under sail, which then slopped below a bucketful at a time. Damn!

7. Flex leaks are caused by excessive movement of hull/deck components as the wave action increases. Getting hit by large waves flex (and crack open) things. Even worse, is getting the boat rudely shoved under water by a sweeping sea. This is why most broken pilot house windows occur on the leeward side, not the windward. (Watch carefully in a gale; the greater impact is caused by the boat hitting the water, not the water hitting the boat!)

Part of the problem is how much modern fiberglass boats flex. *Wild Card* flexes far, far too much. She is like a plate of Jello or a balloon in a major storm.

Many years ago, I was over-tired at the height of a gale and thinking about reefing rather than doing it. I was sitting at the nav station, resting my weary head on my palm, when I heard the roar of a particularly large wave. I lifted my head up in concern. The wave hit the hull hard. It flexed. This caused the nav table to hit my elbow with a sharp blow—and I punched myself hard in the chin.

"Okay, okay," I screamed in alarm and shock, "I'm awake! I'm reefing! Just don't punch me again, okay?"

Carolyn just rolls her eyes at such moments, obviously amused to be married to such an idiot.

But leaks are no joking matter.

My father told me to never drill a vertical hole in my deck, but I did one time

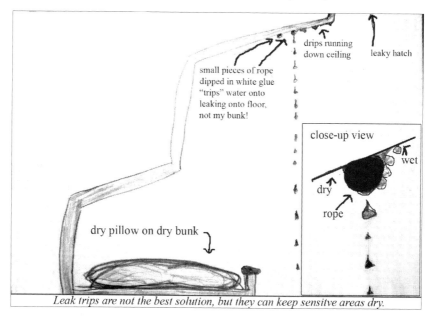

Leak trips are not the best solution, but they can keep sensitve areas dry.

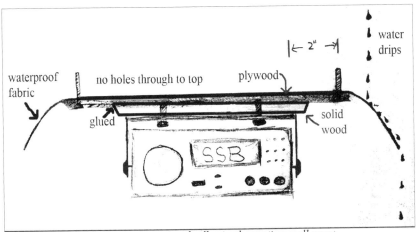

Constructing equipment umbrellas is always time well spent.

when he wasn't looking. ("Take that, old man!") I put large pad-eyes on the side decks to use to sheet my inner staysail. I sealed it well and it didn't leak, even in the roughest blow. I was pretty smug—until winter. In cold weather, condensation collected on the nuts inside the boat and dripped onto my head

while I was reading in the port settee. Each horrible wet drip made a sound that said, "Told you so," in my father's voice.

Properly mounting electronics isn't an easy task. Obviously, it is best not to mount your VHF radio under a known leak. But what about a *future* leak? Or water perversely running from a known leak to your radio?

These issues are why we hear endless sea stories of "everything was fine. Then the gale hit, and our lights/radios/instruments blinked off!"

Electro-stuff getting wet on a small boat isn't something that isn't the captain's fault—because *everything* is the captain's fault, remember?

It is predictable and, thus, preventable.

We use water "trips" to reroute water drips from dangerous areas into benign ones. Thus, if I find that at 34 degrees of heel to starboard my VHF is getting dripped on, I take an eighth-inch piece of string, soak it in white glue, and place it on the headliner in such a manner that it either causes the water to fall harmlessly on the cabin sole well before the instruments, or routes it somewhere safer.

With critical gear, I take even more precautions. Example: We were going to leave on our first circumnavigation without an SSB, but the good people of St. John gave us an Icom 710 at our going-away party.

It was a wonderful thing to do. We appreciated it greatly. Obviously, I didn't want this unit to get wet, especially since we make our living through it (by sending off our manuscripts via the connected digital Pactor modem).

Thus we "umbrella-ed" it to keep it dry. We firmly mounted the radio to a larger sheet of waterproofed, epoxied plywood, paying particular attention to sealing the vertical holes. Next, we rubber-cemented an even larger piece of waterproof Sunbrella Plus over that. (Yes, there are at least two types of Sunbrella fabric, waterproof and water resistant.) Then we mounted it on the underside of the deck.

It has lived there, dry, through (almost) two circumnavigations. Why? Because the vertical holes to hold the unit to the plywood aren't the same as the holes that hold the plywood to the boat. They are outside the radio, on the far edges. If a deck leak develops under the plywood, the water is just harmlessly shed off by the ply and fabric. The fabric in the front of the unit drops down, so even if a wave hits it, the radio won't take a direct hit. To easily see/operate the radio, we just tuck up the fabric.

Note: radios have to run cool when transmitting. This is why the fabric is "draped" over the radio by a couple of inches—so it doesn't inhibit the radio's cooling ducts.

None of this cost a penny—only time and thought.

I didn't want the expense ($600 Ouch!) of having high-tech, heavy, expensive "marine" insulators on my backstay, and I'd heard that some of them had failed during unintentional gybes anyway. Naturally, I didn't want my installation of the SSB to make my boat *weaker*, only better. So I ran an ordinary stranded 12-gauge electrical wire from my antenna tuner (inside aft, under the cockpit by the stern rail) to my (almost) masthead. (I used a five-foot piece of small braided Dacron line to run to the masthead and act as the upper insulator.)

I can't report that this is particularly pretty but it has worked fine for more than a decade, so I can't complain, especially since it cost me nothing (as I'd just retrieved the used wire from the dumpster of a bankrupt restaurant).

Most $600,000 yachts have SSBs that are far more expensive and modern than mine that fail often (some fail almost every time they go to sea!) because of poor, ill-thought-out installations.

This is why I believe a $3,000 yacht can be safer than a $600,000 one, if the owner has taken more time and put more blood, sweat, and tears into his decisions—than his more pampered counter-part.

Plywood acts as umbrella. All potential drips away from unit.

My father was old-school and was involved with wooden boatbuilding prior to WWII. He taught me many practical things—like how to build a hatch or companionway.

"Water wants to leak, son," he told me long ago. "We know that. So we carefully build as watertight a companionway as we possibly can. And then we add a water-trap or air moat or trough to catch and reroute the few smart-ass drips which have managed to get through despite our best efforts."

The hatch carlins I constructed on *Carlotta* were at least two inches high, with a water-catchment trough two inches wide and one inch high. The collected drips drained aft.

Yes, to paraphrase our founding fathers, "The price of liberty is eternal vigilance." And that's the secret to preventing deck leaks too.

Final leaky note: Occasionally, leaks start suddenly in unexpected places while at sea. The problem isn't fixing them later—that's easy. The problem is fixing them now, during a gale, at night, before your bunk becomes a swimming pool.

I use old fashioned toilet bowl "ring" wax for this purpose. It sticks like crazy to wet surfaces. I once had a butt-block on my old wooden boat open up while sailing offshore in late autumn. I temporarily put up too much canvas (sail area), tied a rope to my ankle, and crawled down the "high side" of the topsides, past the boot top, until I could reach the obvious leak. I then rubbed a palm full of toilet wax on the wet slimy area, before having Carolyn hoist me back on deck. This stopped the leak instantly. The following spring, we hauled and my palm print was still plainly visible in the wax.

In an emergency where a seam has opened up on a wooden boat, I mix it with antifouling paint and use it as the best, cheapest underwater "miracle" seam compound.

My buddy Larry Pardey uses "silly putty" for deck leaks.

John Smith, the infamous madman of the famous *Mermaid of Carriacou*, uses bicycle tire patches for emergency underwater repairs.

All three methods work—who would have *thunk* that the best "miracle cures" are almost free?

Hatching Problems

For some reason, it seems as if there is a glut of used or brand-new-but-discounted hatches on the market. This is wonderful. Just make sure to mount them on a completely flat surface when you install them, as the slightest racking is too much.

I prefer aluminum, as many of the plastic hatches are just too flimsy for live-aboard use.

Of course, if you require an exact replacement, that's pricey. But you can often buy a just slightly bigger hatch that is cheaper, and then widen the opening slightly. (Yes, you can use a smaller hatch but that's often more work.)

Don't Waste Money On

...expensive gear when cheap gear is better.

The cheap Davis radar reflectors have proven to be far more effective than many of their competitors costing ten times as much.

Don't use any exterior iron or galvanized iron (except anchor and chain) on non-ferric hulls. It is false economy, especially rigging.

A $150 Maximum wind speed indicator intended for your house will both outlast (and usually out-perform) all those crappy marine ones costing upwards of a $1,000.

But Don't Be Penny Wise and Dollar Foolish

Yes, you can try to use soft plastic hose in place of canvas-covered rubber dinghy guard, but it won't do nearly as good of a job.

Don't be stupid like I was when I purchased six soccer balls to use as yacht fenders, and then had them all pop at once when smashed into the dock by a mini-wave. Damn it!

Ditto, port-a-potties with squeeze pumps. The bottom line: you'll end up wearing it!

Forget transom-mounted outboard brackets on sailing vessels with counters. The running outboard will be plunged underwater the moment the boat starts hobby-horsing—and quit running.

Yes, you should have sails made out of genuine Dacron, not those blue FEMA tarps masquerading as Spectra.

While you don't need exotic, expensive "specialty-core" lines for your running rigging, stick with braided Dacron and nylon, not polypropylene, manila, cotton, or hemp.

(Don't even *think* about smoking the hemp rope because it isn't that type of hemp, you idiot!)

Never get a "white gas" stove anywhere around a boat unless you are a Buddhist monk intent on self-immolation.

Rugs have no place on the sides of the inside or overhead of a boat. If you want to walk on them, fine. But don't allow them to become condensation-and-bug magnets.

Be wary of automotive or truck hydraulics on a boat, especially as a steering system. I've worked on a few—all of which were pieces of crap.

Most steel cabinets don't do well aboard, especially anything resembling a file cabinet.

Contact paper doesn't *really* look the same as a teak deck. If you can't tell the difference between a teak deck and some wood-grained shelf paper—consider gardening as a hobby.

The only difference between fake stuff ashore and fake stuff at sea is that your life has to depend on the fake stuff at sea. That's a *sizable* difference.

Yes, golf shoes are great on the course. No, they don't work as well at sea.

While it is true that pot-metal (or Zamak) doesn't rust, it corrodes at an even a faster rate. Forget pot-metal outside. (You can often tell these cheapy boat bits intended for freshwater runabouts by their smooth round casting marks, which are completely unlike brass or bronze casting marks.)

Plastic through hulls should only be used above the waterline and with careful backing. Forget them anywhere close to the waterline, as skim ice will pop 'em like thin balloons.

Yes, steel electrical connectors will work—for about 2.5 seconds. Once they start to rust, your negatively-charged electrons are gonna have to battle their way through rust. Is that what you want?

Never allow steel wool within ten miles of your vessel, as ten minutes of use will create more rust than you can clean off in ten years.

Read the above sentence three or four times, until you are sure you understand it.

If you need steel wool, buy some bronze wool from your local chandlery. It seems pricey but it isn't so bad really, because a single plastic sack lasts for many years.

Don't ever mount a transducer on a stick over your transom or run the transducer cable *outside* your vessel. Both are just too tacky for words. If you can't afford to haul and haven't the guts to do it while in the water, wait.

Don't be like me. Once a Maine shipwright came up to me when I was a young, struggling boatbuilder, and said sincerely, "There are limits to shoddy, Fatty, and you obviously have no idea where they are!"

Oops.

Belowdecks

The only two stove fuels to consider are kerosene and propane. We use propane, but it can blow up faster than a Southern Baptist, so be careful. (In a pinch, butane can be used in a stove designed for propane *but not the other way around*. Do not use propane in a stove designed for butane.)

We went decades using propane RV camping **stoves** instead of stainless steel marine ones. These work, if you can keep excessive rust at bay. Just a few months ago we came across an almost-new $2,000 Eno stove for $200 because, in the words of the owner, "First one burner went, then a month later—the other one went too! Now neither work and I can't be bothered with it. I'm going electric and eliminating the problem!"

I'm not sure how well his "electric" solution worked, but it took me about two minutes to clean out the burner orifices with a sewing needle and the stove has been "happy as Larry" ever since.

If you use an electric solenoid to shut off the fuel at the tank, make sure you have a manual override that enables you to switch on the gas without 12 volts. (Repeat: propane can be dangerous. Consult and follow marine industry guidelines.)

We like a deep, double **stainless steel sink**. There's no need to get a marine one.

We don't use a pressurized fresh water system—too expensive and prone to failure. We use a foot pump instead, which meters even small amounts of water perfectly.

In addition to the **foot pump**, we have a tiny little inline Whale pump (which must be mounted below the tank) to electrically pump water to fill the kettle, etc.

With a flip-of-a-valve, this turns into our cockpit shower as well. (I used to be a filthy hippie, now I'm a very, very clean one!)

Garbage bins are a big problem on small boats. Ours is under the sink. Some are mounted on the backside of the galley doors—so when you open them, they come out a bit for easy use.

One of the best systems I ever saw was designed by Larry Best aboard the 52-foot Perseverance. It had a lovely foot operated "pop-top" that has been working flawlessly for almost 40 years now.

Cabin lights are expensive in marine supply stores. I make most of mine. If not, I buy them in automotive and/or camping stores. I'm gradually increasing my LED lights, which draw almost no electricity. But I'll never eliminate my incandescence ones totally. I like to eat and smooch under their warm yellow glow. (Yes, Carolyn and I smooch often—like, every time we tack! I can't help it, she's hot!)

Headaches are often caused by marine heads. I use a Raritan PHII which looks like a piece of garbage and isn't. Plastic holding tanks stink. Even if you use a heavy metal tank, the hose still stinks. My head is plumbed so that it can be converted from "full sea use" to "no overboard discharge" with a minimum of fuss and feces.

A **Kindle** book reader only costs about $100 bucks now. I have over 3,000 (almost all free) books on mine; Carolyn has a bit more space left on hers. We get the New Yorker magazine every week—which is like oxygen to a writer!

Digital Devices

There's no denying that boats are carrying more cameras, computers, and electronics than ever before. The good news is that many of these electro-gizmos can save you both weight and money. My iPad is so cyber-speedy that it receives my color copies of *"Cruising World"* magazine even before our Stateside subscribers see them. My large-screen laptop serves as my "poor man's chartplotter," and my tiny 12-volt netbook holds the ships inventory (which consists mostly of rice and beans).

I don't know of a single boat currently sailing around the word that doesn't have a computer aboard. We did meet one traditional Jack Tarr transiting the Indian Ocean who bought a sextant in SE Asia, learned to use it, and tossed away his GPS. But even he had two computers aboard.

In addition to saving money, many digi-thingies help me earn my living under sail as well. My Olympus digital recorder allowed me to produce the series of radio shows that recently aired over NPR. And, of course, my word processors enable me to produce books like this one while underway as well. Yes, I have two DSLR cameras aboard, as about 20 percent of my income is from supplying "art" to accompany my various writings.

In order to market my writing and photography, a complicated gaggle of cell phones, USB sticks, Wi-Fi-routers, and SSB modems are needed as well.

Of course, some people love this cyber age and some don't. But the bottom line is that it allows me to *earn more money than I ever have before*, while remaining naked, shoeless, and afloat in some distant paradise—which is what being a sea gypsy is all about.

But there's no denying the fact that I now carry an astounding number of "electro-bits" aboard.

Sadly, these digi-thingies don't like the moisture-attracting (hygroscopic) qualities of salt water—especially cameras. Within months of residing on a boat, mildew begins to grow inside a camera lens. Often, within six months or so, the cameras are either useless or dramatically impaired. Yet, my Canon DSLR is now over ten years old and working perfectly.

Why?

Because I keep it in a "dry box." Dry boxes are worth their weight in gold.

A dry box not only keeps out water, it keeps out the excessive humidity as well. Thus, my onboard cameras have the same "dryness" as if they were being stored in the dry Arizona desert.

You can, of course, go into a camera shop and spend big money on a fancy dry box. Or you can just get a large, air-tight, resealable kitchen container, drill a tiny hole in it, super-glue a $2 hygrometer over that hole, toss in a small dehumidifier—and you're done.

Once the dehumidifier is "charged" using your 110-volt onboard inverter (overnight or when motoring), your cameras will be safe for many months from excessive moisture, depending on how often you open and close the container.

Yes, in the tropics (especially near the equator) our shipboard humidity is often hovering around 90 percent. But a glance at the hygrometer on the dry box assures me that my cameras are still "desert" dry at 35 percent relative humidity.

I have two dry boxes now, one for the cameras and the other primarily for digital storage media.

Fatty's home-made dry box keeps his cameras dry.

Disk drives are, basically, a spinning platter of "micro-swiss-cheese" magnetic media—a perfect incubator for mildew. Of course, if you use your hard drive daily (like the one in your laptop), the heat it generates kills the mildew almost instantly and you can go for years without a problem.

But if you don't use the disk drive for awhile in a marine environment and it isn't in a dry box, it won't work after a distressingly short period.

We have (I'm ashamed to say) 12 portable hard-drives aboard *Wild Card*, mostly related to the photography part of our freelance writing. These all live happily in their dry box, completely mildew-free. If we leave the boat for more than a week, we put almost every (non-marine) piece of electronics in our dry boxes—so it all works upon our return.

The bottom line: ship-built (homebuilt, but more fun!) dry boxes are cheap and save a ton of money.

Music

Most boats don't have a cassette or CD player anymore—just an **iPod** wired into their amp/speakers.

I prefer to play my **guitar** that I have mounted within easy reach on the main bulkhead. My axe is carbon-fiber—which is practical if I want to snorkel and play at the same time. (Washing your hands before you play and wiping the strings down with kerosene triples their life.)

Hidey-Holes

I used to have a **built-in safe** aboard *Carlotta*. (This was in the days before ATMs were found almost everywhere in the world.) It was very well mounted and couldn't be carried off without hours of work and many tools. I went to a lot of trouble to buy and install it. It was a total failure—worse, actually. Customs officials always came across it and aggressively demanded it be opened. Word often spread that it was aboard and probably contained millions in cash and/or drugs. I was more worried about being killed because of it than having my paltry "valuables" protected by it.

Now I have two built-in "stash" boxes to hide money and jewelry and one large hidden area to hide all (or most) of the valuable stuff on *Wild Card* if I have to leave her for a long time.

Obviously, it does not behoove me to go into specifics.

On *Carlotta*, there was a hidden false floor under the dinette. It was almost impossible to spot and difficult to get into (unless you realized some "bolts" were actually disguised, easily-removable pins).

This worked well, except for the time we were leaving for a week and I hid all the stuff within. I was closing the companionway slide when we heard the just-wound Eight Day Ship's Clock beginning to chime, as it did every half hour—a dead give-away to our stash. (Grrr..!)

Spycraft can be useful to a sailor. Spies know about hiding stuff. And they know that any room can be thoroughly searched if given enough time. Their solution is to hide their most important items outside in plain sight.

I know one guy aboard a very modest boat that has $250,000 vacuum-sealed in his mizzen boom. (No, I don't know why, nor have I ever asked.) When the guy's boat with $250,000 in the boom started to sink during a daysail, his puzzled charter guests were amazed to see him frantically disconnecting the boom rather than handing out PFDs!)

Spinnaker poles are hollow. Has anyone ever lifted up the pile of anchor chain while searching a boat? I doubt it. There sure is a lot of unseen space in an inflatable, isn't there?

The point I'm trying to make is to think-out-of-the-box by not putting stuff in the box where the searchers will first look.

Getting the Water Out

Bilge pumps can't be undersized nor shoddy, but there's still plenty of ways to save money here as well.

I've made many a "quick and dirty" ultra-cheap float switch by taking a hinged toilet bowl float and tying a household mercury switch to it with waxed twine. Once you get the angle of the mercury switch correct so it turns on and off at the right level of bilge water, you're done.

I've had these last for years. (Okay, I'll admit Rule float switches are better because my house-hold cheapies don't like getting repeatedly splashed by salt water. But I've put them on many dock queens with great success.)

It costs almost nothing to plumb your engine's raw water pump to act as an emergency bilge pump as well. But you better have a great strainer on it or your engine will overheat with clogged bilge debris.

My bilges are deep in *Wild Card*, so I have a "bilge pump pod" that I stick down into my very narrow aft bilge. This allows me retract the whole mess to work on it—something I usually have to do at least once a year.

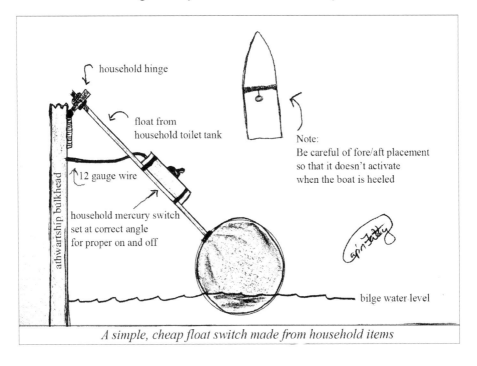

A simple, cheap float switch made from household items

I also have a Whale Gusher Ten manual bilge pump mounted in the cockpit.

Please bear in mind I've been living aboard for more than 50 years and have seen hundreds of boats sink, many of them needlessly. Thus we also carry aboard tiny *Wild Card*, a large Edson manual pump mounted on a portable board which will "pump a pair of trousers" through it without blinking. Many a vessel afloat today owes its existence to this portable "instantly available" pump that throws a lot of water (five-foot handle!) in the hands of a scared man. How many $600,000 yachts in this world carry around a giant pump that is intended, hopefully, to help others out?

Not many.

That's because they have money and don't need the good karma as much as I do!

Fatty with his very large manual bilge pump

More Power

Batteries are expensive. We buy American (Trojan) despite the high cost of shipping. We have two banks. These work well. However, like any lead/acid wet cell battery, if the charging voltage/rate is too high, they boil away their water rapidly, warp their plates, and fail prematurely. If the charging rate is too low (many solar chargers are set far too low), then the batteries sulfate. Both conditions dramatically shorten the batteries' usefulness.

Never deplete your batteries below 50 percent.

If you are replacing your batteries every two years, something is wrong. You should be getting four years out of Trojans.

If you custom build your **battery box**, make sure it won't allow acid to escape, will accept a wide variety of shapes and sizes, and can be latched in such a manner that your batteries can't fall out in the event of a 360 degree roll. Allow for a place to keep your acid-dripping hydrometer. With no electrical drain, your batteries should read 12.6 volts. Check your water weekly in the tropics, monthly elsewhere. Only use ionized distilled water, never tap water. Clean your posts and cable clamps once a year with a wire brush.

The Trojan battery company has a very informative website, with a detailed

PDF file for the prudent mariner to download. Reading it carefully will save you tons of money.

One more hint: I've noticed that old batteries often fail a month after going to sea. I didn't know why, but have since learned that, in layman's terms, powder is shaken off the plates in lumpy seas, puddles at the bottom, and adds to premature failure.

I wouldn't head across the Pacific with 3-year-old batteries. There's too much risk they'd fail before New Zealand. I'd buy new ones before I shoved off.

Speaking of batteries, make sure you don't leave any dry cell batteries in any small electronic devices while circumnavigating. They will leak, and ruin the unit. I've lost thousands of $$$s to cheap, leaking foreign batteries. Don't be fooled by the Duracell or Energizer label in S.E. Asia as many of these batteries are faker than a politician's smile.

We carry high-quality rechargeable AA and AAA batteries as well. These are extremely economical, and have the advantage of never leaking (that we've experienced). These rechargeable batteries are so important to us that we have recharging units in 110, 220, and 12 volts. (Our daughter Roma and I have worked our way through our Gameboy addiction but not Carolyn. If her nose isn't in a book, it's softly illuminated by her Nintendo screen.) (Update: I'd rib her more about this, except now I can't get her away from her iPad 2!)

Cabin fans are an absolute necessity if a crew member is going through menopause and the Indian Ocean at the same time. Trust me on this one, pal. If you don't have a cabin fan for the hot-flashing wifey on the equator—you're both better off dead!

Why an SSB Isn't an Extravagance

I went the first 40 years of living aboard and cruising without an SSB radio. I used my short-range VHF sparingly, and that seemed sufficient to me. However, the wonderful people of St. John in the U.S. Virgins thought differently. They banded together on the sly, and, over the course of many months, purchased an almost new Icom 710 with antenna tuner, ground, and antenna for us. They even sent electrician Chris Angel down to install it. (Chris also taught me to always put a loop in any wire I'm routing into my vessel—so water can't run down it into the instrument.)

Thus, despite my plans, I began my first circumnavigation with a *great* SSB radio.

The first thing we noticed was how many new friends we suddenly had. Instead of just getting to know the boats in our harbor, we began (on the SSB nets) to "meet" our fellow boaters from all over the Eastern seaboard. We might or might not chat, but we'd get to know them as real people. So when they'd finally drop their hook next to us in some nameless harbor, we'd row over and eagerly introduce ourselves because, well, we were already old friends—we'd just never met. Next, we realized we were learning a bunch of stuff from the exact areas we needed to— those directly ahead. Best of all, we were able to avoid a lot of heavy weather by not leaving, slowing, tacking, heaving-to, and/or reversing direction.

The most important thing we learned via our SSB was how to avoid hassle and needless expense. Example, to clear into Male, in the Maldives, it currently costs $200 initially, and then the chase is on for the rest of your wallet. For whatever reason, the office of Customs and Immigration isn't particularly friendly there, and often view yachts as irritating cash-cows.

About 80 miles away (we learned by SSB) was the tiny island of Uligan, where they love boats. They don't attempt to "surprise" the skippers with hidden costs, but charge them a flat $20 for the first three days. Guess which place we went?

In the Philippines, the officials are so corrupt that most visiting sailors just can't deal with it. So nobody, not one single yacht that we knew or heard of, cleared into Customs. They just visited Immigration and the Harbor Master, period.

Other countries, like Samoa, are different—with the Harbor Master being the evil entity.

The only way to learn which is which, when, and where is via your daily, up-to-the-second reports on your SSB.

Cruiser nets abound. The more primitive the location, the more likely it is to have an active, helpful "yachtie" net. Many of them focus on saving you money. They are run, completely for free, by people exactly like you.

Our SSB radio **saves us its cost** almost every two years or so.

Of course, there are advantages other than dollars and sense.

We left the Cook Islands at the same time an old duffer with green crew (young, attractive, female) did. They were bound for New Zealand. Within three days, they were in a moderate winter gale. The old guy had a heart attack. Within two hours of hearing his distress call, we (dozens of people helped) had him talking directly to a heart specialist sailing off PNG. This allowed him to be stabilized enough to make it into Auckland and the waiting ambulance. (The young lady is reported to have returned home and bought an inland farm.)

A few years later, we added a Pactor modem to our SSB so we could send and receive emails. This not only saved us money, it allowed us to earn far more money as well.

Our radio, which I foolishly wasn't going to have, has turned into a win-win-win. I completely understand if you don't want the intrusion of random, unasked-for communication with shore. But sailing around the world without an SSB will cost you greatly in money, time, and vexation.

Don't Forget To Track Your Progress

The entire time you are outfitting your vessel, you should be expanding your marine contacts and visiting various "non-traditional" outlets such as pawn shops, junkyards, and salvage operators.

Pawnshops? Yes, especially in port or naval cities. My father used to bring them pictures of sextants and Astro compasses and tell them he was interested in any "surveying" instruments they might come across. We purchased and resold many marine sextants this way. I've continued this. The last sextant I resold was an old but perfect Plath—for $2,000 to a lawyer with a nautical-themed office.

Shipyards

All shipyards have boats that aren't paying. If they don't pay long enough, they get "seized" and sold, so the yard can recover its debt. The trick is to get advance warning so you can scoop the deal before the auction. This is often as easy as going into the yard office and asking, or buying a yard worker a couple of (dozen) beers after work.

Unfortunately for the yard, not all vessels that aren't paying can be sold. Some aren't worth the trouble to legally seize and auction off. I know of a couple of yards which, thus, offered a local yachtie a trade—their labor and time to "remove" the yacht or disassemble it in place.

This can be tricky. You have to know exactly what you're getting into. But in St. Thomas at least, some of the Lagoonies (the local sea gypsies) have made a touchdown by chain-sawing and burning a hull and then selling its keel and bronze for scrap in Puerto Rico.

The point I'm trying to make is that shipyard owners, managers, and yard workers often know who has stopped paying (and why) a year or so before the boat might come up for auction. Often it is in their best interest for the boat to exchange hands as soon as possible.

In any event, picking the brains of people scraping off barnacles is always fun and often profitable.

Check Out the Daily Newspaper

I once stumbled across a tiny newspaper ad in South Florida that read "Garage Full of Boat Stuff cheap." I dashed over in a van—praying I'd beat Chuck Fitzgerald from "Sailorman." It was an estate sale. The ad was placed by two very wealthy kids who didn't know anything about boats, or care. They just wanted to be able to garage their new Porsche.

The garage was stuffed from floor to ceiling with marine gear—much of it exquisite antiques.

One visible item was a very large Chelsea clock.

I'd just purchased a Chelsea Clock the month before and had been studying up on the company and its wonderful products.

I knew the large clock (it turned out there were four other large baro/clock sets I couldn't see) was worth more than a thousand dollars.

"Gee," I said, "this would take forever to go through item-by-item—and we'd make a mess too. Wanna just sell the whole pile of crap for $800?"

"Sure," they said, "Why not?"

A month later, Carolyn and I shoved off for a year in the Bahamas.

Buying and Selling Used Boat Gear

This can be profitable and fun. I used to manage "Marine Discounts" on Seventeenth Street in Fort Liquordale and I had a ball wheeling-and-dealing.

While managing that very busy store, I had a lot of used gear piled on a weird, wobbly wooden table. I decided to throw the table away, but it took me a while to clear it. A woman walked in, glanced at me, yelped, and ran out the door. Yes, Fort Lauderdale is a strange place. About 15 minutes later, she was back towing an elderly well-dressed British man who bee-lined for the dirty, scratched table.

"Do you know what this is?" he sputtered. "It is the original gimbaled table—custom-made for a Nic 65 (as in, I knew, Camper Nicholson) which we just happen to have! Will you take $500 for it?"

"$1,200," I shot back.

"$1000?"

"Done!" I said, and we both grinned wide.

Stanley's Marine, a used boat bits store in Whangerei, New Zealand

I'm not suggesting you stop outfitting your boat and go into business. I merely point out that you entertain the logical idea that there's no reason not to make a profit on some of the marine scrounging you're engaged in. Just keep your eyes and ears open.

When we mistakenly hauled up that 500 pound giant ship's anchor in Puerto Rico, we knew a seafood restaurant would pay good money for it. It did.

Cape Town shops are filled with marine antiques that they consider "old junk" that never sold and thus, worthless. Ditto, Hong Kong.

I once was on the bridge of a Russian warship with the captain (who was looking at the bikini-clad girls on a nearby beach). I was amazed to have him turn to me and say, "Everything here is for sale. See anything you'd like?"

"How 'bout the folding spyglass you were just looking through?" I asked. "Ten bucks?"

He smiled and handed it to me. I gave him ten bucks. I was with Will Ferry of the catamaran *Cat's Eye* at the time. He was astounded at what had just happened.

"Er..." Will said, "do you have any more of those?"

The skipper grinned and said, "I have one more. But that one is, I'm afraid, twenty dollars!"

Will quickly agreed and we all shook hands—marveling at the beauty of capitalism run amok. (The Russian sailors hadn't been paid in months.)

I could go on-and-on. Buying and selling was relatively easy in wealthy, mobile Fort Lauderdale. People were constantly moving around and reinventing themselves—merrily spilling money as they went. I had a simple rule—never buy a bunch of anything, from which I didn't think I could recover my money within 72 hours *from a single item.*

Fort Lauderdale in the 1970s is the only place I've ever been that rained money—so much money that even I was able to collect a bushel full!

Summing Up

In order for a wealthy person to circumnavigate, they have to buy, outfit, and steer a boat around the world—just like us poor folk. The challenge is almost identical. To circumnavigate, we both have to spend time, spend money, spend energy, spend creativity, spend talent, spend courage, spend knowledge, spend heart, spend... lots.

And the rich and the poor will both suffer at times. We will both experience fear and doubt—two of the coins which make eventual victory so sweet.

The sole difference is the amount of money the wealthy can, and will, spend. So, of the dozen things it takes to circumnavigate, the wealthy have only one single advantage over the poor.

And, believe it or not, there are drawbacks to having too much money.

Extremely wealthy people are always afraid that others are trying to take away their money—probably because other people are always trying to take away their money. Wealthy people often feel a burden to help others—and yet don't know how. This conflicts them, sometimes mightily. Wealthy people feel they should be happy (because they have all that money!) and yet they aren't happy—which is enough to piss off a saint. Eventually, wealthy people realize that money only buys convenience. But, alas, they can become so accustomed to such convenience that, if they're not careful, they start treating their fellow humans as servants. This is not a good formula for forming close personal relationships. In addition, wealthy people have "all the options in the world" and thus, often can't decide what to do next. Boredom is a mental condition that is easy to obtain with a pocket full of gold. Poor people are seldom bored because they're struggling to survive. This gives them a nice, clear goal. Ditto, being neurotic—the poor just don't have time for such self-indulgent mind games.

Plus, wealthy circumnavigators don't have the joys of working as they go, getting to meet the locals on buses, getting assisted while lugging water jugs—none of that fun stuff.

I bet you never realized how disadvantaged wealthy people are, did you?

I have a lot of compassion for my well-heeled friends. Their opportunities to smile are far fewer than mine.

Money really doesn't buy happiness. Sure, it can buy such things as sex. But buying a prostitute (regardless of his/her social standing) isn't love.

Poverty is the common, nearly universal condition of much of the world. Most of my friends live on $2 a day. Poor people around the world welcome me into their homes and hearts with open arms—in part because I am like them, a working man struggling to survive.

I've happily squatted ashore in Asia and ate the offered rice of the desperately poor while staring offshore at the anchored mega-yachts. I don't know what the poor Asians think, but I know what I think at such times: pity the sad rich person locked away in all that solitary splendor, desperately seeking to reach out and touch another person thousands of miles away via modem, Internet, tele-conference, Skype, Facebook, and/or satphone—and so often failing. Everyone needs to be smiled at and touched. We're all just humans. Castles keep the rich in at the same time they keep the poor out. Many mansions are really gilded jail cells. What a shame the wealthy don't have the courage to escape their floating plastic palaces and mingle with the true wealth of this planet—its fascinating, big-hearted people.

Wild Card sails away

Section III

Sailing Around the World On the Pennies Scotsmen Throw Away

Okay, you've now purchased a boat, fixed its major problem, and carefully outfitted it to sail around the world. Even better, you've concentrated on the "strength and safety" issues so that your vessel has a better chance of surviving a circumnavigation than the average $600,000 one.

Congratulations.

The hard part is over. It is almost pure fun from here. You've paid your dues. I doff my hat to you with sincere respect.

You now have to learn to sail your boat. "But I already know how to sail," you might say. "I've chartered twice in the VI and did an overnighter with Uncle Bert!"

Okay. Fine. Maybe you're up-to-speed on the sailing. But I'm talking about sailing your boat in specifically, not a boat in general.

Please note: If you learn how to ride a bicycle one day, you shouldn't join the Tour de France the next. It takes more than a day to develop the muscles, stamina, mental strength, knowledge, and experience the Tour de France requires.

Ditto, circumnavigating.

Take it slow. Learn the ropes of your boat in flat water and light winds. Then, inch-by-inch, move further afield. Sail all day. Sail a couple of hours at night. Set off on a deliciously-exciting over-nighter. Take off for a three day holiday. Spend a week gunkholing. Make a three day (and night) passage, etc.

When do you know to move on? How fast should you progress?

That's easy—keep it fun and a tad exciting. The "fun" will slow you down and the "exciting" will drive you forward.

Don't do what John Caldwell did—fall overboard on your first sail, clamber back aboard, and then set off across the Pacific without returning to shore. (No, his boat didn't make it, but he got the girl and a highly entertaining book called "Desperate Voyage" out of his well-deserved shipwreck.)

The whole point of cruising is to enjoy yourself. Oh, sure, there will be plenty of agony and pain as well, but the joy should easily overpower the misery.

Keeping it **fun** is the key. Anchor in a quiet cove and make every sexual fantasy your spouse has ever had come true. *That's* cruising. Take up knitting. Learn to play the bagpipes. Learn to fish—on a million different philosophical levels. *That's* cruising!

I'd recommend at least a season of sailing locally before shoving off for Mexico (if you are a Left Coaster) or the Caribbean (East Coaster).

Once you've sailed for two years and more than 4,000 ocean miles, you can make your own decisions based on experience rather than hearsay. (Frankly, I think you are completely crazy for relying on *any* of my sophomoric advice!)

Money, Honey!

Let's say you now have a good boat that is well-outfitted and well-traveled. You believe you have enough experience to start to sail around the world, and you're itching to begin.

How much money should you start off with?

You are asking a "dollars and sense" question.

The answer is: as much as you can. Nobody ever started any four year complex goal hampered by too much money.

Many well-heeled circumnavigators spend $50,000 a year on their Big Fat Circle —and a few spend far more than that.

If you're looking for a bargain-basement figure, I'd say $5,000 dollars is the bare minimum, in part because your boat isn't untested. If you and your boat haven't sailed for two years and 4,000 ocean miles, you'll have to find another $10,000 or so because you'll need to make initial changes and adjustments to turn your "dream" boat into a real, practical, ocean-going home.

That's why the two years and 4,000 miles are so important—to gradually get the skipper *and* vessel adjusted to the reality of life at sea.

But let's stop for a second and reconsider this "$5,000 minimum" figure. Five Gs ain't much money. And watching it ooze away can be stressful. I mean, it is hard to have fun circumnavigating when you've just spent all of your money and you still have 80 percent of the world left to go.

So we need a completely new mindset. Let's take a fresh look at the "money-honey" issue.

Carolyn and I have cruised for a long time—almost without cessation. But that's not exactly true. We tend to sail hard (around 8,000 miles or so) for two years, and then "nest in snug harbor" for a year. During this "nesting" year we refocus on our income and refurbish the boat at the same time. This is what just naturally works best for us. Other cruisers have slightly different rhythms.

And we try not to think of the "amount of money" we have as a static concept. We work as we go. This frees us from the "penny in, penny out" hassle of watching our money slip away. We don't. Instead, we meter our spending in relationship to our income. Thus, we're not held to any cruel "you can't have desert tonight" rules. Our rules are flexible. As long as we're spending less than we make, we can spend as much as we want.

This means that spending massive (relative to living aboard) amounts of money snow-skiing in Europe while our boat is moored in the Med is an option *if* our income allows it.

Our lives, and our spending, are in our hands—and we don't have to live by too-rigid a rule.

We work this out very simply on a day-to-day basis: if we have more than $5,000 in our cruising account, we smile and keep on working as we sail. If we have more than $10,000 in the bank, we loosen the purse strings and lessen the work load—knowing that we can go a year if need be without further income.

If, however, our bank account falls below $5,000 (which it has three times in the last 20 years), then we tighten our belts and refocus on earning more money.

Thus, nothing is static.

This works for us. Yes, we have an additional $5,000 invested Stateside (which is difficult to tap into) for "emergency medical use only."

Please bear in mind that, if all else fails, *Wild Card* can go to sea (in the right season) and stay there until she reaches US soil once again.

So this concept of "leaving with $5,000" isn't so you can "forget about it" and go X number of miles before having to work, but merely a figure you don't want to fall too far below as you sail and earn.

You can't sail around the world on $5,000. But you can sail around the world nicely by working and not allowing your account to fall too far below that amount.

The reality is that a poor man *has* to work as he goes. There is no other option.

Legality of Working in Foreign Countries

I'm not a lawyer—I'm a sailor. I don't know how the law works—nor am I really sure we should be blindly following all these silly shore-rules anyway. I'm a citizen of the world, aren't I? I deserve to eat, don't I? Who has the right to draw an arbitrary line in the sand and tell me what I can and cannot do on one side of the line or the other—oh, the big ugly guy with the gun?

That's what we call civilization?

I'd call myself an anarchist if it didn't sound so organized.

Seriously, the reason a visitor can't legally work in a foreign country is usually fairly logical. They don't want you, the passing yachtie, to take a job which could/should be filled by a local.

I agree with this.

Nor should a foreign vessel arrive at some remote island and go into competition with the local charter vessels.

I agree with this, too.

But there are a hell of a lot of very wide "gray areas" in between.

For instance, there is a resort in Micronesia that regularly allows foreign charter boats to operate from its premises because there are no local boats that want to. The money isn't much and it's erratic. The local craft are mostly open fishing boats—and stink-to-high-heaven anyway.

So a passing yachtie often charters out of the resort for a while to replenish his freedom chips. (That's how I think of money—as freedom coins.)

To make his job easier, the sea gypsy hires a local cook to supply his guest's meals and he also employs a young island kid as deckhand/host on the days he charters.

Everyone is happy; the resort, the guests, the passing sailor, and the local islanders.

Is the yachtie in technical violation of the law? Sure. Could he be arrested and fined? Sure. But, most likely, if there's a problem and someone complains, the yachtie will simply be told to "cease and desist."

All he has to do is fold his business tent along with his awning, hoist his anchor, and move on. I have never heard of any yachtie ever getting in serious trouble for working—who stopped breaking the law immediately when notified he was doing so—not one single one, in all my years of monitoring these "gray area" entrepreneurs.

Do some people get in trouble? Yes. The scofflaws do. The "you can't tell me what to do" guys who get "in the face" of the local folks. Yes, they do get in trouble.

And should.

But many a yachtie has sailed around the world picking up the odd charter, doing the odd yacht delivery, and generally being an "artful dodger" as we call them.

The bottom line for me is this: working ain't too terrible a crime. Stealing is. Mugging is. Cheating people is.

But a man trying to feed his family by washing dishes? I don't think that man is evil—no matter what the law says.

Look at it another way—the USA has millions and millions of illegal workers. There probably isn't a country in the world that doesn't have some of its people illegally working in America.

So you can think of sailing around the world and "working on the sly" as a sort of—well, that you are an "uninvited exchange student," so to speak.

Reminder: if you earn one penny illegally overseas, you can never again look down your nose at an honest un-green-carded Mexican worker again! Right?

How to Earn As You Go

The key to earning as you go is the same as the key to buying, outfitting, sailing, and to having a fulfilling life—hard work.

First, take stock of your skills. Some of them might be worth more in Oceania than they are in Silicon Valley.

For example, I would never tell a techno-geek in California that I know a lot about computers because, in comparison, I do not.

However, there are resorts and tiny businesses on small islands scattered throughout the world that have computers and don't know how to wire them together into their printer. Or set up their Wi-Fi. Or test the UPS. Perhaps they speak a different language than the manual is printed in and just need someone to translate and explain the basics.

Yes, someone who is barely "computer literate" in NYC might be hailed as a computer genius in PNG or Vanuatu.

I'm not suggesting in any way, shape, or form that you rip off unsophisticated people or pretend to be what you are not. If you did so, I'd hate you forever. That's bad karma to the max.

But I am pointing out that the computer help many Third World people need is pretty basic: installing software, hooking up wireless Wi-Fi, getting rid of viruses, decrapifying a new computer, unchoking a porn-stuffed hard drive.

One sailor who loves computers and accounting sails around with legal copies of Quicken (and QuickBooks) to sell and set up. He feels really good about what he does because he feels good accounting is so central to financial success. He is "profitably spreading the word" about the importance of number-crunching in the Third World. (Obviously, many people prefer that I be a little vague about their name, understandably so.)

Many sailors trade their cyber know-how for freedom chips—especially in far-out out-islands.

I carry a lot of tools on *Wild Card*, from wood planes to machinist tools. I have every wrench socket in both US and metric sizes and all the ratchets and extensions to match. Need a tap-and-die in either/or? I've got it aboard, in stock, along with the nuts and bolts too.

Now, I would never consider walking into a machine shop in Auckland or Sydney or Cape Town and asking for a job, but I'm not against doing a little tropical nut-twisting if the price is right.

If it is an emergency—I don't even think to charge.

If the fellow is a nice guy with empty pockets, I also might not charge either.

But if the owner of a $600,000 yacht wants a **mechanic** to fix his diesel engine while he drinks Gin-and-Tonics in the yacht club ashore—yeah, I charge.

And I don't lose any sleep about it being against the law, either.

A circumnavigator can easily make his living working solely on yachts and never go ashore to suffer the vexations of their many weird land-centric laws.

Do you like to **sew**? We know probably a dozen vessels that are movable canvas and sail lofts. What to do with the scraps? Why not make wind scoops and fender socks for your fellow boats—or kites and windsocks to sell ashore at flea markets? (Bring a large purse and if anyone official-looking asks for ID, just "stuff and go" before you see the badge!)

Do you play **music**? Busking is popular (and, occasionally, legal) in Auckland, for example. Hey, there's even an official NZ Busker Festival which is very liberal and understanding of musicians—and isn't "hung-up" on silly concepts like nationality.

I often play my guitar in bars for food-and-all-the-booze-my-wife-can-drink. If I was going to do more of this, I'd toss some of the MP3s I've made aboard the boat into an album to sell. In bars, bring a large pot labeled "BIG TIP JAR." On the street, just leave your guitar case open, and pre-seed it with some coins and a couple of dollar bills so the dumb ones get the idea. ("What, me? No way, officer! I didn't ask them to toss in that money, no sireee! I thought it was some kind of weird local ritual, and I didn't want to embarrass anyone by asking them to stop. HONEST!")

Barbi Devine (oh, she is devine!) is a classical pianist who has an electric piano built right into her Whitby 42 *Pago.* She **teaches** music as she sails the world—giving the odd recital (sometimes very odd) here and there to drum up business.

Note: If you play guitar, don't forget to save your used strings and give them

to penniless islanders. You will be their hero for years to come.

David Wegman is a classic "Yankee trader" as he circumnavigates aboard his funky engineless Cowhorn schooner named *A Frig'n Queen or African Queen* (depending on his mood). He pulled into San Blas, and carefully selected hundreds of molas (local embroidery) to buy. (Hint: the transvestites make the most beautiful ones.) By prior arrangement, he shipped them back to a very exclusive boutique gift shop on Fifth Avenue. This paid for his next year of crossing the Pacific.

Josh Sutherland of *Lorca* likes to carve things. He started out working primarily with wood but soon got into carving the swords of swordfish and marlin in the Pacific. His knife handles are utterly unique and in high demand.

There's a South African fellow cruising around the world on a boat called *Shoestring,* not only because of his limited budget, but also because he used to be a cobbler. Thus, he didn't even think about it when his stainless steel helm felt cold to the touch; he just got some lambskin and neatly sewed it onto his wheel. The moment he was done, other yachtsmen in the harbor asked him to do theirs. Now he has a successful business doing custom yacht sewing on wheel covers, turnbuckle covers, you-name-it-covers.

Some sailors are really into "macho stuff" and have figured out a way to earn a living with it as they circumnavigate. Tyler on *Blue Horizon* often tosses over a baited shark hook attached to 50 feet of chain shackled to a 45 pound CQR when he's in deserted island anchorages. Almost every time (in certain locations, like the Bahamas) he ends up with a shark. If he's able to, he gives the meat to the locals, and then cuts away the jaws with a Sawz-all. (I know, Sawz-alls aren't romantic, are they?) He then places the jaws on a local ant hill, and allows the ants to clean it until spic-and-span. Then he sells the scary-looking shark jaws along with the sea shells he collects.

This isn't for everyone, and there are some legal, environmental, and ecological questions raised by such a practice. But Tyler has been successfully doing this in a low-key way for many years.

I've earned a lot of money over the years by **splicing** rope and doing fancy ropework. This is easy and relaxing. Splicing three strand is dead simple. Splicing braided isn't too bad if you practice (and only use brand new line, as used line is almost impossible to splice).

Lots of small island businesses need very basic stuff they can't get: digital pictures for their adverts, for instance. Translation work. Copywriting.

Web masters abound on boats. HTTP isn't that hard to learn, and the resulting web site doesn't have to be state-of-the-art, just handsome and functional.

Bartending is an easily transportable job. Many island bartenders earn extra money booking daysails, in various above-board and under-the-table ways.

If you're **chartering**-in-a-low-key-way, get the local bartenders on your side by giving them your boat cards to distribute (with *their* name on the back). The moment someone charters with you from one of those cards, dash back to the bartender and kick-back generously. Word will get out fast and you'll soon have a "stealth" sales force working tirelessly for you, all at no upfront cost.

The sky is the limit, really. Most English speakers can **teach English**. Most swimmers can teach kids to swim and drown-proof the local babies at the same time. (Every day 55 children drown in Bangladesh, mostly in mud puddles.)

Yes, you might be paid in "pennies and dead fish" by their struggling families. But dead fish are tasty with a touch of salt and a little garlic. And besides, earning money is just part of the joyous pay-off of helping out in the Third World.

Do you **draw**? Our friend Lizbeth, when she isn't being a mid-wife in Greenland, sails the world aboard a lovely little double-ender from Sweden and paints along the way. Occasionally, she has a major show in a wealthy country—and counts the cash with her paint-splattered fingers.

We first met her on a small island in the Tuamotus (French Polynesia) where she painted a wonderful picture of the church. A local couple stopped by to admire her work and the husband came back alone to purchase the painting for his wife. Liz wasn't sure she wanted to sell it. The man owned a large pearl farm with over 100,000 oysters in the water. Eventually he managed to trade Liz a large bag of nearly perfect pearls for the painting.

She is still giving the pearls away and selling them—depending on whim and financial status.

Many of our friends make **jewelry** as they go. Some are quite slick—each piece is artfully "certified" to be crafted on a boat at sea.

I **write**, of course. Last year, $40,000 flowed out of my pen alone. To be honest, my income would *drop* if I stopped living like a king in paradise and writing it down.

Is writing easy? No. I work at it four hours a day, every day we're in port. I write 40 articles and columns a year—plus at least one book. (Sometimes, two books.) I write advertising and do catalog work as well. I also write for a men's magazine under the name Condor Van Harding, and my female side is *Carlotta* Carlson.

Occasionally I give **seminars** on writing and/or sailing—whichever is easier and more profitable. Sometimes I hustle my books at boat shows, if someone wants to fly me there to give a talk. (See fattygoodlander.com for more info.)

In the islands, you don't have to be Stephen King to earn money from your pen. Lots of local folks know about email and have email addresses for the relatives they'd love to contact but don't have, nor want, a computer. You don't have to have a degree in English to help them write a letter and send it over your computer. Sure, you'll get paid in local goods, but that's what you buy every day, isn't it?

One fellow in the Western Pacific who was "thinking about freelancing" to the marine magazines just happened to shoot a lot of pics to accompany his future stories. He put them into a slide show and started writing a feature story. Instead of submitting it to a fish-wrapper (our disparaging name for half the marine pubs in the world), he shopped it to local breweries. (This guy really thought out-of-the-box, eh?) One regional brewery bit. He earned ten times the money he would have from a magazine for the digital CD "Guidebook of Vanuatu". The following year, he paid for his next trip with a CD "Guidebook of New Caledonia." (This is a perfect example of how imaginative thinking and not-following-the-conventional-wisdom can succeed.)

There are a million ways to imaginatively milk the chartering industry: rendezvous dives, underwater video, windsurfing lessons, beach-combing tours, and nature walks are just a few.

Some boats have cockpit name cloths that say something like "Handy Man" or "Jack of All Trades." One boat has a sign hanging from the lower life lines with the boat's name and hailing port on one side and (upside down) on the other side "DIESEL MECHANIC." Thus, he can flash that he's available for employment to his passing marine prospects, while not drawing too much attention to himself.

One important caution: working as you go is fine, endlessly attempting to exploit your fellow cruisers is not. There is one well-known, greedy, disliked idiot-of-a-cruiser who passes out price sheets each time he meets you. He also pretends to be a journalist to better con the locals. He's always trying to sell you something—and/or to get in between you and the service you need. He has no friends and only a few customers. Every time I bump into him and his pathetic price sheets, I remind myself sternly to never turn into such a floating money-grubber.

Clerical Work

Working in an office usually isn't a good idea for an undocumented worker.

But who says clerical work has to be office-related? Why not galley-table related? Or nav-station related?

Just because you're not a professional writer doesn't mean you can't make money massaging words. Translators and "letter writers" are in demand everywhere. You don't have to be Hemingway. The hookers in Thailand need scribes to pump out an endless supply of "Dear John, please send money!" emails. Why not assist such an important service industry?

Can you proofread? Edit? Create ads? Put together a newsletter? (I produced the "Dockside Bookshop" newsletter for years while anchored in the Virgins.)

Right now, I regularly do copywriting for businesses which have no idea I'm surrounded by betel nut chewers in Micronesia as I type. They only know the important things: I work faster, better, and cheaper than my competition.

The Internet has made location a limiting factor only to the unimaginative and cyber-impaired. The rest of us can easily work in the jungles of PNG and still get paid in NYC greenbacks, truly the best of both worlds.

Truly Odd Jobs

We met a cruising balloon-twister in Oz who was making a fortune. He'd just find a kid-or-young-family event, grab a ten cent bag of balloons, and watch the money roll-in.

I've often thought a clown outfit would be worth its weight in gold aboard a vessel with a husband-and-wife acting team.

I've also considered bringing fun PSA (public service announcements) to the outer, more remote islands of the world. Sure, most people in Cape Town know what AIDS is and what a condom is—but do Fijians, Malagasy (from Madagascar), and the Ni-Vanuatu?

We love Asia, and many Asian companies are launching products to be sold in America and Europe. Thus they need Western models for their brochures, print ad, promotional videos, etc.

Smart members of their PR department know that if they need western models locally, the nearest marina is a good place to start.

Which reminds me of one of my favorite "earn a few pennies ashore" stories.

I became friends with Rolf and Anna in Langkawi because they lived aboard a Peter Ibold-designed Endurance 35, the same design boat that I built in Boston as a teenager. They were German. Rolf was an engineer who designed shipboard watermakers, and a decidedly strange person. Anyway, one day Rolf sees a notice on the marina's bulletin board (This all takes place in Malaysia) asking for Western actors and models. It says not only will they be handsomely paid, they'll be treated to a lavish three day weekend at a fancy local resort, and wined and dined as well.

So Rolf spreads the word and, along with another three other yachtie couples, signs up.

Everything goes well. A nicely dressed man from the government comes down to audition them, and happily says they are perfect. A brand new government van meets them on a Friday morning and whisks them to the spectacular dream resort where they are greeted like visiting royalty by an adoring audience—but only for a minute, as they are quickly sequestered from the crowd.

Rolf is happy as a clam, but his wife is acting puzzled. Things aren't adding up for her, and she mentions this to Rolf.

Rolf tells her to relax. "You're being paranoid," he says. "What have we got to lose? Enjoy yourself!"

There's lots of talk about snakes. Rolf finally puzzles out that there is a snake charmers' convention going on at the resort. This strikes Rolf as way-cool. He can't wait until his modeling job is over, so he can converse with the snake fans. Snake charming has intrigued him since he was a young lad in Germany.

The guy that invited them is getting more and more nervous. They aren't allowed to leave their room.

Suddenly, a release form is thrust into Rolf's hand. He is told to sign it. It says that, basically, if Rolf should die because he was bitten by a poisonous snake—well, the organizers can't be held responsible.

At this point, the other yachties start getting nervous and leave. The whole scene is too bizarre for them. Snakes? Dying of poison? No, thanks! But Rolf stays. He's intrigued. The nervous guy soon confesses: He has been give a large sum of money by the Malaysian government to organize a world-class snake charming demonstration. But, instead of spending it to do so, he... er, embezzled it. Over the course of an entire year.

But he had to do something, somehow to produce the World Famous Snake Charmers which had theoretically cost so much money. So, in desperation and to buy a little more time, he'd put up the notice at the marina... and... and...

At this point, the embezzler bursts into tears and begins moaning, "I'm going to jail! I'm going to jail forever... forever and more... unless... unless..."

"Unless what?" Rolf asks.

The guy frantically makes his pitch. "If you'd just consent to going on stage for a few tiny moments and *pretend*," he says to Rolf. "We'll give you a venomous-less, drugged-to-the-gills Cobra and... well, you could put on a quick show for a couple of seconds, then you kiss the cobra."

"Kiss the cobra?" asks Rolf.

"Kiss it, like, on the lips?" asks his wife in astounded amazement. "No way, Rolf! You are not going to..."

"Shhh," says a beaming, smiling Rolf to his wife, then turns to the embezzler who's peeing his pants, "Why not!"

The wife is hustled out into the audience, while Rolf is coached on the steps to impersonate an honest-to-goodness snake charmer.

The key thing is to not flinch during the final kiss.

Suddenly, Rolf is on the stage and they are taking the tops off wicker baskets filled with snakes. Rolf is fiddling with his flute.

Rolf's wife can't believe this is happening. A couple of minutes later, a man who she has seen back stage is standing next to her—a guy who was conversing with the embezzler.

"Thank gosh," she whispers to him. "They drugged it."

"Don't be silly," says the man irritably. "A drugged snake won't perform. That snake isn't any more drugged than you or I. And it certainly hasn't had its venom drained, which is a very laborious, time-consuming, and expensive process."

Just as Rolf's wife is about to slump to the floor with fright, there is a thunder of applause. She looks up. Rolf is kissing the cobra—hell, he's damn near *French*-kissing the cobra!

Oh, yes! The sailing life is an exciting one.

Think Out Of The Box For Income

The ability to make money while cruising under sail is only limited by your imagination.

I had a weakly... er, weekly radio show on WVWI Radio One, St. Thomas for more than 17 years—even as I circumnavigated.

Of course, producing and starring in a radio program takes a bit of time, especially initially.

Most of my week would be spent in preparation for "going live" at 8 a.m. on Saturday morning. But, hey, that's how I earned my weekly pay check.

Eventually, however, I gradually reduced the amount of time it took to produce a radio show—mostly by making Carolyn my executive producer.

Every three months during our first circumnavigation, Carolyn would announce something like, "Tuesday is a radio day, okay Fatty?"

She'd then line up 12 to 14 "radio guests" (mostly my sailing drinking buddies) and run them through *Wild Card* every 40 minutes or so, beginning early in the morning. Then I'd edit the tapes and Carolyn would package them up and Fed Ex 'em off to my station. And I wouldn't even *think* about radio for another three months. (But, ah, how sweet it was to see those weekly direct-deposits in my account!)

I was, at one point, away from the station so long (five years) that when I returned and mentioned my name, my co-workers didn't recognize me. They said, "Fatty's not here. He's off sailing in Africa or somewhere."

Since I didn't broadcast from the studio, my show was listed in radio-talk as a "remote." And at my station all the DJs were listed under "talent."

Thus, my direct bank deposits were labeled "remote talent."

"That's perfect," cackled my wife Carolyn, "because sometimes your talent is very remote!"

Radio is an interesting business. Mostly it is a "medium without content," which is perfect for an airhead like me.

Making A Massive Deposit In The Karma Bank

We know dozens of doctors, nurses, midwives, and dentists who "practice" for free as they go—to the immense benefit of all. Hell, Canadian surgeon Ken Bradley of the *Ken B* always carried a set of scalpels in his back pocket—and would slice and dice when appropriate. "Hold 'em down, Fatty," he'd say. "This will only take a second!"

The Right Reverend Jim was given Also Island (his boat's name is *Also*, also) for teaching the local youth shipwright skills in Fiji.

Harry of *Cormorant* engineered solar and water-powered 12-volt, extremely low-tech and easily repaired electrical systems for remote islands—and often secures the NGO funding to have them constructed as well.

We met a New Zealand single-hander who buys the cheapest reading glasses imaginable in bulk and then hands them out in the most remote harbors of Asia and Africa.

Most of these sailors, admittedly, aren't operating on the slimmest of shoestrings. You have to *earn* before you can *give*. But should a desperately poor sailor help out in some non-monetary way, if possible? Absolutely. "May you always do for others, and let others do for you," says Bob Dylan in "Forever Young."

Deposits in the Karma Bank are always counted, whether large or small.

Traditional Jobs

Obviously, there are certain jobs that sea gypsies naturally gravitate towards: shipwright work, bartending, electrical work, house painting, mechanic work, rigging maintenance, teaching, nursing, fiberglass repair, surveying, boat cleaning, welding, etc.

My father and Dave Lovik opened "Davey Jones' Locker" in New Orleans when both were attempting to raise cruising funds after their Mississippi River trip.

Gwen and John of *Two Captains* fame hustled (in a delightfully low-key way) Spectra watermakers as they wandered the Pacific.

While it probably wouldn't be a good idea to blast into Sydney and announce you are an undocumented yacht broker, it might be highly profitable to form an "understanding" with a local broker—and feed him contacts, listings, and sales.

My racing buddy Peter Thurlow of *Antares* has repaired outboards for years. "It's easy as pie," he once told me. "I don't do much repairing, really. Mostly I just clean the water out of the carbs, that's all."

I've already mentioned canvas and sail repair.

One clever, sexy seamstress didn't work on sails or dodgers, but rather made rather arty and sexy bikinis which she modeled and sold to the bored wives of international yacht racers (while their husbands were on the race course).

I'm often asked to do electrical work. Many yacht owners are intimidated by electrical matters. This is silly. Twelve volts is dead simple. Anyone with a volt-ohm meter and half-a-brain can find and fix most problems within minutes.

Onboard generator repair is another lucrative area for the moderately handy. Lots of local grease monkeys feel they are competent to repair a diesel engine but are intimidated by the electro-gen-side. But, if you can repair a diesel, everything you need to know about the gen-side can be learned in a single day.

And the tools required are minimal.

Sextant and compass adjustment used to be a good business. I once carried a WWII astro-compass aboard to professionally "swing ship." The only tool required to adjust a sextant is a screwdriver—the lubricant is free! (The famous "nav-man" of Fort Lauderdale, Jim Sullivan, taught me to use my nose oil for the very best in human lubricants—just squeeze!)

Perhaps the wealthiest "floating repairmen" have a vacuum-pump, a pressure gauge, and some canisters of refrigerant. Yes, the marine refrigeration experts are always busy and rolling in dough.

Sailing gel-coat repairmen don't do too badly either.

My friend Robin is called, affectionately, the Head Hunter because that's how he makes his living. "My job stinks!" he says, with good reason. He's a funny guy. "I'm #1 in the #2 business," he jokes. "Your s#*t is our bread and butter!"

You see, the ability to make money off, and from, a small vessel is unlimited.

We met a guy who developed a "yacht watch alarm" which is specifically tailored to the offshore sailor. It is infinitely adjustable, and can be set to blink dimly at, say, 15 minutes. If you hit the large button once, it resets and begins again. If you don't, a low audio alarm goes off—just loud enough for you to hear but not loud enough to awake your partner. If you still do nothing, it waits two minutes and sets off a loud siren that a dead man could not sleep through.

First, he started building them as favors for friends, but soon had so many orders he couldn't fill them all without stopping his cruise— something he didn't want to do. So, he sold the rights to his gadget to an American company. I last time I saw him, he was grinning and counting his money in Vava'u, Tonga.

In a sense, the best part of sailing a $3,000 boat around the world while earning your living is that you'll be forced by economic necessity to have a lot more fun than your wealthy counterpart. Lucky you!

Sign painters can always pick up a few bucks in nearly every port. This is how my father supported us while cruising aboard the schooner *Elizabeth* in the late '50s and early '60s.

Haircutting is popular. The young mother who cuts hair on the train tracks behind the Opua Marina in New Zealand is making a fortune. Ditto, the woman off *Forever Young*, who snipped her way to mega-bucks in Chagos. A pair of scissors and a comb don't cost much nor take up a lot of room, and yet can earn a lot of money in the right hands.

One final note on working-as-you-go. Some judgmental people, usually wealthy ones, are very upset by this. They scream bloody murder that honest working men and woman shouldn't earn the money to feed themselves outside the United States—that only rich people should be able to travel abroad for any length of time.

I respectfully disagree. There are a lot of gray areas here. Am I, as a freelance writer, on a higher moral plane earning my living aboard than a bartender ashore? I don't think so. When Walter Cronkite covered Viet Nam, did he apply for a work permit? I don't think so. We capitalists import/export all the time. It's just when the little guy wants a tiny piece of the action that people get upset.

Yes, I consider myself a "workingman." My father considered himself one, and my grandfather, too. I'm proud Goodlanders don't steal nor beg. I've been on my own since 15 years of age and never asked nobody for nutt'n.

I pay my way the old fashioned way—by earning it from the sweat of my brow.

I'm proud that I work as a go, not ashamed of it.

Of all the crimes being committed today, washing dishes to feed your family surely doesn't rank high on the despicable list.

Never Get Behind the Eight Ball

By that, I mean never get in debt. Don't get in debt to buy the boat or you won't be able to afford to fix it up. Don't borrow the money to fix it up because you won't be able to afford to sail over the horizon. And, lastly, don't borrow money to complete your circumnavigation. Why?

First off, it is discouraging to start out with an "I'm going to fail and will have to borrow money from Dad at the end" attitude. It is nearly always fulfilled. Second, once you start sailing "on credit," your spending might sky-rocket (with no increase in pleasure or a small decline). Third, our life as sea gypsies is all about freedom. You will be far freer debt-free than in-debt. Debts have to be paid back. I don't think of them as debts, but as chains. Who wants chains? Many circumnavigators go home for a few weeks, celebrate, look at the job market, look at the home market, vomit, and head back out to sea again.

Keep your options open. Keep yourself debt-free. Never spend a penny you haven't already earned. Chop up *all* credit cards and use only debit cards. Paying interest (except for income tax reasons) just makes you a rank sucker. Why would you pay to use someone else's money? I don't. Are they *that* much smarter than you? Are you *that* much weaker, that much *dumber*? I use my money. I "self-finance" my adventures. I self-insure my life. So can you.

Your Route

I strongly recommend an east-to-west route amid the Trades for your first circumnavigation. This is called the **Coconut Milk Run**. Most West Coast American sailors begin with the **Puddle Jump** from Mexico to the Marquesas. East coasters go through the **Panama Canal.** The advantage of taking this tried-and-true tradition route is that the winds and currents will be in your favor 99 percent of the time. All the routing decisions were (correctly) worked out a hundred years ago. Basically, all you have to do is leisurely drift downwind and pull into the next perfect harbor—while paying careful attention to the seasonal shifts of weather. ("Be in the right ocean at the right time," is the best ocean-sailing advice I've ever received.)

Wealthy people often cheat themselves of the main attraction to cruising (the lovely languid laziness of it) by spinning around far too fast (a two year "speed circ") and flying home too often. Luckily, you (the penniless pauper in the filthy yachting cap) won't have such a problem.

Figure six to eight years, with lengthy stops in New Zealand, SE Asia, and Cape Town to replenish the cruising kitty.

Yeah, you can go up the Red Sea if you want, but please be aware that cruising the Med ain't cheap. You can stay a week locked up on your boat in France (unable to afford to go ashore for fear of buying a croissant) for every month you spend traveling inland in Asia like a Raja—while freely sampling all the delicious delights of the most exciting cities in the world.

Let's Dispel Two Emerging Myths

One live-aboard myth is; If you can afford it, you can have it all—all the conveniences of home *plus* all the conveniences of a yacht. Bullshit.

While it is true that boats can be very comfortable things in port, even the largest, most luxurious vessel can be uncomfortable and inconvenient at sea. If you want convenience and comfort—if those are your two priorities—don't go to sea to find them.

Boats are boats—not movable condos.

The second Modern Emerging Myth is that, if you are careful, you will never get in heavy weather. Not true. Yes, you can avoid most of the heavy weather around you. But if you sail enough sea miles across enough oceans, you'll have to go through some. It is unavoidable.

If you think you should not be in any heavy weather—that makes it worse when you are. If you fear the weather, that again makes it worse. If you truly dreaded it, that's triply worse!

I used to fear heavy weather and "pray" that it would somehow magically "go away" as it approached. How silly. My "prayers" had no effect of the weather system and a lot of negative effect on my mental attitude.

Now I'm in a "completely different headspace" as we used to say in the 1960s.

Just before I head offshore, I remind myself how much I love cruising, sailing, and circumnavigating. This is easy, because I do. Then I remind myself that love and life are package deals—we love our spouses *with* their flaws. In essence, we have to love it all. And so, we should also love all the aspects of sailing offshore, including the nice breezes, the calms, and the storms. It is all part of it. Without the storms, it just wouldn't be the same.

As a result of this new mind-set, I no longer fear the storms; I actually look forward to them. I embrace them. I hug them to my chest. What a wonderful thing it is to see Mother Ocean in a grand mood!

Is Sailing the Farm Realistic?

No and Yes.

Yes, in the sense that there are still places left on earth where you can live for years completely unmolested by civilization. We went four and a half months without reprovisioning in deserted Chagos. While there, we bumped into a number of "survivalist-type" yachties who managed to live off the sea for years at a time without major provisioning.

How? Well, they are classic hunter/gatherers. They catch fish, lasso lobsters, and trap crabs. Coconuts are well-packed gifts from a benevolent God, and they make full use of them in every regard. When the tide toppled a palm tree into the water, they were there instantly to machete its heart of palm. What little fruit they could gather was dried in the sun. Most of these sun-bronzed people had amazingly sophisticated gardens aboard their vessels. I'm not talking about just sprouting some seeds—I'm talking about cucumbers, green peppers, tomatoes, etc.

Carolyn catches lunch in Chagos

To preserve their eatables for a rainy day, they air-dried them in the sun, salted them, canned them in a pressure cooker, or smoked them.

A few took vitamin supplements—just to make sure they were getting all the nutrition they needed.

And they ate some pretty strange creatures—land crabs, etc. (There was even talk of eating rats, birds, and bats.) Some even experimented with eating various types of seaweed as well. (Never, ever eat anything off a boat's bottom. The poisonous anti-fouling paint makes that an absolute no-no.)

So, yes "sailing the farm" is possible—but it isn't practical. And it is very labor intensive. Working from sun up to sun down is a daily occurrence. And you can forget about maintaining your craft or playing volley ball on the beach.

Despite this, I personally am fascinated by living off the sea, and want to do more of it. Certainly, many cruisers stretch their provisions by trolling as they go. But I believe it isn't for everyone—just too much bloody work.

And don't end up like the famous (well, in the Indian Ocean anyway) Chicken George who pulled into Cape Town on a 28-foot wooden sloop that was home to him and 16 chickens! "Yes, George was the most chicken-shit sailor I ever met," one fellow told me with a grimace. "There wasn't a square centimeter of his boat which hadn't been... er, *christened* by the dirty birds."

The South African officials refused to clear him in, as they didn't want to go aboard. George attempted to tie up to the marina to complain—but both restaurants in the marina evacuated because of the stench. People never anchored too close to George, to put it mildly. Yes, George had eggs a'plenty but friends a'few!

"We heaved a sigh of relief," the harbormaster of Darwin told me wryly, "when Chicken George finally flew the coop!"

Speaking of Diet

It is far, far easier to provision today than in Josh Slocum's day. UHT milk is now everywhere, as is powdered whole milk. *Yeah!* Freeze-dried products are everywhere, as are canned goods. Box juices are cheap. We have a dozen MREs (US *Meals Ready to Eat* Army rations, jokingly referred to "Meals Rejected by Ethiopians" by the army grunts forced to consume them) in our "shipwreck" supplies.

We carry our 40 pounds of Thai jasmine rice stowed in separate dried plastic soda bottles—so that any bugs which have cleverly stowed away, don't contaminate the rest of our supply.

Eggs last a long time, if dipped in scalding water or waxed, and turned regularly.

Cheeses can be preserved for many months just by floating a little oil over the top in their jars to inhibit airflow.

Many boats today have a small refrigerator and a large freezer. This is especially nice if you catch a large fish—none of it has to go to waste.

Carolyn and I "can" (preserve in old-fashioned glass jars, actually) our own meat in half-pint, pint, and quart containers. It's easy if you have a pressure cooker. Just buy the jars and extra tops and follow the recipes in "Joy of Cooking," or check out the many canning sites on the Internet. We can chicken, beef, pork, buffalo, lamb, turkey, etc. These last more than a year. We've never had a health problem. But if a jar top doesn't "pop" as we open it, we immediately throw away the contents. This doesn't happen often, less than once a year. We carry 120 of these jars when we head off to Chagos or live for months within a landless atoll. (This is one of our favorite things to do. We love Beveridge and Minerva reefs in addition to dozens of uninhabited and unexplored atolls in Micronesia.)

Of course, canning is a technical thing that must be done right. People can die of botulism. We're extremely careful. If the jar doesn't audibly "pop," we deep-six it.

What NOT To Bring

If you're poor and going to work your way around the world—you cannot bring any debts or expense with you. I don't mean to be discouraging, but you cannot. You are going to have to work hard to put food on the table and antifouling on the bottom. You can't be paying off old credit card debt too.

Wanna keep your house? Wanna put your car in storage? Wanna keep your Harley Hog because it brings back such pleasant memories of smoking dope with Hunter S. Thompson?

Well, you can't. Not with empty pockets.

Chances are you won't "turn a profit" on your first circ—maybe later, but not out-of-the-box.

I know, I know—all that old stuff you have is precious and priceless and absolutely cannot be discarded.

Here's how I did it after selling "American Paradise Publishing" and setting off on my first circ.

I sold things. I donated things. I "gifted" things. And I threw things away until I ended up with a large pickup truck full of my most prized personal possessions—things that I literally couldn't live without.

I drove to the town dump on Gifft Hill, St. John.

I picked up a box of yachting trophies I'd won over the years—the first one when I was nine years old and competing in the Optimist program in Vinoy Basin, St. Pete.

I shouted aloud, "Do I want to keep these trophies or do I want to sail around the world?"

I was paralyzed for a couple of moments—then managed to fling all the silver out of the truck while screaming, "I want to sail around the world, damn it—not have a bunch of *stuff*—not be prevented from doing so by material *crap*!"

Soon I was just shoveling all the junk out of the truck.

Now, I really can't even remember what most of the stuff was—just junk cluttering up my life, really.

One more important hint: don't bring any dogs or cats, either. They cost a fortune and are a huge hassle to quarantine in such places as New Zealand and Australia. And they simply shoot a dog on sight in Muslim places like the Maldives.

I know, I know! We loved our shipboard pet, too. But we gave Joker of *Wild Card* to Chris and Elsa Angel of St. John—with whom he lived in the lap of shore-side luxury for an additional ten years before he died peacefully last year at 21 years of age.

When we sailed off, people would ask us about Joker because I had written so many stories about him. I used to say, "We gave him to the Angels"—and watch their faces drop. Now he *is* with the angels. Rest in peace, Joker-Boy!

Wait To Take On Weight—and Then Don't

The cruising sailor is often conflicted. His boat is small, so space is a problem.

The smaller the boat, the more weight sensitive it is. So, if he's smart, he realizes that it can't carry too much stuff—just about the same time that he's figuring out all the safety stuff he has to take with him!

While this isn't a big issue on a 50-footer, it certainly is on slender *Wild Card*, which is designed to weigh 13,000 pounds and actually weighs 16,000 when fully loaded. That's a significant difference. Carolyn and I both realize that we can't take on more weight without slowing the boat down too much and lessening its ability to rise to a large wave.

Strength is important, but so is **buoyancy.** Boats that are too heavy sail poorly and are dangerous in a blow.

We knew one weird guy in Fort Lauderdale who purchased a 22-foot boat to sail around the world. He was well-heeled and he loved teak as well. He crammed every imaginable piece of gear aboard this boat and ordered a custom teak bracket to hold it as well. This went on for years. Gradually, the boat sat lower and lower in the water. Eventually, he set a departure date. Alas, the USCG caught wind of it, came down, inspected his vessel, and declared that taking it to sea would be a "manifestly unsafe voyage." Game over!

This is why many sailors recommend a "moderate displacement" craft for circumnavigating—knowing it will end up a "heavy-displacement" one.

We've lived on *Wild Card* more than 20 years now. Everything we own is aboard. We have nothing "stashed on the dirt." We are on the verge of weighing her down **dangerously.** Already her ability to right herself has been compromised by her heavy wind generator because of its height. (Betcha didn't think about that, eh?)

We'd love to carry more fuel, water, and batteries but cannot. In fact, we

Carolyn finding places to stow canned meats and lots of other stuff.

both agree we need to "lose 500 pounds" as soon as possible.

Ultimately, the problem is this: Each year, we make improvements and take aboard gear that enables us to cruise more safely and more comfortably. But we have to keep the boat at the same weight. So gradually, over the years, we've had to prune the useless gear to a minimum. Sadly, the "useless" gear are our personal belongings which we have to keep shrinking. This isn't easy after 20 years. My wife still demands an underwear drawer and I'm not about to give up my Playboy collection!

So we're extremely weight conscious. We used to have hundreds of books aboard, and now we have a couple of dozen and two Kindles. Our CDs have been tossed in favor of MP3s, podcasts, and audio books.

Since we live in the tropics but occasionally sail in higher lats, we have to have both winter and summer clothes. We are, thus, very miserly with our cold weather duds, because they spend most of their time stored under the forepeak. (Yes, we could ship them back and forth to save weight, but that costs money, doesn't it?)

Obviously, when provisioning we avoid heavy glass containers in favor of cardboard and plastic. (Of course, we're forced to use heavy glass jars for canning.)

Singing with Tongan friends on the island of Niuatoputapu

Every year Carolyn sternly forces me to go though our tool box and toss any extras I've accumulated during the year.

I often wear pareos only—which turns Carolyn on and saves us time as well. (Blush) We limit ourselves to three pairs of shoes each.

We do a lot of entertaining and enjoy our meals more with real crockery and glass—not plastic. But we have to make up for this extravagance elsewhere.

I don't carry any extra copies of my books anymore. I now closely monitor our ship's stores, so we always have two of everything (oil changes, fuel filters, etc) but seldom more than two.

We no longer collect heavy rocks nor shells.

If we bring 20 new paperbacks aboard, we have to take 20 old ones off at the same time. Our once-mighty sound system has shrunk to my guitar and an iPod.

I deep-sixed the extra 50 feet of spare chain I carried.

In essence, we *weigh* our decisions very carefully in terms of *weight.*

The Easiest and Best Way to Save Money

I once heard an extraordinarily dumb statement uttered in India. A hotel owner said to me, "We're too poor to do maintenance."

This is exactly wrong.

The wealthy yachtie on the $300,000 boat doesn't have to be so careful about some chafe on his running rigging because he can buy a new jib sheet in Tahiti and a new halyard in Bora Bora. But a penny-pinching sailor doesn't have that option. He *has* to make his gear last as long as possible.

Preventive maintenance equals money-in-the-bank for the careful sea gypsy.

There is no reason to allow your **cordage** to chafe other than laziness. Be vigilant.

Anchor lines and chain snubbers should be covered in hose where they run through the chock and/or bow roller.

Rope anchor rodes will, eventually, get severely chafed in one spot. I simply cut out the area and resplice the three strand nylon. Braided line is more difficult; I cut out the chafe and tie a double-carrick bend to rejoin it. So the bitter ends don't catch on stuff, I sew them back to the standing part with an awl. People laugh and belittle me for using such a rejoined rode—but most of them are laughing from ashore. Who cares what a landlubber thinks?

Some boats back the jib when they **heave-to** and this can result in serious sheet chafe against the forward lower shroud. We use a portable piece of chafing gear made out of poly webbing and Velcro if this is a problem.

Never sheet in your **working jib sheet** so hard it hits the shroud—allow it to float just off it, even an eighth inch is fine.

Headsail **halyards** often chafe on the spreaders, radar, lights, etc. I have to replace the halyards forward of my mast three times more often than those aft for the simple reason the forward ones get blown into the mast while the after ones get lifted off it.

The solution to this is:

1. Minimize anything sharp aloft.

2. Whip the area with waxed twine so the cheap replaceable twine suffers,

not the expensive halyard.

3. When not in use, lead the ends of the halyard forward of the mast and put them under considerable tension so they don't hit or, worse, drum on the mast.

Biminis and dodgers often move quite a bit in a blow. Double-check they aren't rubbing on anything as Sunbrella isn't chafe resistant at all. (We love Sunbrella. Our dodgers, bimini and sail covers are all made out of it and have all lasted for more than a decade of continuous exposure to the tropical sun. But there's no denying that Sunbrella is one of the most easily chafed fabrics we have aboard.)

The **sun** is another enemy of the frugal. We always use our **sail covers**. Sure, we might have to take them back off in a couple of hours, but this is far better than forgetting them for a whole day or, gosh forbid, longer.

Our working jib has been around the world (almost) twice and has lasted for more than ten years of hard use. But we re-stitch its sun cover every three years as a matter of course.

If you're careful with your running rigging and your sails, they should be good for at least one circ. If you aren't—well, we know people who have replaced their "rags and strings" three times during their first planetary loop!

Everything on your boat needs to be *exercised* every so often—even while in port. So every Sunday I turn on all my electronics (which heats them up, dries them out, and self-lubricates them). Ditto bilge pumps and all motors. I also test my bilge alarm by lifting its float to ensure it is working.

I spin all my winches and run my windlass. I either run my outboard or spin it. Ditto, all my seacocks and engine valves. I partially unroll my headsails. I pump and lube the head. I snap and unsnap my few bronze snap shackles, so they don't seize up. Ditto, the four pins on my two whisker poles. I exercise my engine controls as well, and allow the wind gen to take some spins. Speaking of spinning, I turn on the radar and flip through its ranges as well.

We carry a minimum of five laptops aboard. Don't forget, we are a floating business as well as two people permanently-on-vacation. I have a large, fast laptop that stays aboard and an iPad to carry ashore. Carolyn has a big laptop and small netbook as well. Plus, we have a "nav" computer solely dedicated to that purpose—it never gets hooked to the Internet nor accepts USB devices. (Tape over the USBs so you don't forget.)

Yes, we annually inspect all our emergency life raft supplies to replace batteries, etc, and confirm nothing has leaked or exploded. Ditto, our fire extinguishers.

Basically, it is "use it or lose it" as Carolyn likes to say with a grin.

One final word: Our goal, of course, isn't to sail around the world while spending as little as possible. Our goal is to sail around the world and spend as much as we earn—and never more.

But we aren't penny-wise and pound foolish. We often buy the most expensive gear in the world—because it is the best buy over the long term. Our Harken roller furler, Monitor windvane, and Max prop are three perfect examples.

I *really* like to sail and it is very important to me that my boat handles well and is able to claw off a lee shore. Thus I have a Max prop despite its obscene cost.

There is nothing worse than an engine that isn't dependable. I'd rather have none at all than one that leads me into danger and leaves me in the lurch. Our **Perkins M30** has never failed to start nor ever stopped while running—well, the only times it has stopped is when an idiot (me) ran it out of fuel.

In order to keep my Perkins purring for these last 15 years, I religiously follow its maintenance manual. I dutifully change its lube oil every 100 hours, using the highest quality 15-40 diesel-rated lube oil available. (Be careful in India. My ultra expensive oil, in perfectly sealed and printed containers, was actually re-refined crap with clumps of garbage floating in it!)

But there's more to maintaining a diesel than changing the lube oil in the crankcase and transmission, and tending its filters. We flush out the cooling system once a year, and every three years "acid wash" the heat exchanger coils and re-torque the head.

Yes, each time we refuel we add a few drops of Biobor JF to ensure no "bugs" grow in the fuel. (Once, before I learned to do this, my fuels lines clogged so bad my diesel wouldn't run.)

Every minute and penny spent maintaining your diesel engine saves you thousands in future repairs.

I religiously run my engine for an hour every week, just to dry it out and keep it lubricated. It is preferable to run it under load, as this allows the cylinder head temperature to be higher, and thus prevents glazing of the cylinder walls.

The bottom line: Occasionally, someone calls me cheap. I smile, knowing that I am not cheap. I spend every penny I earn in exactly the way I want to. I just don't waste my money foolishly and thoughtlessly.

So when somebody calls you "cheap," they're really accusing you of being aware and intelligent.

I'm fully aware my life is in my own hands. Every decision I make has a cost and consequence. I'm cool with that. I have a choice: lead a low quality life or a high quality one. I choose the high quality one.

Geography and Saving Money

Things cost different prices in different places. A dinner out in Tahiti usually costs more than $100 and often tastes like crap. A dinner out in Thailand often costs $3 and usually tastes like heaven.

I once paid $8 for an awful-tasting cup of lukewarm instant coffee in Bora Bora, which, after one sip, I attempted to unsuccessfully return.

Currently, we're in Turkey. Tea at my favorite "free Wi-Fi" cafe here costs 33 cents. Yes, you can bring in your computer, plug it in, and stay four hours for that price.

Carolyn did exactly this for five days at Sultan's Café in Fethiye and got chatting with the staff while editing one of my manuscripts. On the fifth day, the owner came over and gave her "on the house" an additional cup of apple tea for being such a good customer. (Go figure!)

Yes, we spend a lot more time in restaurants, teahouses, and coffee shops in Thailand and Turkey than we did in French Polynesia.

The simple reality is that there are places on this planet that are dirt cheap and places which are ridiculously expensive—and it is up to you, the cruising sailor, to determine how much time you spend where.

On our second circ, we were ready for French Polynesia. We seldom ate ashore except at the delightful "harbor trucks" of Papeete. We never stopped for coffee—not with the many pounds of fine brew aboard which we'd just picked up in South America.

But we did buy bread and frozen chickens —both of which were delicious and subsidized by the French government. (And a couple of Tin-Tin comics, too.)

The point I'm trying to make is that even the most expensive places on earth have some good deals, but you have to both research them and search them out.

For example, Madagascar is a great place to trade stuff. You will regularly be approached by families (sometimes entire villages) in dug-out canoes yelling, "Change! Change!" by which they mean they'd like to "change" what they have for what you have.

They really really love resealable containers. They are so poor, they don't have garbage. So any jar or bottle with a lid or cap is highly desirable to them. Even empty tin cans are precious. They make stoves and lanterns out of them by re-shaping and re-soldering them.

The trick is to buy your food in cheap places with income earned in expensive places. That is simple but true. In large part, it is why we're able to live such wonderful, rich lives on so few pennies— because our pennies are always buying ten times the stuff they would if "cashed in" where they were earned.

This delightful geo-shift is at the core of any successful "mini-buck" circumnavigation.

Another simple trick: If we've been a tad too extravagant, had a financial setback, or need to engage in a major haul-out—we just sail off to a deserted place like Chagos for a while, where we can't spend money.

We stayed four and a half months in Chagos and never spent a penny. All the while, we were working and earning our regular income. Thus, at the end of the most idyllic and most romantic time of our wonderful lives—we had a pile of money too.

What Not To Buy Where

Basically, don't buy any imported items as you sail. Buy only items made, grown, or manufactured in your host county.

I suppose the most obvious aspect of this is the often-repeated advice, "Buy local and eat what the locals eat."

Basically, frugal sea gypsies adapt their diet to their location. They seldom buy anything from the US in the Third World because it is wildly expensive.

Culture and religion plays a part. Toilet paper in many countries is almost difficult to find and extremely expensive. (We knew an American lawyer who married an Indian woman and was perplexed by his mother-in-law crying at the wedding and complaining he was going to teach her daughter "to dry clean!" He attempted to reassure the mother-in-law that his new bride wouldn't have to do the laundry—completely unaware the mother was talking about what she perceived as the perversion of using toilet paper.)

And don't visit a Hindu temple in hopes of being given some beef stew.

Is it possible to live on a dollar a day? Sure. Many of our friends do. And many of them are healthy and happy and raising wonderful, caring, loving families at the same time.

Generally speaking, I find that shoe-less fisherman in Bangladesh are far happier than NYC stockbrokers by any reasonable measure.

Currency Fluctuations

We seldom have enough money to worry about this. The good news is that a rising American dollar floats all US boats!

When the US dollar was extremely strong in relationship to its Kiwi equivalent, we headed down to Auckland for a delightful summer tied up at the posh West Haven Marina, just a short walk from the Central Business District.

Our buying power was more than double what it is now. Once this monetary imbalance corrected itself, we headed back up to Tonga, Fiji, and Vanuatu—places where your average citizen doesn't even know there is such a thing as currency trading.

But I must say I was saddened by the bad luck of a friend of mine in Thailand. He'd just purchased a large, newish Swan for $500,000 or so. He was consulting with me all the improvements he wanted to make on his new dream boat. I was anchored off Yacht Haven in Phuket at the time. Then, I was startled to watch him anchor right next to me—and flabbergasted to hear him say he could no longer afford the dockage after having invested every penny with a fellow named Bernie Madoff in NYC.

Oh, how fast and far the mighty can fall!

Yes, we had him over for dinner a couple of times and allowed him to cry in our beer.

Trading and Gift Items

We bring dozens of gifts to give away as we go, and stuff to trade as well. On small primitive islands, right after clearing into Customs, we search out the local teachers and give them some pencils, paper, and crayons for the students. It usually takes about 2 seconds for the word to get around—*you*

Tongan kids love to go for a dinghy ride.

went out of your way to help *their* kids.

Often, on our first visit ashore to an island teeming with kids, we bring a large plastic garbage bag full of freshly popped popcorn. This is *always* an instant hit with the local youngsters (and much less of a hassle for us to stow than teeth-rotting candy).

And yes, believe it or not, you *can* make popcorn without a microwave!

Fishhooks are the single most requested item. We purchase ours by the thousand in India—for only a buck or two. I'm sure they're cheap Stateside as well. Don't get too big or too small ones. Get two medium sizes instead. Snorkeling gear, especially "looking glasses" (masks) are in great demand—

ditto tools, especially vice-grips and screwdrivers, and also reading glasses. Bras are wildly popular in Polynesia.

One of the most sought after items by primitive fishermen all over the world is perfume. They will trade anything for it—to give to their wives and girlfriends. You don't have to give them too much or anything expensive. They don't want perfume that has a subtle fragrance; they want the stuff that reeks! We buy it in large bottles at dollar stores, and then decant it into tiny crack vials (ask any drug dealer on the corner where to buy 'em) for easy transport and exchange.

Surgical tubing for Hawaiian slings (traditional spear fishing devices) are always in great demand. In fact, string and fishing line of any type is priceless.

Carolyn used to make jewelry along the way and gave it as gifts to the local ladies as well as selling it.

Guitar strings are much appreciated, even used ones.

Most islands have at least one DVD player. Thus we bring Disney movies for the kids and "Mister Bean" episodes for all ages. (Be careful about giving "racy" materials to Muslims, etc.)

One word of caution: We never give alcohol to Polynesians. For whatever reason, they can't handle it and instantly turn into aggressive zombies. (Trust me on this, I've learned it the hard way.)

Just before we leave a small island or village, we often give them a DVD slide show (with music and commentary) of our visit, mostly featuring them, of course. It is hard to describe how much they love these very special, very cherished gifts. (We occasionally make 'em videos, but have found the DVD slide shows are more treasured.)

Sometimes I record a "special" music CD for them that leads off with a loud, goofy song I wrote about them, and performed for them. (Anything "special" for them is greatly appreciated, and often marveled at for years.)

Intoxicating Freedom

Freedom, like slavery, has its own mindset. Having the world as your oyster takes some getting used to. If you've applied yourself in school, succeeded in the market place, and then laser-focused on making your escape to paradise via a modern cruising boat; then this might be the first time in your adult life when you have a wide menu of choices but no set goal to narrow them.

Many cruisers dash down to the Caribbean, gush how wonderful it all is, grow bored, and return to the rat race. This isn't because freedom isn't attractive, but rather that they're recidivists, like penal lifers suddenly given parole. They long for the structure of work, death, and taxes. They've had their blinders on so long, their peripheral vision scares them.

Most sailors come down to the Caribbean, (understandably) go a little crazy on the booze and ganja, right themselves after a few months, and become highly effective, fulfilled individuals.

A few folks fall into a rhum bottle and never recover.

The trick is to be proactive. The idea isn't to set up your life so you don't have to do anything—and then do nothing. But rather it is to set up your life so that you don't have to do the mundane, silly things which clutter up most lives, and then allow yourself the freedom to do all those millions of things you've always wanted to do but couldn't afford the time for.

One is positive, the other negative.

My primary love is learning. Thus I write a lot, because writing is one of the primary ways I learn. (I realize that sounds a bit weird but it is absolutely true: I don't really "know" something fully until I've written about it. Only then, have I carefully considered all its facets.)

I also read a lot. I'm self-educated, having only gone to school for five years (three years grammar, two high school) while cruising aboard the *Elizabeth*.

I'm a bit of a fitness freak, as I've found regular exercise makes me much more facile as a writer and calmer as a person.

I love music. I primarily play guitar, but also pound on pianos and burp into harmonicas. (If I wasn't a prose writer, I'd be a songwriter.)

I enjoy singing, and believe it is good for the soul.

I'm very interested in the law. (By *law* I mean the way mankind organizes itself.)

I am very poor at drawing, which is frustrating since both my sisters are fine artists, taught by my father who was a sign painter and graphic artist extraordinaire. Having spent so much time helping him and being with them, my graphic criteria are extremely high. This, coupled with little natural talent, is a sad, ego-bruising combo. However, despite this, I try to spend a few minutes drawing each day.

I'm intrigued by organized religion and all other forms of mass delusion. I'm particularly intrigued with eastern thinking, Zen, Buddhism, Hinduism, etc.

The point I'm trying to make is that the sailing lifestyle can be (and should be) an extremely active and intellectually stimulating one. Most folks are simply too busy earning a living to actively learn how not to have to.

The funny part, the ironic part, is that by not working, you can afford yourself the time and perspective to not *have* to work for someone else (you *always* have to work for yourself). Or, to put it another way, when I pursued the publishers on Madison Avenue, they hid from me. The moment I stopped chasing them and headed away over the horizon, they set off in hot pursuit. For ten years I tried to figure out how to get my "sea gypsy" report broadcast over NPR. Again and again, I pitched them intricate proposals. Finally, I gave up and sailed off to Micronesia, where they contacted me and begged for ten summer spots.

I could go on and on. But there's something about Mother Ocean that conspires to nurture deep, heavy thinking. If I was going to study something totally foreign to me, (let's say gold or monetary trading) I'd go to a deserted atoll for my competitive edge.

For me, there's just too much "noise" ashore to truly focus. The sea, on the other hand, has all natural sounds. It is there, where a man can truly think.

Booze

I'm not going to tell you if you should or should not drink, nor how much. But the reality is that the sailing life is, traditionally, saturated in booze.

Once upon a time, I loved to drink. It was never a problem for me. But around the age of 48 or so, the health negatives started adding up; hangovers, the hint of a beer belly, etc.

In essence, I discovered a note written in the bottom of my beer bottle, and that note said "Quit."

I hope you never get this note or need this note. Carolyn has never gotten it or needed it. It is a joy for me to buy her wine, uncork it, and lovingly decant it into her wineglass. But I got that note. And I heeded it.

This wasn't easy, especially since I was (perhaps) the most famous **lush tropical vegetable** in the Caribbean.

But if you can't keep a promise to yourself, who can you keep one to? The only reason I bring this up is because so many newbies on the yachting scene go off the deep end with alcohol.

Forewarned is forearmed.

Drugs

I've heard there's a drug problem in the Caribbean. Not true. We've got plenty.

Seriously, I won't lecture you about drugs any more than I'll tell you to stop drinking.

But drugs are very dangerous in the sense that very serious people toss you in jail for them.

My life is in pursuit of freedom and fun, both of which would be in short supply in a foreign jail.

I've been absolutely flabbergasted to be sitting in my cockpit in Malaysia, duck down below to make my guests a cup of tea, and reappear on deck to be offered a joint. (Marijuana cigarette)

The fact that *Wild Card* would be confiscated immediately if found with even a tiny bit of drugs aboard doesn't even factor in. The penalty for drugs in Malaysia is **DEATH**!

That's right: death as in D-E-A-D forever!

No, thanks! Maybe medical marijuana is all the rage in California, but they haven't got the word in Kuala Lumpur.

I do not allow any drugs aboard my boat *ever, anywhere*. That's a pretty simple, basic, easily understood policy.

Cosmetic Considerations

People are going to judge you by your vessel. There's no getting around that. It's just human nature.

If a landlubber glances at *Wild Card*, they see a shabby boat. But if a sailor glances at *Wild Card*, they see a shabby *well-found* boat.

There's a world of difference, if you're a sailor.

Each of us carries his own set of prejudices. If I see an absolutely pristine yacht, I consider its owner a great ship's husband—who probably isn't into sailing. People who are really into sailing and putting miles on their vessels generally don't travel around on gold platers, as there are just not enough hours in the day to do both. So, in a sense, I'm prejudiced against too-fancy of a boat. I immediately dismiss it as a "dock queen," which is, in my opinion, a derogatory term.

But shabby and hard-used have nothing to do with sloppy and screwed-up.

There's a good excuse for having faded topsides—you can't afford a new Awlgrip job. But there's no good excuse for a dirty boat, a wavey boot top, a misaligned cove strip, or a vessel with halyards slapping, or bags of reeking garbage in the cockpit.

Sea gypsies are poor in money but rich in time. So avoid *sloppy*, and embrace *hard-used*.

There is a certain cosmetic level that I don't ever want *Wild Card* to fall below. I think of her, in some ways, as a long-haul truck. She might be covered with mud and bugs, but there's always tread on her tires and gas in her tank. She might look world-weary, but she also looks ready-to-roll as well.

This is important. The moment a boat anchors next to me with numerous topside scrapes incurred at different times. (Yes, I can tell from a distance.) I think "Anchor dragger! Beware!

Once you become a competent seaman, your boat sort-of (for better or worse) morphs into you. It isn't just a representation of your personality, it is your personality.

If you're attempting to slide in under the radar on any level, make sure your vessel doesn't call unwanted or un-intentioned attention to itself.

Of course, some people want their vessel to do just that. Larry Pardey makes his living doing high quality work on old wooden vessels, and, thus, he uses his lovely Talisman as his very effective calling card.

I'm just the opposite. Sometimes I work on other people's boats but only on a "beat it to fit, paint it to match" basis of assured crudity. I used to proudly call my Boston company, "Bozo Boat Works." Our motto was, "Cheap but not chintzy." Our slogan was, "We don't clown around." Not many people hired us. Those that did, had a sense of humor and never wasted time trying to find the complaint department. Why bother?

Spare Yourself the Heavy Expense Of Heavy Spares

It used to be that a frugal circumnavigator had to bring along as many spares as he could possibly fit aboard his boat. If he didn't, he'd regret it.

Not so today.

In fact, to save money, only bring the items you normally will need and none of the heavy, bulky items you *might* need.

Why?

It's simple—most of this "deep storage" stuff will be damaged by moisture than actually used. I used to carry a spare starter motor, spare alternator, a spare gasket set in my bilge. Hell, at one point I even carried a spare head for the motor. Now I do not. I carry the standard spares, sure: filters, belts, impellers, a head-gasket, three injectors, but little else. I air-freight it in if I need it. Communications are now easy world-wide. FedEx and/or DHL are everywhere.

No matter what it costs to ship, this is ultimately cheaper than having a bilge full of rusting components that won't actually work when you need them.

Reincarnating Your Outboard

Sooner or later your dinghy's outboard engine is going to go for a short, vertical swim. This isn't a matter of *if*, but *when*. If you are Bill Gates, I recommend buying a new one. If you are, alas, only moderately wealthy and happen to be in a civilized country, I recommend you have someone dive it up and immediately bring it to an authorized repair facility.

If you're like the rest of us, often in the wrong place at the wrong time with empty pockets, don't despair! Time is of the essence, true, but perhaps not as you think. It is absolutely critical to get the engine cleaned and started ASAP after it is brought up from the seabed. But it can stay down there for a couple of hours or even a couple of days if, upon surfacing, it is immediately taken care of.

Here's the step-by-step procedure for a small two-cycle outboard.

I begin working on it the moment it surfaces by removing its cover, rinsing with fresh water, if possible, and heavily spraying it with WD-40. Then I whip out the spark plug and drain the carburetor of water/sludge. I WD-40 it again. Then I connect a fresh tank of clean gas/oil mixture and squirt some 3-in-1 oil

Fatty working on his outboard in Paros, Greece

directly into the cylinder. I pull the cord a couple of dozen times with the throttle wide open, while someone else WD-40's the entire engine again and again. Then I shut off the gas and give it ten more strong pulls to clear the cylinder of any remaining water or grease. Then I put just a dollop of oil in the cylinder (to increase compression) and slap a new spark plug in. After reconnecting the (WD-40'd) plug wire and opening the fuel, I attempt to start it. Occasionally it starts right up but usually it does not. I then re-drain the carburetor, re-dry out the spark plug and try again. This time I shoot starting fluid in the carburetor opening as I'm yanking on the cord. Once it shows any sign of starting, you've won! It is just a matter of getting it to fire again—more and more often—until it "sort of" runs. (You may have to "play" the choke to keep it going. Do so, as playing the choke is a lot easier than yanking on the cord). Once it starts—don't stop it. If possible, cast off and circle while continuing to WD-40 the engine. Run it (with a moderate and varied throttle) for more than ten minutes after it starts to "purr" cleanly. Give yourself a break, then WD-40 it and run it again, four or five times in quick succession.

I've done this routine dozens of times (for myself and others) and have never failed to get the engine to start. (If the engine is old and stubborn, I angrily take apart the carburetor.)

I've had modern outboard engines underwater more than three times, for up to three days, which have run longer than three years afterwards. (Noisy buggers, though!)

Caution: be careful! Sparks, gasoline, WD-40, and ether can be a fiery combination.

Four stroke outboards are a different kettle of fish. I don't have much experience with them. However, the main difference is that their crankcase has to be repeatedly flushed—first with fresh water (a couple of times), then kerosene (if available), and finally oil.

Once it runs well, I'd still change the lube oil at least two more times over the course of the next few days. (Don't just run it once for an hour and think it is fine. It is not fine until you've run it numerous times and all the salt crystals and moisture have worked their way completely out of the system. This takes time. The trick is to allow the engine to run a long time without freezing up. Keep shooting it with WD-40, too. You have to totally displace all the saltwater residue or the engine's life will be greatly shortened.)

Monitoring Your Monitor Wind Vane

The best thing to do with all your marine equipment is to maintain it according to the manufacturer's instructions. But some people can't seem to let well enough alone, and try to do a teensy bit better. This often results in a bad outcome.

For instance, it isn't recommended to oil or grease your Monitor windvane. But people often have problems in light air (usually from less-than-perfect sail trim) and blame it on the Monitor or Aries. Thus, they "help it out" by oiling it with WD-40, CRC-66, 3-in-1, silicone spray, Teflon grease, lithium grease, axle grease, etc.

The result is that the Monitor factory constantly gets back units that are so gummed up with lubrication that they'd barely work in a hurricane.

First off; different types of lubricants work in different ways and are not compatible. They turn into cement if mixed, and adding more of both only increases the problem. Two, many thin spray lubricants are intended for metal and actually "swell" Delrin and other plastic bearings. This not only binds the parts, but causes increased wear. The result is less performance for a much shorter time.

My Monitor instructions say to "rinse with fresh water" when I pull into a dock, and I do. (This happens to be about once a year, sometimes two.) The way I figure it, if God thinks my Monitor needs rinsing, He'll make it rain. Thus, my Monitor went almost ten years and 70,000 miles without needing to be rebuilt.

It only takes an afternoon to rebuild a Monitor. But I strongly suggest taking it off your transom so all those tiny bits bouncing around won't escape.

Yes, use only that amazing Marlow cordage that came with it, as its inner core isn't braided. (This is one of the reasons why it stretches so little.)

If my control lines (to the tiller) haven't been used in a bit, I have to tighten them a few times during first use. Normally you don't want too much slack in the line, as it results in wasted motion and increased inefficiency.

However, in light airs, don't over tighten the control lines as this increases the friction on the bearings. Allow a little sag. I also custom-made three different sized, thin plywood wind blades to use in very light air, moderate conditions, and very heavy air.

Some people don't take off the top wind blade or fold up the bottom rudder when anchored or docked. This results in excessive wear.

Accurately Inventorying Your Inventory

It is important, on a small boat, to know what you have aboard it—so you don't leave without what you need nor think you have what you do not.

So we have a base list of spares and supplies that gets a tad more complex with each year (as our memories fade).

What was I saying?

Oh. Yeah.

Your engine isn't the only thing that requires spares. Don't forget your pumps, stove, outboard, head, folding bikes, blocks, windlass, etc.

Nothing underwater? You sure? We need to have a certain type of grease aboard to lube our Max prop. Yes, we carry a spare cutlass bearing and two zincs aboard as well.

Extra ball bearings for the roller furlers? Traveler? Wind Gen?

Can a boat have too many O-rings? Yes, if its crew doesn't know where they are.

You have to know what you have aboard to know what you need before you shove off. Some of this can be kept in your head—but less and less as it turns gray.

This can be as simple as stapling an index card onto the back of each cabinet and bin to mark what you put-in and take-out—to snapping open a handy netbook.

The bottom line: not knowing is expensive. Bill Gates and Steve Jobs are right—knowledge really is power.

Pamper Your Diesel

The most expensive thing on your boat is probably your diesel. This means it has to maintained exactly in accordance with the manual. (Yes, re-torque-ing the head and adjusting the valves as per the factory specs are important!)

No excuses. Modern diesel engines will run almost forever if you never run them hot or without oil. Chances are, you *can't* run your engine long enough to wear it out. Only by *not* maintaining it correctly *can* you cause it major, life-threatening trouble.

Remember the Immortal Words of my favorite BVI grease-monkey, a lovable guy with eternally-bleeding knuckles named Diesel Dan Durban: "Nirvana can only be obtained through the rigorous application of periodic maintenance."

How true! (Editor's note: Every time Fatty tells someone to "pamper their diesel," Carolyn starts angrily demanding, "What about me, Fatty, what about me?")

Pedaling Your Ass Around Town

The cheapest, healthiest, and best way to see a cruising destination is by bicycle. The vigorous cardio exercise (which is so important to an aging mariner) is only part of it. You can stop at will, explore, and converse. It is just fast enough and just slow enough. You can really see when bicycling. Bikes

Cap'n Fatty and Carolyn riding their folding bikes in Langkawi, Malaysia

and boats are silent as they move. Both aren't just great transportation devices—they are physical manifestations of Zen.

The best boat-bike in the world is the folding Brompton. It is extremely compact, very ruggedly constructed, and rock-solid on the road—but, alas, it ain't cheap. (I purchased my ($1,350 retail) Brompton used, for $200. It lasted for more than a circumnavigation—until it was pan-caked into twisted metal by a multi-ton tide ramp... boo hoo!)

If you buy a folding bike to stash in your cockpit locker, decide if you want a "marina" bike to ride short, smooth distances or a road bike to ride for miles.

Only a few folding bikes are suitable for any distance—and they don't give them away. But there are other, less expensive options. Some sailors buy a full-size bike, disassemble it, and stash its various parts where there is available room.

Others buy a bike when they stop somewhere for a long time. In Australia, I purchased a wonderful full-sized bike for Carolyn for $10 Aussie ($6 US) at a resale shop and gave it away six months later when we left Brisbane.

I've seen a couple of full-frame bikes hack-sawed up and joined back together with metal sleeves because most boaters only need their folder to fold when taking it aboard—so if the process takes ten minutes versus ten seconds, big deal.

We don't even think of them as bikes. We call 'em "land dinghies." We met one old duffer in South Africa who had mini varnished trail boards on his Brompton, and cute, tiny fenders to toss out when he stopped as well!

Why not pedal around on your quirky sense of humor?

Idiot-Proofing Yourself With Waterproof Cases

If you live-aboard year after year, you have to learn to protect yourself from the sun and your electro-gear from water.

You have to be eternally vigilant to keep your computer, camera, and mobile phone dry.

The problem isn't falling in. You shouldn't be doing much of that once you get your sealegs. The problem is wind, rain, and salt spray in the dinghy.

Our solution is covers-within-covers. When we get a new netbook, Carolyn makes a very tight-fitting, almost splash-proof soft fabric case for it and we put it into a plastic waterproof container on rough days.

The Pelican containers are the best. They are super-strong, watertight, fashionable, and convenient. Needless to say, they are pricey, too.

We often used Tupperware-type kitchen products to accomplish the same thing. In some ways they're even better—lighter in weight and leaner in size than the crush-proof Pelican cases.

We have a number of **dry bags** for use in the dinghy as well. These are soft and flexible, and we've never had one leak. However, you have to be very careful when you open them. If your hands or hair are wet, your gear will be too.

If we're ashore with our computer or both our Canon DSLR cameras and it kicks up or starts raining, I just run to a grocery store and grab a fistful of large plastic garbage bags. If you tie and clinch them, they are watertight after three layers. (Our cameras are within a bag, which is within a bag, which is within a bag: three layers of bags are usually sufficient.)

There's a bit of irony here, though. I know one sailor who bought a used netbook for $100 and then spent $150 on an airtight case for it—which made it even bigger and bulkier than his large laptop! Is this progress or insanity? (I ponder this question often.)

Conserving Diesel: Don't Be Fuelish!

Ideally, your diesel engine should be run under load for a minimum of an hour a week for maximum longevity. Since we never have to crank up to charge (because of our solar array and wind generator), we do this every Sunday, especially when at sea.

But we're currently in Turkey, where a gallon of diesel goes for $10 US. This strikes me as absurd. I used to bitch about the cost when it was 29 cents! In any event, cranking up isn't free.

I'm not going to tell you how much to run your engine on passage. That's between you, your accountant, and your conscience. But we don't normally crank up until our speed has fallen below three knots for more than an hour. Occasionally I refuse to run the engine at all—just for fun. (This back-fired on the windless 250 mile trip from Ado, Maldives to Boddam, Chagos which took 11 days, anchor to anchor.)

If we run our diesel flat-out, we get over 6.25 knots in smooth water, and burn almost three-quarters of a gallon an hour. If we throttle back to five knots, we get *better than twice* the fuel economy. That means we can save twice the money or go over 80 percent further.

That's a considerable savings—and much better for the planet as well.

Speaking of our planet, to prevent any oil weeps from getting in our bilge; I toss a large Kotex (female napkin) in my drip pan that soaks up an enormous amount of fluids.

Tweaking and Light Air Sailing

The best way to save fuel on passage is to shut off your engine. Most people fail at this because their resulting boat speed is low. For example: They are powering along at five knots and shut down their diesel. Their speed immediately drops to 1.8 knots. They feel this is far too slow. Thus, they soon crank up again. This used to happen to me often—until I was in Europe where diesel fuel costs $10 a gallon and powering with the "iron jib" was simply too expensive.

The result was an entirely new policy of shutting off the engine for a *minimum* of half an hour. At first, of course, I'd be going 1.8 knots like everyone else. But I'd soon find that if I headed up or down a bit from my rhumbline course, my speed would increase to 2.1 knots. Then I'd watch my headsail telltales and play with my sheets, my jib car placement, and my jib halyard tension. This would add another half a knot to my speed. Then I'd check my weather helm via my tiller—was it a tad too much? Was the rudder acting as a brake while steering me? Could it be eased simply by moving the traveler to leeward? Finally I'd turn my attention to the mainsail: foot, Cunningham, and halyard tension first, then traveler placement and mainsheet adjustment. Is my mainsail's draft too shallow or too far forward? Was the boat pitching too much because of a full water tank forward and/or all the chain/anchor gear forward? Why not gravity-transfer the water aft to my now-empty saddle tanks and physically transfer the chain/anchor belowdecks to the base of my mast? (We never cross an ocean with the chain in its locker, only secured to the mast base in the head. Yes, this is an awful, dirty job—but one of the reasons we're fast and also heave-to so well.)

All of this doesn't happen in five minutes. It is an hour's project of tweaking, tweaking, and more tweaking. But I often get my boat speed from 1.8 knots to 3 knots in this manner. Three knots, for me, is fine. That's 72 miles a day—plenty for a laid-back sailor who loves to be on passage.

Light air sail trim isn't magic, but it takes consistent, considered, quantified practice. I often have *Wild Card* beam-reaching at over three knots on a "ghost wind" which barely ripples the surface of the water.

But it takes time and perseverance—two traits of a good, economical sailor.

Morphing Your Fast Greyhound Into a Slow Pig

This is easy to do. In fact, about 50 percent of all liveaboard cruising boats do it eventually.

The first thing to do is add weight: generators, freezers, ice-makers, washing machines, and massive battery banks. The more weight, the merrier. If you can distribute it high (like bookshelves near the hull-to-deck joint), so much the better. Since you probably want to live in the middle of the boat were the space is greatest and the motion least—put all the real heavy stuff (anchors, chain, propane tanks, anchor buddies, life rafts, outboards, fuel tanks, etc) at the ends. This will increase your pitching magnificently. Why, if you put enough weight at the boat's ends, you can totally eliminate your ability to sail to windward!

If your design waterline is about a foot under water, you are on the right track. If you have to do a compression dive to see if—*perfect!*

Next, increase your vessel's windage by adding fixed dodgers, massive traveler arches, windshields, and immense "towers of power" aft. (Don't forget to glue various television and Wi-Fi antennas onto your masthead—the added weight and windage really pay off when they are high!)

Ditto, radar and windmills.

Bow thrusters not only dramatically increase your drag, the weight of the unit and its batteries so far forward will dramatically increase your pitching moment as well. (I average about 8,000 miles under sail per year and dock once or twice while doing so. Surely the negatives of an expensive, prone-to-failure bow thruster outweigh its occasional advantage.)

If you really want to kill all performance, put a roller-furler behind your mainmast for the "convenience" of standing still with ease. (This can dramatically decrease your mainsail's efficiency so much that the much smaller, less efficient (no battens) sail becomes utterly useless.)

Since large jibs are tough to tack, don't buy 'em. Instead, fly tiny storm sails in light airs while complaining that the bubbles in the water aren't moving.

If, after all of the above, your boat is still able to crawl downwind at half a knot, use a fixed three-bladed engine propeller and toss over a giant, water-powered, 12-volt generator prop to kill any attempt at forward motion.

Oh, yeah—line your side-decks with jugs of fuel. With their weight so high, it will help with being knocked down, broaching, and even rolling 360 degrees. (The chances of pitch-poling can be increased immeasurably by having two or three massive anchors on your heavy bowsprit, and the chain to go with them just behind the stem.)

Does the above sound harsh? It isn't. I regularly visit fine sailing boats that have been ruined by all of the above—and more!

Knots

The three most important knots a sailor needs to know are the bowline, the reef knot, and the clove hitch. The bowline, in particular, is useful. A sailor should not only know how to tie one, but be able to tie one in the dark, on the other side of piling, or behind his back.

A double-carrick comes in handy for joining two ropes together.

The rolling hitch is extremely useful for clearing a jammed winch or transferring an anchor rode (while under strain) to another cleat. It is simple to tie—and can get you out of a major problem fast.

I probably know fifty knots, but only use about a dozen on a daily basis.

But I find marlinspike seamanship fascinating and will happily show anyone my "joke" knots; like the trailing bowline, towboat bowline, thief knot, and Spanish handcuffs.

"Ashley's Book of Knots" is the ultimate authority here. But there are at least two very good copyright-free knot books available for the Amazon Kindle reader—totally without weight or cost. (How can a literature-loving sailor beat *that*, eh?)

Marine Showers and Conserving Water

Most boats over 42 feet have a stand up shower aboard, and a few even have a sit down one (or even a small bathtub). But many boats below 32 feet do not. They either use a portable Sun Shower or a two gallon garden-style, pump-up insecticide sprayer. Both systems work well in warm weather, and the insecticide one is particular stingy with the aqua.

I usually go swimming first, clean myself thoroughly in the saltwater, rinse in the sea—and then just rinse off with fresh water at the end.

If I can't swim first, I make sure I use a rough "scrubby thing" to scour off the dead skin and very little soap. (It doesn't take a lot of water to wash, it takes a lot to rinse the soap off.)

I recommend Joy dishwashing liquid. Never use ordinary soap in saltwater, as it coagulates into a lard-like mess. Afterward, I splash with Avon's Skin So Soft, which keeps the no-see-ums away as well. (If you're bothered by mosquitoes on the beach, just toss some coconut husks on a campfire—and they're gone within minutes.)

Boatyard Blues

We average 24 months between haul-outs and we've been lucky that none of our haul-outs have been emergency ones.

This allows us plenty of time to plan. And planning is what saves us money.

Yes, haste really *does* make waste.

The first, most important thing to do is gather your materials together cheaply. This means get them at wholesale prices, from sale bins, and from out of dumpsters.

The second thing to do is to make sure you understand the yard rules and the yard prices. Bear in mind that the yard and you should never become enemies. But also bear in mind that they are hoping you're a cash cow and you're hoping you're not. You have different objectives. Therefore, the rules become all important.

Can you live aboard during the haul-out? If not, forget it if you're on a budget.

What does the haul-out include? In *and* out, right? Power wash? Blocking? Jack stands? Electricity? Scaffolding? Ladder? Is there a re-blocking charge? Is the voltage in the yard 110 or 220? Are there voltage converters if your tools don't match? What's allowed: Sandblasting is good if you are trying to strip the coal-tar epoxy off your steel hull, but not so good if you are trying to re-varnish your mahogany cap rail. How much is storage by the day, week, month, season, year?

Can you do all your own work? If not, get gone!

I once hauled very cheaply in Malaysia during the height of their monsoonal rainy season. Not only did I not get much work done on my boat, I was scared it might be swept away in the floods!

What time can you start working? When must you stop? This is often a problem with "resort shipyards" attached to both marinas and hotels.

In Tonga, for instance, you will be arrested if you begin stirring a paint can on the Sabbath. Ditto, if you crank up a grinder on a Friday in certain Mideast countries. (Madagascar is the worst. Each village has elaborate rules for a visitor's conduct of which the sailor is completely unaware until he is "arrested" by the chief and typically fined a cow or pig for the upcoming feast.)

The best way to learn the answers to these questions and many others is to ask. Ask in the office and ask the strangers laboring in the yard. Then check your bill daily for the first couple of days. One yard we hauled at in Asia just added on every silly thing imaginable to our bill. Every day at lunch, we'd

Cap'n Fatty enjoying life in the shipyard

come in, smile, check our bill, and demanded it all be removed. They did so also with a smile—knowing that many of the others outside in the yard weren't smart enough to do the same. Nobody lost face and we gained their respect.

Shipyard prices vary greatly from location to location and from yard to yard. It isn't difficult to find out which operation is trying to *earn* your money and which one is attempting to *steal* it.

Here's a truism: The less time you spend in shipyards, the less money you will spend in shipyards. ("Brilliant," says Carolyn sarcastically.) We work from dawn until after dusk every day while in the yard.

Recently, we discovered a bunch of unexpected fiberglassing we needed to do. Within hours I was twirling resin-dripping sheets of bi-axial at the boat—working by flood lamp until midnight. We soon hit the water, only a couple of days and dollars shy of our original plan.

We had plenty of time to recuperate aboard during the following season in Micronesia.

Careening Toward a Tidal Berth

Careening a vessel and hauling out on the tide are two different things. Let's talk about careening first.

This is done where there's little or no tide—in the Lesser Antilles of the Caribbean, for example.

The boat (as the pirates used to do) is brought into a quiet cove or river with absolutely flat water and zero wakes. It's best if you can be tied from side to side via strong palm trees, although it can be done with anchors to seaward and the vessel heeled toward land.

Basically, you "pull" the vessel down (from the masthead) and over on its side to expose as much bottom as possible, one side at a time.

Yes, there's a trick: The lines you tie to prevent your vessel from moving towards the haul-down line should go from the same side as the haul-down line, down into the water, and then under the hull! (*see illustration.)

Let's see if I can make it clearer. Mentally picture the boat from astern. Now visualize a line running to starboard from the masthead to some palm trees ashore. If we pull on that starboard line, the entire boat would move to starboard, right? To prevent this, we take a line (actually, two to six lines) from the starboard rail and lead it down into the water, and to port under the vessel. (Careful of the rudder and prop!) Now when we pull the boat to starboard from the mast head, it can't move to starboard—so it heels to starboard. Clear?

There's an angle problem. Pulling down the vessel gets easier and easier up to 45 degrees of heel, then gets harder and harder as the pulling line gets straighter. One solution is to move the pulling point towards the boat so that, ultimately, it is 90 degrees from the mast when the mast is parallel to the water.

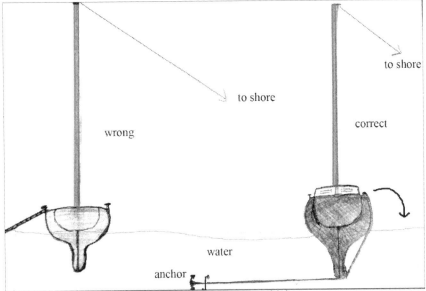

Careening is simple. If the pirates of yore could do it, so can you.

If the boat isn't jostled, she is stable in this position. Many beamy, light displacement craft can get one entire side out at a time. Most heavy displacement craft can get only about 80 percent or so out of the water.

Of course, there's always danger when heavy things are under load. A large ski boat coming unexpectedly into the cove can do a lot of damage, maybe even strain your chainplates.

But if the pirates regularly careened their heavy craft, so can you.

It is actually a lot of fun.

Hauling out on the tide is much easier, but the time is all-too-brief. You have less than six hours to both dry and paint your boat. This isn't much time. Many folks scrape and inspect on the first tide, then dry and paint on the second.

Obviously, the tidal range has to be sufficient—you can't haul a boat drawing six feet on a five-foot tide.

If you have a wall and/or some pilings in a tidal berth to go against, it's dead easy. Just lash your boat solidly (and slightly heeled) to the wall and allow the water to leave. Many marinas in Australia and New Zealand have a free passive "hauling station" on premises. All you have to do is ask to be scheduled.

Sometimes, only a beach is available. This best bet is to get a bunch of truck tires from the junkyard and place them under the turn of your bilge as the tide goes out on your sharply-heeled vessel. Positioning these tires is much harder than you might think—make sure you have plenty of lines available to hold them in place as the tide drops. There should be absolutely no wave action when you bottom out or float off.

Most boats float off without a problem, but not all. Some are improperly designed, with large cockpit lockers that take on water before the boat has enough buoyancy to rise and break the suction of the sand or mud. Make sure your boat will float off without problem, or it will be the most expensive "free" haul-out of your life. (Yes, close head and sink seacocks as well.)

This method only allows you paint one side at a time. But it can be a very fun, very interesting thing to engineer. See all the nauti-joy the wealthy folks miss?

P.S. Don't leave a mess on the beach and return the tires to where you found them. Your free haul-out should not be at the expense of the environment. All "organic" haul-outs and careening should be *revenue positive* in the Karma Bank!

Saving Money While Hauling

Regardless of whether you haul out in a shipyard, on the tide, or careen, here are some simple ways to save money.

We paint our topsides with small nap paint rollers, often using industrial epoxy versus a major marine brand. I use the roller almost 100 percent of the time. I use a small brush for only a few areas to "cut around" certain objects on the topsides. This comes out with a tiny "orange peel" effect—that I find sexy. Many people don't. And so, they work as a team: one person rolls and the other is right behind to "tip" the finish with a brush. If done properly, this creates a smoother, more mirror-like finish.

My friend Juicy Jack who rehabs yachts in Malaysia uses a cheap electric spray gun, and manages to get wonderful results.

If you use the right paint thinners, you can catch a free buzz as well. (Oh, gosh! I wish I could stop making such sophomoric 1960's jokes!)

Most shipyard dumpsters contain dozens of discarded pieces of wet and dry sandpaper that are barely used.

We collect various plastic bottles and large-mouthed cans during the month before we haul, so we have plenty of paint containers and don't have to buy any. We also buy the cheapest "throw away" brushes (find ones that don't shed), and then clean them instead of tossing 'em. We use cheap masking tape, not which super expensive blue stuff, and only allow it on the boat for hours—never, ever overnight.

While it is always impossible to find a paint stick if your epoxy is starting to set up, it is easy to find dozens of free paint sticks (well, twigs and such) during the month before you're on the hard.

Obviously, since you're usually paying by the day while hauled-out, it behooves you to be quick. Carolyn and I work from the crack of dawn until dark until *Wild Card* splashes.

Fiberglassing is, even in the hands of skilled professionals, a wasteful task. There's often a lot of "ruined" cloth, matt, and roving around a large job. Make sure you ask politely first—but the workers are often happy to allow you to satisfy your itch. (Oh, no! Not another pun!)

Zincs can often be found discarded in the shipyard mud, some of which are barely used. Just wire brush 'em back to shiny and save a bunch of money.

Since most yards charge a hefty "re-blocking" fee to move or shift your vessel's supporting poppits, it is good to carefully consider their initial placement. This can save between $50 and $100 in many yards.

Use small rollers and trays; they don't waste as much paint.

Yes, I'm a cheap bastard who pinches his pennies hard—but I'm not foolish, either. I pay to have my boat power-washed, and I use good quality antifouling paint when I can afford it.

Anti-fouling hint: Many paint companies have a "yacht line" and a completely differently branded line of "commercial" products aimed at fishermen. Most of the time, the products are identical—just the price is vastly different.

Generally speaking, fishermen pay far, far less for the same stuff we yachties use simply because they're more careful, intelligent shoppers.

I never pay to have an engine hoisted aboard nor a mast pulled, because it is safer and quicker if I do it myself.

My father used to be a professional sign painter, and I know there's nothing better to set off a classic boat than a nice lettering job on its transom, trailboards, and life ring. But, alas, good quality sign painters aren't cheap.

If you're semi-tight with your pennies, you can go to the nearest "computerized sign shop" and get your name and hailing port in vinyl for around $80 bucks or so—which is a hell of a lot less than a sign painter would charge.

But if you are super-tight with your pocket change like we are, you order the name and hailing port over the Internet a month in advance and get the same quality vinyl letters for only a fraction of the price. (We just paid $27 for both *Wild Card* and our dinghy!)

While it is true that you are normally not hauled out long enough to scrounge all your materials from the wasteful boaters around you, this might not be so difficult if you are hauled for a long time and/or anchored near the yard.

In that case, a month or two before your haul-out date, start casing the boats on the hard. You'll soon meet some great folks. Tell 'em you are "hauling on a shoestring" soon, and you're interested in any paint or materials they might want to recycle. We've gotten tons of brushes and trays and "half-cans" of paint this way, which saves us from rescuing it out of the dumpster. And, hey, it was all gonna be thrown away anyway. Plus, boaters with money don't want to lug around an extra gallon of antifouling on the race course. So you're doing everyone (and the planet) a favor by recycling the stuff.

Pat yourself on the back, you Artful Mooch!

One final note on painting: A high quality topside finish is 99 percent prep, and 1 percent application. We sea gypsies are wealthy in time. Chances are, your $200 paint job ain't gonna look as perfect as a professional $12,000 Awl-grip job will—not if you really really look hard. But, hey, nobody looks hard.

After a certain point, people don't care how "like glass" your topsides look. Why should you?

The last word on haul-outs: Shipyards are great places for a sea gypsy to network. I often make great trades and acquire needed gear cheap while hauling. It is also a good place to find a job, since everyone can see if you do good work at a fast clip.

Never Confuse Salvage With Stealing

In many ways, your house and your car are the same. Let's say you parked your car on a hill and, while you were away, your emergency brake slipped and the car rolled downhill a couple of hundred feet, and slid into the ditch.

It would still be your car, wouldn't it? Of course it would. You wouldn't be happy if someone stripped it, would you? Of course you wouldn't.

Don't think that a vessel that has been driven ashore is the property of "anyone who claims it." It is not. Boats have owners. You can't strip or claim them unless they are truly abandoned.

I know one sailing idiot who thinks that if he sees a dinghy that hasn't been used for a long time, it is okay to borrow it, use it, and then maybe, claim it as salvage.

This is stealing, plain and simple.

Salvage laws are among the most misunderstood in the world.

Protecting Your Vessel From Being Salvaged

The flip side of all this nonsense is, if your vessel ever appears to be "salvageable," you must take precautions to protect it from such silliness. Never, ever leave your vessel aground or driven on the shore if you can help it. Stay with it, or leave someone else to stay with it, while you go for help.

If you must leave it to go get help, then: 1. lock it, 2. write in magic marker in large letters on the topsides **NOT ABANDONED! I WILL BE RIGHT BACK. DO NOT TOUCH!** 3. put out an anchor (even if you're high and dry).

These three simple steps will ensure no one "mistakenly" thinks they can steal all your stuff—or will force them to make restitution if they do so, at least in the States.

Of course, in many Third World countries it is best not to rely on the "rule of law" because there is none. I've heard of incidents in Africa and South America where it was the local Coast Guard and police who looted the vessel.

San Blas, Panama may be the worst. The Kuna Indians there, nice as can be most of the time, are absolutely convinced that they own your boat if it goes aground.

One elderly Irish couple ran aground in front of a village and was delighted to see help was on the way—only it wasn't help. With the Irish owners aboard, loudly protesting, their vessel was stripped before their amazed eyes because it was "aground and anyone's game" according to the local looters.

Just the word "salvage" strikes terror into my heart. I've seen so many horrible crimes committed in its name, so many world cruises come to unexpected grief.

If you are interested in the subject of maritime law, reading the evolution of marine cargo regulation is both fascinating and ironic because the original intent of many of these "salvage laws" was to protect the ship owner, not the person finding the ship.

I'm Pro Propane

There's no question propane is cheaper than any other marine stove fuel. Another big advantage is how compact and light in weight it is per BTU. But there are still plenty of problems circumnavigating with propane.

Some countries don't have it—only butane. This normally isn't a problem, despite the fact that a stove's orifice needs to be adjusted for optimum efficiency when changing fuels.

The main problem is a physical one. Every country has its own tank fittings.

This would be easy if you went to one country. You could simply change to the new type. But traveling along an "endless highway" of different fittings is a royal pain in the butt. I know. This situation has cost me dearly in blood, sweat, and tears as well as money.

One way to deal with it is to pay *someone else* to deal with it. This someone else in Asian is usually an old guy trying to make a couple of pennies by decanting his local bottle into your foreign bottle.

If the price-is-right, let him do it.

Unfortunately, there are an increasing number of places in the world that double and triple the price of the propane decanted into any "foreign" bottle. The premise here is, hey, they can afford it and they ain't us—so why not gouge 'em?

I don't like being gouged. So I just rent a "local" jug of propane and decant it into my tank with a hose.

This isn't difficult if you take a few simple precautions. There are dozens of sites on the Internet that will tell you exactly how-to do so—which your widow can sue if you get it wrong.

Basically, gravity does the work s-l-o-w-l-y.

But you either need a country-specific fitting at the "local" end of your reinforced plastic hose or a number of different sizes of hose-with-adapters to step-up and step-down in diameter and an unregulated fitting on your tank end.

Plus, some tanks require a piston to be depressed before gas can flow. This can be tricky if you don't have the correct adapter. I've hacksawed off a square-shanked screw driver, and "walked" it down the hose with a series of hose clamps to depress the valve.

This was laborious (figuring out a way to depress the inner valve) but eventually I got the gas to flow in deserted Chagos with only some hoses, hose clamps, and stray bits. This proves the old saying that "necessity is the mother of invention."

This isn't particularly fun but it has saved me as much as $40 dollars a tank, perhaps a hundred times. That's a lot of dough, pal.

Oh. Yeah. It's best not to smoke anything legal-or-non while messing with explosives. Sparks should be avoided.

Losing (and Finding) Your Marbles

I love live-aboard kids. One 5-year-old on the dock was playing with a truck one minute—and nothing the next. I smiled at him, went over, and asked if he'd lost his truck. No, he hadn't. He knew exactly where it was, he said as he pointed down into the harbor water.

Eventually, all of us drop stuff overboard. The problem usually isn't diving down to the bottom to retrieve it, but rather *finding* it.

The first thing to do *immediately* is to throw four or five small, easily seen items into the harbor water at the exactly same spot. Don't think, just do it: your coffee cup, spoon, cookie plate, pocket change, whatever. Watch them sink, noting if there is any visible current.

The idea here is to quickly mark the spot and get a small, concise area to grid search. (Hit the MOB on your GPS as well, if appropriate.)

If you're tied to a dock, your boat can't have moved much. But if you're at anchor, your boat can be continuously crabbing sideways, back and forth, without you realizing it.

Don your snorkel or scuba gear ASAP, and try to find the lost item while being extremely careful not to stir up any sediment from the bottom.

If you don't find it within five minutes, return to the surface, borrow four white dinner plates, and place them in four corners, fifty feet out from ground zero. Do everything possible to find it as soon as possible. As the minutes tick, your chances plummet.

Search methodically, in a grid pattern. Make some passes about three feet off the bottom for a good wide view, and other passes with your mask almost touching (but not stirring up a single grain of sand).

If it is late afternoon and the light is failing, try again tomorrow at midday.

Patience is a virtue here. You might not see the small gold wedding ring the first ten times you swim over it—until the eleventh when it winks in the fading sun.

As a child growing up on the schooner *Elizabeth*, we were fortunate to be tied up right across from a busy daycharter boat named the *Ranger III*. It was amazing how often the guests lost wedding rings, wristwatches, brooches, charm bracelets, wallets, tie clips, and other crap while strolling between the boat and the shore. The instant something was lost overboard, I'd be called. Thus, I've managed to find many rings, etc., on a murky, cloudy bottom. I made a lot of money in tips this way.

When I was six years old, I'd just dive down and get it. But by the time I was eight years old or so, I realized it was much more fun for all concerned if I took a little more time to earn a lot more money.

Why to Avoid Marinas

Most of my life I've been living like a King afloat, but one of my few forays ashore resulted in a brief sojourn in a trailer park. I'm not a big fan of trailer parks. However, even the meanest, cheapest, most "red-necky" trailer park in Hicksville has a reasonable amount of space between the trailers.

Many marinas are more crowded than trailer parks.

Not so a marina. Usually, your boat is within three or four feet of another boat in a marina—unless you're in the Med, and then it is actually touching the neighboring boat. (If an uncaring sailor wants to join the fun in crowded marinas in France, he just wedges the bow of his steel boat into the pile, and gives it full power while wiggling his transom. He's soon able to wedge in, after (perhaps) a Bavaria or Beneteau is crushed to dust!)

The point I'm trying to make is that marinas offer a very low quality of life. You're cheek-to-jowl with your neighbor. It is noisy. You're much more likely to be bothered, hassled, and ripped off. There are ants, roaches, and rats. There are rules, rules, and more rules. Your home will be hotter than at anchor, because your vessel can't pivot into the wind. If you plug in (we never do) and run air conditioning, you've effectively walled yourself off from your natural environment. I've been having a great time visiting with my neighbors at a marina—joking, and talking, and goofing with them. But then, once they've turned the "air-con" on, it is as if they've disappeared. They completely fall off my fun scope. Carolyn and I joke, "Hey, they probably died in there and no one will know because the bodies are refrigerated!"

A boat is a marvelous freedom machine at sea and anchor, but it is a stupid apartment when being held in humiliating bondage at the dock.

Besides all the disadvantages above, it is easy to get into the wrong mindset in a marina. Money can seem like the solution to everything. Since most of the people you meet will be scared of the sea and ashamed of their inability to anchor, it will seem a bit "scary" to do something as rash as leave the dock.

However, there are times when going to a dock is required. If the job is a small one, say loading a heavy transmission aboard or some new chain, do you really have to pay for a night's dockage?

Instead, I cultivate the dock jockeys hanging around the marina fuel pumps.

If they like you, they can be a big help.

The key here is preparation and consideration.

I have *Wild Card* all set to go—her halyard ready, etc. I wait for a slow day and the slowest period of it. Then I swing up to the dock and ask for water, diesel, ice, outboard gas, outboard oil, etc. And I make a point of saying, "No rush!" As they're just unrolling the diesel hose and Carolyn is grabbing it to refuel, a couple of my friends just sort of "happen by" dragging a cart with my transmission aboard. In the blink of an eye, I swing it aboard. I might get a glare, but that's usually it.

While coming down the Ditch (the U.S. East Coast Intracoastal Waterway system), I often pulled into fuel docks in the early afternoon when nothing was happening. I refueled and then asked, "Hey, my wife wants me to help her grab some groceries—okay if I pull my boat to the end of the pier where it's out of the way? I'll be back in 30 minutes, max."

Most of the time (especially the more southward you go) they say okay. I've had the guy say, "Don't worry about it. I'm not busy until five. Our town's pretty nice. If you want to stretch your legs, go ahead. Just be back before 4 p.m."

Please don't misunderstand me. I'm not suggesting taking advantage or screwing the boater waiting to refuel—not all at. What I am saying is that if you buy something and the marina has already made some money off you, then they are often pre-disposed to be nice. Allowing a crewmember to load *something that doesn't slow up the transaction* is being nice, so is allowing you to take up a few feet of a mammoth, totally vacant fuel dock. No, they don't have to do so and you shouldn't expect it. But there's no harm in trying, is there?

When Is a Dock Not a Dock?

It used to be far easier to "wiggle" into a dock for free than it is now. But we still do it occasionally. Let's say there's a fleet of tugboats or fishing boats. Often they'll allow you to raft up alongside for the night. (We do this in the Mississippi and along the Gulf Coast all the time.)

If you hit it off, they might ask you to stay. Often, there's a place at the dock that actually isn't a dock, not strictly speaking. And sometimes you can wedge your boat in there. Why, nobody hardly even notices! We call these spots the "Free YC" because they're often available if you really need 'em to be. The trick is to just "invent" your own space, not take an existing one. (Lines to shore, anchors out, etc.)

They're not free, not exactly. You have to give value. Help the fishermen lug their catch or roll their grease tubs down the dock. Keep an eye out for theft. If somebody's boat suddenly started running its bilge pump continuously, notify somebody. In essence, be a good citizen that people like to have around. You have to pull your own weight. We ultimately get what we deserve. If you deserve a free dock and if you really really need one—you'll be amazed how often fate will deliver one to your doorstep... er, companionway step.

This was brought home to me in Jackson Park, one of the loveliest harbors in Chicago. I was illegally using a friend's mooring. Sure, I had his permission but it was against the harbor rules. Thus the harbor master had been trying to find me for months, leaving increasingly strident notes on my boat. I was ducking him with great success.

Anyway, I snuck down to my boat one night by tip-toeing past the harbor master's house—only to discover the lovely old wooden boat next to me was sinking. Not only was it sinking, it was sinking fast!

I dashed back ashore and pounded on the darkened Harbor Master's residence loudly and explained the situation quickly. Within five minutes, we had pumps aboard the stricken vessel and she was saved from sinking.

"You the guy I've been hunting all summer?" the harbor master asked me as I was helping him put all the gear (pumps, strainers, hoses, etc) back away.

"Yep." I said. "But I wasn't going to watch a good boat sink just because of..."

"Well, don't you worry 'bout me finding you no more, son. I reckon I've given up. You can keep that ole double-ender on John's mooring for as long as you want. Deal?"

"Deal!" I said, and grinned.

Special "Mom and Pop" Dock Deals

Many of the marinas in the USA (and increasingly worldwide) are now owned by corporate chains. These don't offer any "wiggle room" to the artful dodger, and are best ignored. But there still are a number of private, "mom and pop" marinas around—struggling businesses where everything is negotiable.

If you're outfitting your boat and not sailing it, or it is in deep storage, you can sometimes greatly reduce your dockage by not taking up a slip and just tying it between two boats that are. Or tying it "inside" the dock at a mud berth (where it runs aground daily on soft mud) at a greatly reduced rate. Or use the ole "stern anchor" trick. Or Med moor with only your transom to the dock.

Often shipyards have docks that they aren't allowed to rent out legally. This means they can be rented cheap "under the table" as long as you're willing to move on short notice should "Johnny Law" start poking around and asking questions.

Should you attempt to get the best possible deal while negotiating for a dock? Of course. Why not? Aren't we capitalists? I am. And thus I'm honor-bound to work the market place. Are there rules? Sure. Should we blindly follow 'em? I dunno. I'm not sure.

One thing I can tell you is this: I've tied up to docks for *years* for free in such crowded yachting centers as West End, New Orleans, Fort Lauderdale, Florida, and Chicago, Illinois, and have never once parted in bad company with the dock folks or my neighbors.

Could I have paid? Sure. Did I? No. Instead, I put all that "marina money" into the boat to make it safer and stronger offshore. If you've only got pennies to spend, you have to spend them carefully. That's what being a sea gypsy is all about.

Free Offices! Free Secretary! Free Parking! Free Car!

It is absolutely amazing the great situations that you can fall into if you're truly deserving and just ask.

What does "ask" mean? Just that. Ask. If you have a need and you want someone to fill it—you have to gently communicate these facts to others.

As mentioned, I write four hours every day, rain or shine. But when our daughter Roma Orion was born, this wasn't easy to do on a small boat. So I decided I needed a free shore office for a couple of months. We were anchored off St. Augustine, Florida, at the time, in the lee of the Bridge of Lions.

"Mrs. Darby will see you now," said the blue-haired woman at the circulation desk of the local library on Aviles Street.

Mrs. Darby was a gray-haired, bifocaled, no-nonsense type of librarian, so I didn't pull any punches.

She cocked her head in amazement as she listened to my spiel, and occasionally jabbed a fat pencil in-and-out of her hair in exasperation.

"Let me get this straight," she said. "You need a quiet office five days a week where you can work without interruption. Do you have any money?"

"Well, no," I admitted. "But I've got a strong back. I could pull the weeds or wash your car or lug some books."

"Do you really expect me to say yes?"

"Well," I said, "I thought that maybe if you were into promoting book reading that, you know, you'd be into promoting book writing too."

We stared at each other a long time. "Follow me," she said, and led me up a narrow stairway to the attic. There were three odd-shaped rooms up there, two of them filled with spilling piles of spine-damaged library books. Our shoes left tracks in the dust. The floorboards creaked. It was stifling hot. Airless. Stuffy. Confining.

"Have you ever read 'The Yearling?'" she asked, as she led me into the final room. It was strangely empty, save for an ancient desk and rickety chair facing the lead-glassed garret window.

"Yes, ma'am," I said. "Margaret Kenning-Rawlings. Pulitzer Prize winner."

"Margaret used to write up here when she wasn't at Cross Creek," Mrs. Darby said quietly.

I felt the hair on the back up my neck stand up. My hands were shaking and my throat was dry. I couldn't believe my good fortune. It was an omen. I was on the right path.

"I'm taking a big risk here, young man," she said as she turned and left. "Please don't disappoint me."

I did not disappoint her. I helped out so much around the library, she even started giving me a paycheck. When she was forced to take a leave of absence for three months because her husband had a stroke, I was able to take over the reins of the county-wide system on a temporary basis—which worked out well for her.

"Saying "yes" to you was one of the best things I ever did," she told me as we finally parted a year later.

A few years later, I pulled the same trick at an answering service called Connections on St. John, in the U.S. Virgin Islands. "How long will it take you to finish up the story you're working on?" asked Cid Hamling, the owner.

"Oh," I said, "probably only a couple of weeks."

Two years later, Cid moved—and I moved with her. (We were fast friends by this point). But about a year *after* that, Cid had expanded her business so much she really needed my desk space for a new employee, and, hey, I'd never really gotten around to paying her. So she asked me to leave.

"That's it?" I said. "No notice?"

"Fatty," she said, "you asked for space to write for two weeks. That was three years ago. You know I'd let you stay if I could. But I can't. I need your desk. So you have to go!"

The phone rang. Cid got busy. The next time she looked around, I wasn't there. She felt bad about giving me the toss, but, hey, it was time.

About an hour later, she had to go pee. She had one of the other three Connectaritas cover for her, and hurried off to the bathroom. (Her offices had once been a branch bank, and the facilities were commodious.) Only, when she threw open the door to the john—there I was, typing merrily away with my laptop set up on the lip of the urinal.

"Fatty!" she screamed with a rueful smile.

"I'll vacate whenever you need to defecate," I reassured her. "No problem!"

I managed to write there for another six months in (what became widely known as) the Head Office before moving into my own place.

Even Cid saw the logic. "It's perfect for the crap he writes," she said resignedly.

Hard Wired, Easy Wired, and Crappily Wired

It would be wonderful to always be able to use color-coded marine-grade wire of the proper size, high quality marine switches, and corrosion-resistant terminal ends while doing any 12-volt electrical work on a boat.

But the reality is that these items aren't cheap nor widely available in the Turd… er, Third World. So if you're going to do electrical work in Tonga or Madagascar or Borneo, you're going to have to make some compromises on component choices.

I look at it this way: Even the finest components poorly mounted won't last long. So I pay particular attention to routing and looming my wires to keep them dry, and mounting my electrical equipment in the driest manner possible in hopes this will cancel out my lack of quality gear.

I carry a limited stock of squeeze terminal ends, for instance. But I carry plenty of shrink tubing and flux/solder. So every end I make is soldered.

Once you are comfortable soldering, it is easy to fabricate different sizes and types of end fittings. Plus, I cannibalize a lot of old parts from discarded gear as well.

I solder with a small 12-volt "pencil" plugged into my inverter, a small "Hot Shot" butane torch, and a plumber's style large torch as well. (The latter is extremely useful getting stuff apart. A little heat and a large hammer can work wonders on stubborn stuff.)

I believe in soldering rather than just crimping, especially for bilge pumps, float switches, and engine components.

A few years ago, I wanted to solder my GPS and AIS wires together but lacked a soldering device, so I used a candle. It worked, despite Carolyn laughing so hard the tiny flame kept dancing with her mirth!

Fixing Stuff, Especially Electro-Doodads

Carolyn and I have a simple policy—if something breaks, we attempt to fix it, or at least take it to bits in the attempt. Why not? If it's not functioning, you've got nothing to lose and everything to gain. Even if you can't fix it, you'll learn why not—which is often a valuable lesson in itself.

Often Carolyn does the physical part and I kibitz on the side. We're both amazed at how often we get the thing functioning again.

Most sailors can envision fixing the mechanical stuff, but don't even try with the electronic stuff. But this is silly. Chances are your VHF radio or depth meter or chartplotter isn't malfunctioning because of a Zener diode or a mal-adjusted variable capacitor, but because of broken mechanical connections between such components as the circuit board, screen, power switch, etc.

In essence, in a marine environment, 99 percent of the problems you have with your electronics isn't really electronic, it is mechanical.

Basically, the job of a modern sailor is to clean gobs of corrosion off stuff and live happily (and inexpensively) ever after.

One more thing: I use a lot of automotive, truck, and RV stuff in my boat's electrical system. True, if I was using top quality gear, my work would probably last twice as long as it does now. But emergency repairs using lamp cord and automotive sockets usually last for a year or two—plenty of time to do it right (yeah, that's wasted labor) when you are in the First World.

Long Passages, Minor Clean-ups

We're often at sea for more than a month, and this means that goose-barnacles start growing on our counter (squatting because of our speed) and submerged topsides on the leeward side. These can start to slow us down after three weeks or so.

Wiping off the topside ones are easy but to remove the ones under the counter (between the transom and the design waterline) I use a thin, strong string passed under the counter with both its bitter ends in the cockpit. I sort of "saw" them off with the thin, sharp Kevlar thread—pulling it back and forth to cut, and allowing it to move aft toward the transom to cover the entire area. This will get 85 percent of 'em—but, of course, takes off some antifouling paint at the same time.

Of course, the hull gets a thick crust of salt baked onto it as well. We had great difficulty removing this very strong, very hard salt build up, until Carolyn tried standard household toilet bowl cleaner. WOW! The anti-lime acid in it washes the salt away with ease. Just make sure you rinse it off well or your plastic boat might melt along with the salt! (It steams upon application!)

Dinghy Painter Cordage

I am not a big fan of polypropylene rope. While it has the advantages of being both light in weight and cheap (two things very dear to my heart) it weakens in the sun, floats, and has little chafe resistance.

But, some highly experienced cruisers use it as a second anchor line, especially in coral. Since it floats when there is no wind, it doesn't tangle quite as easily in the coral—just snags all the water skiers going by! (If, however, it *does* snag on a coral head, then it will chafe far faster than nylon.)

One New Zealand boater in Tonga was experimenting with splicing alternating 20-foot sections of poly and nylon together so that it would neither float (and catch dinghies) nor sink (and catch coral heads)—but instead, it sort of "accordioned" into a "Z" scissors pattern.

His conclusion? "The idea needs more work!"

So many do, eh?

One place where I always use 5/8" three-strand yellow poly is for my dinghy

Fatty uses a float to keep the painter in the dinghy.

painter. Since it floats, this allows me to ignore it when I back my vessel as it cannot (or never has) get entangled in my prop.

I also put a fixed float on the poly painter just about five feet forward of my dinghy's bow eye. This allows me to visually check that my dinghy painter is all the way aboard as I power around the harbor and immediately attracts my attention if it starts to get pulled out. It almost never gets pulled out because of the slight extra weight of the float.

Here's a Flipping Good Idea

Once a year or so, I flip my halyards end-for-end. This allows them to change chafe points and suffer the sun in different areas. Ditto my standing rigging where the end fittings are identical on both ends. This makes sense—since the salt air that is corroding the wire is more concentrated the closer to sea level it is. The vast majority of times that s/s rigging wire breaks just above the terminal, it is the lower terminal. The upper terminal doesn't get nearly as much spray nor does it "hold" the salt crystals as well. Thus I flip my standing rigging every three years or so.

Free, High Quality Cockpit Cushion Foam.

The dense, closed cell foam that high quality cockpit cushions have inside is very expensive. It has to be because it doesn't absorb water and it's very firm, even after years of hard use.

Luckily, Jah (the nice, generous God who gives stuff to Caribbean sailors) will supply you with an endless supply if you anchor off Caneel Bay on St. John, the Bitter End on Virgin Gorda, the Four Seasons in Nevis…

Huh?

The hotel guests rent these expensive floats from the beach concessionaire. But, being landlubbers, they don't think about such matters as tide, vessel wakes, nor wind gusts. Thus, the downwind/downcurrent reefs from these resorts are littered with lost (expensive) swimming floats.

All you have to do is anchor at one of these "collecting points" during a busy time like the Christmas holidays or an Easter weekend—and scan the sea with your binoculars.

I'd say the Virgin Grand in Great Cruz Bay loses, on average, two a day to King Neptune.

What did Bob Dylan say? *"My loss shall be your gain!"*

Yes, there's plenty of free cockpit foam around—and you can salvage or recycle as much of it was you please.

Anchor Chain

Don't buy that cheap Chinese chain nor any "cadmium-plated" stuff. It is false economy. (Most chain sold in hardware stores in the US is made-in-China—and utter crap.) I buy chain made in Germany, Italy, or Turkey—and then re-galvanize it every couple of years.

In order to get the best deal on chain and/or take advantages of sales/gifts—I have a number of slightly different-sized gypsies for my Maxwell 1700 windlass.

There was a funny "chain incident" in the VI back in the late '60s when the National Park and the USCG suddenly placed all sorts of buoys in the Virgins with long lengths of brand new BBB galvanized 3/8' chain!

Of course, the local fishermen stole it all within days, but kindly put old ropes to hold the buoys in place.

These frayed ropes lasted for as long as—well, it took for the local "teefs" to row away!

A similar thing happened in French Polynesia when the government started scattering solar cells (on nav buoys) around the Marquesas. Damn, a lot of fishing shacks suddenly had 12-volt lighting systems!

Of course, anyone who would cause a mooring or nav buoy to drift away or malfunction is beneath my contempt and will be punished severely by the Karma Gods and/or Johnny Law. But such incidences show that the First and Third World really do live in difference moral universes.

Another example is when FEMA went around handing out huge bright blue tarps to protect the VI houses with roof damage after hurricane Hugo. Many houses (of fishermen) required a considerable number of these tarps.

And for years after, all the local wind-borne fishing craft appeared to have high-tech materials in their bright blue sails.

Raising Sunken Treasure Without Airbags

I have had to (for fun and profit) refloat a number of heavy objects off the bottom for various reasons—like large, lost anchors; mushroom moorings; transom-departed outboards, etc.

The easiest way to do this is to rent air tanks and borrow some airbags and even the heaviest object will pop to the surface. However, this isn't an option if you have empty pockets or are in the deserted Chagos Archipelago.

Once I raised an entire vessel (Carl Alberg design, built by Cape Dory) with nothing but a little "chutzpah" as they say in Israeli.

It was sunk in about 12 feet, off the calm beach of a busy island.

The first thing I did was send Carolyn ashore to collect as many empty plastic jugs as she could, from the local resorts, restaurants, and tourist attractions. Within three days, she had collected hundreds of them.

The next thing I did was re-read the opening of Mark Twain's Tom Sawyer, to confirm I hadn't forgotten any of the juicy details of white-washing that fence.

I next borrowed all the floating cockpit cushions, PFDs, and fenders that I could from the hundreds of yachts in the area—oh, yeah, all the snatch blocks I could borrow too, plus, short pieces of old line.

Next I announced a huge "Raise the Titanic" party aboard *Wild Card* on the following Sunday and anchored her right alongside the sunken boat I wanted to raise.

Once all the gear and folks were gathered together, I simply started passing out shots of 151 rhum and then dove overboard with an empty milk jug in my hand.

I swam down to the wreck, swam inside it, and stuffed the empty jug as far forward in the forepeak as possible. Then I repeated the process. People started asking me what I was doing. "Stuffing jugs in that sunken boat down there," I said.

Soon I had dozens of helpers—all swimming down buoyancy to the submerged boat. One of the guys helping was relatively sober and had a fast, high-powered inflatable dinghy.

"Can you get your dinghy?" I asked him.

When he returned, I had a large fender on a long line which ran through a snatch block down to the sunken vessel's rail and also a short three foot line on the fender as well.

"Okay," I told the guy in the dinghy. "I want you to roar away in the dinghy holding on to this line. That will force the fender underwater, and down to the boat's rail. Once it hits there, you'll be able to feel it. Decrease throttle and hold it there for about 60 seconds while I tie the short piece to the boat's rail. Once I resurface, throttle down."

This worked far, far better than I could have imagined. Soon the rail of the sunken boat was lined with fenders.

For a long time, nothing seemed to happen. Then some sand shifted, and I could tell the boat was trying to break the suction. We added more floating stuff inside (until it kept coming back out) and more fenders. Majestically, she stood upright on her keel in the sand underwater.

This got a huge cheer from the crowd and renewed dedication for the task at hand.

Within three hours of starting, we had the boat break the surface (actually, just its fenders) next to *Wild Card*.

I checked my watch—we'd have to hurry or miss high tide.

I quickly organized a flotilla of dinghies to pull her to the beach near where I'd tied a huge turning block onto a palm tree. Once the boat was aground on the beach and pointed at the palm tree, I ran a line from its bow cleat, through the turning block ashore, and then to a large truck which was waiting by pre-arrangement. (Thank you, Mister David!)

As the truck took a strain, we "bounced" and "wiggled" her up the beach as far as possible. This made her awash at dead high tide, and we propped her up with sawn-to-length 2x4s as best we could—and then crossed our fingers as the tide went out.

Once the tide was down a few inches, I started a couple of siphons going and gravity started bailing her out. (The boat had sunk in a storm and had no holes.)

Within 12 hours of starting, just after dark, she was floating once again and we lashed her alongside *Wild Card*—and oh, what a party that was!

The point is—you can do amazing things, even with heavy objects, if you're optimistic, tenacious, and refuse to allow common sense to discourage you.

Sure, it is easier if you have the right equipment, but it is more fun if you don't! (Yes, we were the Heroes of the Harbor for a long time after that.)

Scratching Your Whiskers Over Whisker Poles

Most frugal cruising boats don't carry large symmetrical spinnakers and the giant, heavy poles required to fly them. However, almost every circumnavigating vessel has a whisker pole or two to pole out the jib(s).

I regularly run downwind for thousands of miles with my poles out—which I don't take down even in (mild) heavy weather. (Of course, I roll up the sails. But I leave the poles rigged for future use.)

I recommend a standard pole, with standard ends, and mast-mounted track.

This pole is, potentially, one of the most dangerous things on a cruising vessel. Thus I recommend it be well set-up, and able to be taken down at night during a squall.

Of course, boats sailed poled-out downwind for centuries before the modern equipment we now use was invented and so can you if you're careful and somewhat risk-taking.

The pole usually isn't the problem, as it can be made out of a discarded aluminum pipe or laminated out of wood. It is the track and inboard end fittings that are difficult/expensive to come up with.

One "quick and dirty" way to make a whisker pole is to take a piece of wood, and drive a long, headless bolt down it to created a spike-with-a-knob-on-it for the outboard end.

The spike will go through the jib clew cringle, and the knob will help keep it from falling off when it "pops" in the ocean swell.

The inboard end should be three or four feet longer than normal, and have a six foot rope at its end. Thus, the pole doesn't butt into an end-fitting on a track attached to the mast. It goes beyond the mast a bit and is tied to it.

Yes, this chafes the pole against the mast, but that's easily taken care of. The big problem is the huge forces shock loaded on the pole during a severe gust.

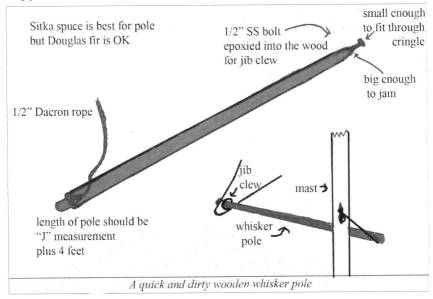

A quick and dirty wooden whisker pole

That inboard rope had better be strong. (If it breaks and the pole drives itself through your chest—well, that will be that.)

Do I recommend the above? No, I do not. Why include it? Because it is possible, and is great food for thought. I recently had a guy tell me, "Nobody crosses the Pacific today without a watermaker!"

"Perhaps that's so," I shot back, "but many have crossed that ocean before watermakers existed, and, who knows, perhaps will after watermakers are forgotten!"

Do you really *have* to have anything on your boat that Josh Slocum didn't have on the *Spray*? I don't think so.

Tuning Into Cheap Tunes

Many sailors, particularly young ones, cannot bear the thought of being without their music. I understand. I need to listen to Bob Dylan, Tom Waits, and Bonnie Raitt—or I will go sane! (Sic).

My solution is to play guitar, and bring a bunch of drums, cymbals, and cheap percussion instruments (metal film cans filled with beans) with me when I play on the beach or in a bar.

However, there's no denying that, occasionally, I need to hear the Stones playing "Sympathy for the Devil" at full volume, and nothing else with do.

I just use a $40 40-watt amp/graphic equalizer connected to two mediocre speaks, and plugged into my iPod.

This is enough to damage my ears—if desired.

I don't have cockpit speakers, and don't like people who do. I love my music, but I do not insist that *others* love my music, knowing full-well they probably love *theirs* more. (I dislike people with loud cockpit speakers who leave their boat and don't turn them off. They should be hunted down ashore and tortured without mercy!)

Another musical option is a modest 12-volt boom box radio and an FM transmitter on the iPod. An added bonus is that MP3s take up little space.

To Shoe Or Not To Shoe?

Many boaters insist on having their crew wear shoes, and many insist they don't. The debate rages.

I agree with both sides.

Yes, shoes protect your feet. But, yes, shoes stink and you don't know when you are going to slip with them on—whereas bare feet give you tactical warning.

Regardless, I've found that wearing no shoes is cheaper than wearing shoes. And I've always been able to afford no shoes—even during my poorest of cruising forays.

Thus I seldom wear them. (But I always keep a few empty tubes of toothpaste aboard—as they make a great splint for a broken toe.)

Unstylish Diving Gear

Never, ever wear goggles for diving. (They are only for surface swimming.)

Our Filipino friends carve their goggles out of wood, and use the bottom of plastic Coke bottles as lenses. These aren't great, but that's how they do it.

Yes, fins can be made out of plywood-and-discarded gym shoes.

Snorkels are easy to fabricate out of discarded PVC pipe joined with hose.

A very good Hawaiian-sling can be made from a piece of wood with a hole in it and some sharpened rebar.

Often a "looking glass" (mask) with a shattered glass lens can be replaced with some discarded clear plastic sheeting. (Ask at a sign shop.)

Timers

We use timers for a wide variety of reasons—to stay awake on watch, to remember to check for ships, to remember when a weather forecast will be broadcast, to remember to turn something on or off, etc.

I like mechanical kitchen timers because they are so easily operated in the dark, but my wife Carolyn doesn't like the loud ticking.

Thus we are always on the scrounge for any small, portable electronic timer, that can be operated easily in the dark. (Many can't be, but a few can.)

The best ones only need to be pushed once to start re-timing—not a bunch of times.

Dinghy Lights

I think we're often exposed to more danger in crowded anchorages while in our dinghy at night than in deep ocean. People can and do get killed at night in dinghies—rather often, actually.

We know... er, knew a number of them.

The secret is being well-lit—I mean well illuminated.

Seriously, we carry small LED flashlights when we know we'll be ashore after dark. We also occasionally carry a blinkie-blink in our dinghy but these are often ripped off by the local kids.

Just to be on the safe side, I hide a small chemical cyalume light stick in the bow for emergency use.

In a pinch, iPhones work fairly well to ward off other speeding craft.

Sail Repairs

It's best to protect your sails from chafe and sunlight and then you won't have to affect any repairs. Modern sails are incredibly strong if they are not abused.

The best way to fix a sizable hole in a sail is to take down the sail and sew a patch on both sides. Using an awl is slow-but-sure, and you can do it on deck and without electricity.

Carolyn and I often stand on opposite sides of a sail or bimini top and pass the needle back-and-forth.

However, for emergency repairs, "sticky back" Dacron insignia tape is incredibly wonderful.

And, believe it or not, I've had good luck with Mystic tape—and plain ole duct tape too.

Lacing and Webbing Stuff Onto Boat and Rig

This is growing in popularity. Metal stainless steel fittings are heavy, and often break. Often boom vales, pad eyes, and plates can be replaced by high tech line or machine sewn webbing. Hey, if your whole boat gets picked up by sewn together nylon straps, surely it can hold the mainsheet block on the boom, right?

The beautiful part of this is, with a little imagination, a spool of Kevlar string replaces a drawer full of spare stainless steel fittings.

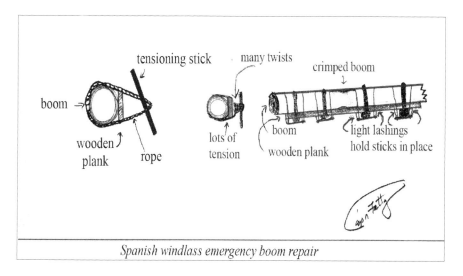

Spanish windlass emergency boom repair

Booms That Go Boom

Booms used to seldom break. Alas, some idiot must have been pissed off at their longevity because many new yacht designs have booms that are susceptible to damage because of mid-boom sheeting and rigid vangs.

Thus, I've recently seen a number of broken or "crimped" booms. One in Fiji was almost broken in half, but the owner needed to get back to NZ. So I went over to help him straighten and strengthen it enough to make that arduous journey.

Luckily, we managed to find a long 2x8 piece of wood on the island. We placed it alongside the boom, and then "winched in" the bend with Spanish windlasses.

What's a Spanish windlass? It is a simple knot trick with a rope that allows you to put tremendous force on something with a bit of rope and a small stick. Basically, you put the two pieces you want to join together alongside each other, wrap a loop of tied rope around them, then stick a piece of wood within the loop—and twist. Then you secure the piece of wood to it.

You keep adding new Spanish windlasses in new spots, and retighten all of them as you go. You can get thousands of pounds of clamping force this way.

Using only Spanish windlasses, we managed to both straighten and "fish together" the almost-broken-clean-through boom and plank together. It made an emergency repair that lasted almost a year in boisterous weather.

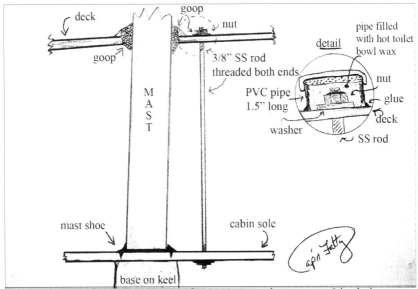

A simple mast tensioning rod prevents upward movement of the deck.

Mast Steps, Tension Bars, and Compression Posts

If you can't keep your mast from leaking where it comes through the deck—especially in a blow—it is probably because there's excessive deck movement. Why? Well, boats loosen up after awhile. And, in a gust, the hull tends to squeeze together just at the same time the mast is driven down into the mast step. The result is that the deck moves upward at the same moment the mast moves downward, and thus this area leaks regardless of what you seal it with.

The best solution is to install a compression rod between the mast step and the deck, so the deck can't move upward in a gust.

Mine's pretty simple—just a long 3/8" s/s rod threaded at both ends, and snugged up just enough to prevent any movement upwards.

A cheaper "quick and dry" solution I've used a number of times, is to just temporarily fiberglass the mast to the deck where it comes through the deck.

"What the hell?" you might say. "You'll never be able to pull the stick!"

Well, it only takes a second (with a Sawz-all) to carefully cut the fiberglass.

Can this create as many problems as it solves? Yeah, it can. There can be corrosion problems at the aluminum-to-fiberglass point. Also, if the mast step gets pounded down over the years (and through the gales), then the deck can be deformed as well.

But it can be a useful trick to "get her home" with empty pockets.

Again, many structural problems of a boat can be solved creatively and practically—for pennies.

Of course, naval architects and marine engineers will howl that you can't do this, that, or the other thing without their blessing—but that's what you'd expect them to say, right?

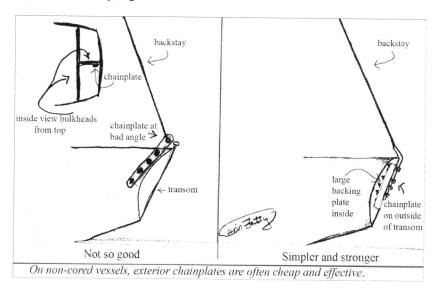

backstay

chainplate

inside view bulkheads
from top

chainplate at
bad angle →

← transom

Not so good

backstay

large
backing
plate
inside

chainplate
on outside
of transom

Simpler and stronger

On non-cored vessels, exterior chainplates are often cheap and effective.

Backstay Problems

Many backstays mounted to chainplates on a fore-aft bulkhead glassed to the transom start giving problems after a decade or so of hard sailing. They start peeling away from the transom, lifting up, and moving forward—and will ultimately fail. (A number of C&C boats have this problem.)

Re-glassing the fore-and-aft bulkhead (in between the transom and the cockpit's after wall) often isn't easy.

A simple solution is to remount the chainplate on the exterior of the transom, and through bolt it with a generous backing plate (if a solid fiberglass hull).

Now, instead of having a tendency to "peel off" in a gust, it is pressed on more firmly. This is a far better, simpler, longer-lasting method.

Courtesy Flags

By tradition (and, sometimes, by law), visiting sailing vessels are supposed to fly the courtesy flag of the country they are visiting, from their starboard spreader. This is nice. On our first circumnavigation, we did this in every single country we cruised. Of course, we saved all the flags.

Since courtesy flags are expensive and often hard to get, we usually make our own—sometimes by sewing and, at others times, by painting white fabric with waterproof acrylic paints.

This is SOP (standard operating procedure) for 90 percent of all cruising vessels.

There is, of course, a security issue here as well. Some cruising sailors don't like an "I'm new here and a foreigner" sign glowing in their rig.

Whether the above is common sense or paranoia is for you to decide. We don't have a problem with flying a courtesy flag in most countries.

Some countries, like Turkey, are truly obsessed with their national flag. You have to have one flying *and it better not be the least bit faded or frayed* or someone will board you and put a new one up!

But the reality is that most countries could care less. On our second circumnavigation, we only flew the proper courtesy flag in six or seven countries.

This saved a lot of time and expense.

But, I need to be completely honest here. Some of my fellow yachtsmen find this despicable on my part and even insulting to the host nation. They may be right. But if I've got a choice between buying a courtesy flag or a spare Racor fuel filter, I know which I'll choose every time.

Adapting To 110 and 220 volts

I have a wide variety of electric plugs and adapters, so I can use my electric cords ashore while in almost any country.

Sometimes I do sanding or metal work ashore, primarily because electricity is available there. (Yes, I've scrounged 110 and 220-volt inverters for *Wild Card*, but power tools running continuously can drain the batteries fast.)

The good news is that more and more modern stuff is now multi-voltage, but that doesn't include power tools with large electric motors. Make sure you know what voltage you're plugging into where.

Of course, if you use someone's shoreside electricity, you need to ask permission and you should offer to pay.

I've had very good luck drilling metal and sanding wood behind bars, fish markets, brothels, etc. In fact, the biggest problem for us working ashore is how nice all the people usually are. It is hard to get anything done while being showered by such kindness.

Yes, poverty is a great common bond. In Thailand, if Carolyn and I are working on the beach or behind a shop house, the local residents will (silently and bowing) bring us food at meal time and tea in between! Of course, we return the favor on as many levels as we possibly can.

The Biggest Problem With Circumnavigating

So many people have been so amazingly nice to us in so many different countries at so many different times. Whew! It is a daunting challenge to attempt to repay all these past favors.

Our solution is to make sure that we are *giving* as well as *taking* and to

Having lunch on Palmerston, Cook Islands with Bob Marsters' family

befriend the thousands of people who are less fortunate than us at every opportunity.

I honestly believe that if I treat people like shit, I will be treated like shit. And if I treat even the lowest of the low with dignity and respect, they will return the favor.

They do.

No one will have fun sailing around the world and ripping off people. I've met a few who have tried. It always ends in meanness and hatred, even for the wealthy.

However, if you sail around the world (even with empty pockets) and are willing to push a stalled car or stubborn water buffalo out of the ditch without thinking about it—just because it is the right thing to do and you are practicing the Golden Rule by reflex—then you will have a fun, fun, fun trip.

And you will deserve to.

We reap what we sow. Thus, it behooves us to sow plenty.

The Joys Of Grappling Hooks

The good news is that we find a lot of lost anchors. The bad news is that we also lose a few, too.

The key here is, again, marking the area ASAP. A small, well-defined area is a lot easier and faster to search than a larger, less defined one.

Our restaurant supply grappling hook

Searches in shallow, clear water are far easier than in deep or cloudy water. I've smashed my facemask into the bottom and into the side of a barnacle-bristling piling before seeing it through the murk.)

Occasionally I locate my lost anchor and rode in 70 feet of crystal clear water, but it is too deep for me to retrieve while free-diving. In these cases I use a grappling hook from the surface to "fish" it back up. (If no grappling hook is available, I use three large fishhooks laced together.) Sometimes dragging for it with a grapple from a dinghy on the surface is the only option. This occasionally works in pure sand but is far less effective (or impossible) in rocks or coral.

Grappling hooks are useful items to carry but they are heavy and hard to stow. We use a miniature stainless steel version made in China, manufactured to hang Peking ducks in Chinese restaurant windows. It is light in weight, works like a charm, and cost us $4 ten years ago.

Rags And Clothes: Is There a Difference?

Barely.

Seriously, the poorer you are, the more important it is to (occasionally) dress well. When Bob Dylan was having the lovely *Water Pearl* built for him on the beach in Bequia, he used to look and smell so bad that the West Indian laborers would occasionally order him into the shower. Only people with bags of gold can afford to appear this destitute. The rest of us, especially those with empty pockets, have to appear to be solvent.

Carolyn and I buy our clothes at resale shops because we can get far better quality threads for far less money than at Walmart. Australia, in particular, has great Op Shops (Opportunity Shops). In the States, we hang with Sally, our code name for the Salvation Army and/or Goodwill.

Africa is a wonderful place to buy pure white dress shirts because international do-

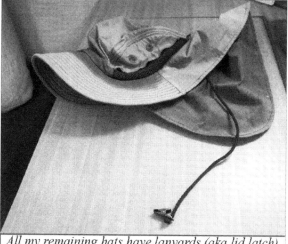

All my remaining hats have lanyards (aka. lid latch).

gooder organizations, such as Goodwill Industries, ship tons of such items labeled as rags (for some legal reason—avoiding import duty, perhaps?).

In the Third World, clothing is generally cheap. But inspect it carefully, as I've purchased great jeans without pockets, with sewed-shut zippers, buttons-but-no-button-holes, etc.

Ditto, shoes. We can't afford leather uppers, and they mildew on the boat anyway. So plastic sandals and imitation Crocs (less slippery and cheaper, too) are a perfect match for our dinghy-on-the-wet-beach lifestyles.

Yes, we're extremely careful our good clothes don't chafe in the hanging locker. My favorite shirt was reduced to see-through lace during our first ocean crossing.

We almost never throw away any clothing. If we don't use them for rags, we give them away to grateful natives in Fiji, Vanuatu, or Madagascar.

To keep our clothes new and fresh, we seldom wear them aboard the boat in the tropics. The minute we get back aboard, we strip and slip on our pareos (wrap-around unisex cloth). Often, in India, Malaysia, Southeast Asia, and Pacifica this is what the locals wear anyway.

This saves time and hassle in the romance department too. (Lucky me!)

Note: The sun is the enemy of the long-term sailor, not his friend. Thus, I only wear short sleeve shirts in moderate climes. Along the equator, I always wear long sleeves. (The Arabs are perfectly dressed for their environment.)

Hats are important, and the only item of apparel I buy new. Yes, I like a wide brimmed hat that provides plenty of shade, but that stays on, too. But if it is blown off, it needs to be easily retrievable. (Larry and Lee of *Osprey* once made "lid latches" for Christmas stocking-stuffers. This is a piece of hi-tech string with small plastic clamps at both ends to attach your hat to your shirt.)

Foulies

Foul weather jackets are called that because of how they smell, not what they protect against.

Seriously, don't buy any of these "breathable" jackets that cost more than my yacht unless you are filthy rich and utterly masochistic. They don't last. They soon leak.

Instead, wear what the local fishermen wear—non-trendy **PVC**.

Old-fashioned oiled **Sou'wester hats** are wonderful because you can keep your hood down, and thus preserve your side-to-side vision while sailing.

Seaboots are useless in the tropics but delightful in the North Atlantic during that last, late-season cruise. Cheap ones are available at places that sell to commercial fishermen.

In cold weather, an aluminum steering wheel just sucks your body-warmth right out through your fingers. I use snowmobile gloves despite their awkwardness. If worse comes to worst, and I'm helming a boat northward from the tropics, I use two rags or towels to protect myself from the aluminum heat-sink of a wheel. (*Wild Card's* wooden tiller is always a joy to hold. Ah, the many disadvantages of owning an expensive, complicated boat!)

Vitamins and Prescription Drugs

I hate adulthood—drugs used to be much more fun in the 1960s!

Seriously, I take the non-recreational drug Lipitor every day. The good news is that it is often far cheaper in the Third World than America, but there is, alas, also a far higher likelihood of it being fake. Thus, we're careful where, and through whom, we purchase it because the merchants of India know the profit margin on placebos can be very lucrative.

We also take vitamins. But in some countries, they are mislabeled and misrepresented. We only buy them Stateside from manufacturers we trust and then have them toted to us via visiting friends. We normally carry a six months supply of Lipitor and vitamins—no longer, for they deteriorate in the tropical heat.

Charting Your Way To Safety

In order to properly navigate, you need to have the suitable charts aboard your vessel for the waters you are transiting. This used to be a big hassle. Charts were expensive, bulky, and easily damaged. Plus, they rapidly go out-of-date. Thus, a large part of our expense budget used to be chart-related.

I'll never forget pulling into Colon, Panama, and paying $35 for a single chart (because that's all I could afford) as I headed out across the wide, wide Pacific—when I really needed about $3,000 worth of charts just to get to New Zealand.

Obviously, we used to trade charts whenever we could. We also used to buy cheaper "yachtsman" versions such as "Charlie's Charts of Polynesia."

We didn't carry many ocean passage charts aboard on our first circ to save money. Instead, we'd carefully peruse a borrowed chart to make sure we'd be clear of all obstructions, and then use cheap graph paper while at sea to mark or progress.

Nor could we afford to have all the "possible" harbor charts we might need if we had to divert to an unintended island, say during a medical emergency. So, instead, we just laboriously copied a series of "safe, from seaward" waypoints into the main harbors we might need.

Certainly, this wasn't ideal. But we felt it was better than nothing.

As a last resort, we'd Scotch-tape pieces of typing paper together and laboriously trace an existing chart. (It took us two days to trace the charts for the Torres Straits. And thank God we did as it was blowing 38 knots as we careened into that very confusing mess off Thursday Island.)

Once digital photography came into being, things got easier. We could, in an emergency, take a digital snapshot of an existing chart. Again, this was hardly an ideal solution but it was much preferable over having absolutely nothing to go by.

I know that "real mariners" will howl in disapproval, but the fact is that I've used the maps in Encarta more than once as an aid-to-navigation.

I know a bit about chart retailing, having managed a couple of different East Coast chart agencies over the years.

My perspective as a sailing *consumer* is a tad different, of course. The thing I used to hate most about NOAA was the government repeatedly double-dipping into the pockets of their citizens. Example: Our American tax dollars had already paid for all those marine surveys so many distant years ago, and now the Feds were attempting to "user-fee" us once again to access that very same data!

This didn't seem fair.

Luckily, this is changing. NOAA now gives away *all* its USA charts in various digital formats (http://www.charts.noaa.gov). And the good sailors who formed the Open Charting program group (http://Opencpn.org) have developed a free, copyright-less charting program as well. This means that US sailors can now have every single NOAA large and small scale chart on the their computers—along with a legit charting program—all legal and for free. If you think eCharts are crazy—consider this: since May of 2001, commercial vessels like super-tankers, etc., haven't had to carry paper charts at all—only electronic ones. Ditto, all ships which fall under the SOLAS regulations. Basically, paper charts are no longer mandatory, and, even more amazing, are rapidly becoming a thing of the past. I used to love chart agencies, regardless of which side of the counter I was on, but these are now all fading from the scene worldwide. Soon you won't be able to buy a paper chart even if you want to. (Ah, but that chart agency in the Panama Canal Zone birthed many a dream, eh?)

Of course, electronic charts require computers and/or plotters, and shipboard electricity. As backups, we now carry our medium-scale paper charts in deep storage aboard *Wild Card*, and rely solely on electronic charts for our daily needs.

One more thing: Redundancy is important here. I have five different devices (called laptop computers) to read my charts. I'd be very wary of putting my eggs all in one basket, regardless of how dependable that basket was.

The last word: The poorest of sailors can now afford better charting than ever before in history. I recently purchased a cheap GPS in Singapore, and nobody even mentioned (ho-hum) it had all the navigation marks in the Indian Ocean and the Med already installed within. (Perhaps the whole world?)

That's pretty astounding to a sailor who has spent days laboriously hand tracing a chart that his life ultimately depended on!

Eating Cheap

The key to eating cheap afloat is eating seafood and eating what the locals eat. We love rice, beans, and pasta. Ditto fish, lobster, shrimp, crayfish, crab, squid, and octopus. We stock up where things are cheap, and consume those cheap items in places where they are expensive.

The result is a more flavorful, healthier diet.

Coconuts are God's gift to mankind and a marvel of packaging too.

There are many places where fruits rot on the ground because it isn't economical to harvest them. They are often there for the taking: breadfruit, yams, bananas, etc. (Always ask, of course. Each fruit tree in Polynesian is owned by someone.)

When the chief's son, Paul, of Kuehi, was attempting to talk Carolyn and me into staying forever, he said to me with great sincerity, "You can have any fish in the lagoon corral, Fatty. You can pick any piece of fruit on this island for free. Why leave? Where in the world is better than where you are now?"

He had a point.

If you go to Madagascar, bring a huge pot. They'll trade you giant mud crabs with claws as big as your hand and full of meat for a faded T-shirt. (Carolyn and I find these crabs far tastier than any lobster.)

One of the things we love best about cruising Turkey is the veggies. We're constantly rubbing shoulders with the local farmers who are amazingly generous with their delicious produce.

Just before shoving off on a major ocean passage, we often buy our food and related household supplies in bulk from a wholesaler and/or restaurant supply house. In the third world, farmers' markets are usually cheaper than grocery stores. Even Cost-U-Less is more price-competitive than most outlets.

Booze is often a good buy. In Madagascar, 151-proof rhum goes for $1 a quart if you bring your own container. (Most yachts use new 5 gallon gasoline cans—just don't get confused!) In Portugal and Greece, wine is inexpensive.

Some places only allow you to bring in two bottles of spirits. One such place is French Polynesia, where the wine is reasonably priced but the rhum ridiculously expensive. We, of course, attempt to obey all laws. And, needless to say, we expect you to obey all laws. However, some people don't. They save their empty box wine sacks from Chez Cardboard, clean them, and then fill them with Cruzan Rhum. They then toss the filled wine sacks into the center of a spinnaker, fold it inside, and stuff it all into a large sail bag which they toss under the cockpit or wherever. Thus, if boarded and inspected by the

French authorities, the sail bag won't clink like bottles and is flexible to the touch—certainly not full of booze!

Saudi Arabia has more moonshine than Tennessee. It is awash in illegal and home-made booze.

Don't even *think* about taking a sip of whiskey in Africa without breaking the seal yourself—or you will be drinking poisonous anti-freeze in no time.

In remote locations where the indigenous folks don't have even a penny, there's still always some way the locals... er, relax.

Even in the far-out out-islands of the Pacific, they have "coconut beer" which bubbles sadistically and really packs a wallop. (Don't plan on doing much except weeping on the morrow!)

Carolyn makes delicious rice wine (the Fatty secret: a teabag at the end) when we're remote and broke. (You can find the recipe in the appendix.)

Exercise

The sailing lifestyle is, generally, a fairly healthy one. But I exercise ashore (or aboard) everyday regardless. The cardio work I do keeps my ticker-ticking, and the light-weights keep me trim.

One of my mottos is, "The best jewelry is a nice body."

Luckily, we're (once again) blessed by our poverty. We're forced to walk long distances, carry stuff, and run after buses.

If I was wealthier, I'd probably look a bit porkier.

Luckily, I'm not.

The Sun Is the Enemy!

Lots of stuff needs to be protected from the tropical sun: you, for instance. I now wear long sleeve shirts, floppy hats, and plenty of sunscreen—because my 59-year-old epidermis has given up from years of sailing abuse.

In all the years I ocean-sailed both *Corina* and *Carlotta*, I never had a bimini or dodger—and now I am paying the price. (Whenever I'm in Southeast Asia, I have the local skin docs slice-and-dice off my skin spots in Thailand or Malaysia for about 5 percent of what it would cost in the States.)

Your sails need protection, too. We never allow our sails to be exposed to the sun needlessly. We cover them within minutes of furling. We even cover our jugs, etc, with Sunbrella to prevent sun damage. Ditto, our dinghy as mentioned.

Shore Vacations Can Be Free and Fun

When we're aboard, we can limit our spending to almost nothing if desired, but not so ashore. But there are a lot of places we want to see that just aren't on the water. What to do?

Our first trick is to route ourselves imaginatively when we're paid-to-travel. Example: The Sint Maarten Heineken Regatta used to fly me in every year to act as their PR spokesperson. I always had them buy me an RTW (Around The World) ticket so I could stop in five continents to visit old pals and revisit old haunts.

If someone wants me to speak at a seminar, I continue to make sure I'm able to route my plane ticket to maximum advantage.

Local sailors in New Zealand, Australia, and elsewhere, who are on limited-time vacations, often need their land vehicles retrieved or delivered. We happily do so for "no pay but limited expenses" and get a free shore vacation.

Normally, I charge $200 a day to deliver a boat. After all, it is hard work and a tremendous responsibly. But, occasionally, Carolyn and I will act as crew for very little money (but a generous living allowance and flexible return transportation).

This allows us a change of scene from *Wild Card* and also a free vacation for doing something we love to do, which is go sailing. It's a win-win for all concerned.

Occasionally long-haul truckers, tug boat captains, and offshore fishermen, etc, are doing interesting things in unusual places, and desire human companionship. We're happy to sing for our supper.

We were in Georgetown, South Carolina, when a friend's Jaguar started to run rough. The guy complained about how there weren't any local mechanics with enough experience to fix his Jag, not like his magic wrench-twister in New York City. I suggested he loan me his pickup truck, put the Jag on a trailer, and I (and Carolyn) would blast it up to the Big Apple for $300, food, drink, and accommodation. He was happy to. We had a ball.

It is best, of course, if you know and trust the people prior to getting too involved with them. But all of our experiences have been positive thus far. Just make sure that everyone is on the same page from the outset.

The same sort of thing can be done with boats, rather than land vehicles. I have a friend who is a very experienced seaman and was a very popular charter captain in the Caribbean who also did a lot of transatlantic deliveries. Now he lives ashore and his focus is on his business. But he still loves to sail and likes to keep his hand in the delivery game. So he still retains a few charter boat company clients. He will occasionally deliver a boat back to the States if time isn't a factor. (One delivery started in St. Thomas, paused in Antigua for Sailing Week, and then checked out Sun Splash in Jamaica before pulling into Fort Lauderdale six weeks later.)

Here again, it is a win-win situation because the charter company received a cheap, high-quality delivery from someone they trusted for a boat delivery that wasn't time-sensitive. And my friend got paid a small sum to take his "charter vacation" to someone else's chosen destination.

Single-handers and Other Special Circumstances

Did you ever notice that single-handers never talk about what they're doing with their other hand?

Seriously, there are some important social areas that need to be discussed here. Some cruising couples shun single-handers for fear of the "*glom-on.*" The "glom-on" is when you're nonchalantly waving-in-passing at a single-hander and he abruptly heaves-to and swims over with his knife-fork-and-bib while asking, "What's for dinner?"

If you serve him said dinner, he spends the whole night speed-rapping about how much he enjoys solitude, and you can't get a word in edgewise.

Generally speaking, single-handers talk a lot. I told one exactly that. He became so incensed he rowed over to my boat and ate an entire pig while denying it "most vehemently!"

Carolyn and I love most single-handers. Once threatened with the muzzle, they usually settle down and become fairly docile.

Sure, they like to eat, but so do we. Carolyn loves to cook for a crowd. Since we usually are only having rice-and-bilge-scrapings, they're welcome to join us anytime. They do. Often.

One of the hobbies (or obsessions might be more accurate) of many single-handers is efficiency. They're always trying to shower with vinegar (to save water) while stomping on their trousers (to save laundry time) and mashing grapes (to ward off sobriety).

I had one chasing me around Indonesia for years, yelling at me about how to preserve my razor blades in water so they'd "last damn-near forever!"

I wasn't convinced, as it looked as if he hadn't seen a razor in years.

Yes, they've got some weird habits. I'll admit I was amazed how well WD-40 took beach tar off my feet. But I'm not ready for it as a deodorant, regardless of the dire need! Ditto, as a breath-freshener.

We met one ole codger in the Philippines who was in his 80's and single-handing around the world in a giant old steel schooner he'd built eons ago. This boat was so big, it should have been manned by *cadets*—a bunch of them! But it was just him and his yellowed beard, squinting into the distant horizon.

Our friend Lindsay, formerly a cop in the rugged NW Territory of Australia, loves to single-hand his rusty steel vessel in the Indian Ocean. One day he "just barely" missed the channel into an atoll—and sailed over the reef instead. This bent his rudder so badly it dimpled his vessel's counter. "Lucky for me," he said, "there was a large, barely submerged rock in the lagoon as well." Lindsay soon had his boat spider-webbed with anchors directly in front of the rock—which he backed into with great force eight times before his rudder was straight again.

Frankly, I find "can-do" single-handers like Lindsay fascinating, rolling across oceans with only their wildly spinning brains for company. Many are extremely knowledgeable seamen and handy Mister Fix-Its. Yes, it takes a tad more energy to befriend a speed-rapping single-hander, but we often find their extra joy worth it.

They are intense.

We like intense.

Thus, some of our best, dearest friends are single-handers.

Shoving Off

At some point, if you are going to circumnavigate or sail across an ocean, you are going to have to cast off and head out to sea. This is the moment that separates the men from the boys.

Only you can decide when this moment arrives. Leave too early with no experience on an ill-prepared boat, and you will come to grief.

Wait until you're completely ready and you will wait forever and ever. You will never go. There will always be something else to buy, install, and test. Something else to learn. Something else to consider.

The sweet spot lays somewhere between.

I believe that I am safer offshore during a gale than I am walking the streets of NYC at night, but both are dangerous. It is easy to come to grief either place—just ask Dave and Irene Winters or Colin Craig or Peter and Carmen Tangvald. Each were dear friends of mine. Many of them were far better sailors than I'll ever be. But they are gone. King Neptune took them. They sailed away, but not back.

They're in Fiddler's Green now—where the sailors dance a merry jig and receive Sunday duff seven days a week.

I don't tell you this to be morbid nor discouraging. I tell you this because it is true. The sea is an indifferent mistress. You can love her for a lifetime but she won't blink when she smites you for breaking her few rules. (Air in, water out.)

The trick is to seek to understand her world and not attempt to fight against it. We are but mere mortals—a few bizarrely arranged molecules in the face of a magnificent one million ton breaking wave.

We can ride the wave but we can never steer it.

Praying doesn't help either.

But if you're careful and thoughtful and always prepared, then you can ride on the back of Mother Ocean in safety and comfort for a lifetime.

It is up to you. That is why you are now called Captain.

Stone Soup

Occasionally a circumnavigator gets a bit discombobulated. He arrives in a strange port with lots to get done and no prospects on how to accomplish it. Perhaps he even has an empty belly and wallet. In this case, there's only one reasonable thing to do—make Stone Soup.

I rummage under the galley, find the stone, place it in the pot, pour some water over it, set it to boil, and say to Carolyn, "Stone Soup tonight! I'll be right back."

I then dinghy around the harbor and invite all the local yachties over for a party. Ditto, the crews of the dock-huggers in the nearby marina. It doesn't matter who I invite as the jerks will just naturally stay away. Many people will ask me what to bring. I suggest they bring whatever beverage they'd like to drink, and explain to them we're making soup. Would they happen to have some carrots or potatoes aboard?

Later that evening, we gather aboard *Wild Card*. Sometimes there are so many people we can't fit them all. If the weather is calm, they just hang in dinghies off the sides near the cockpit and form an additional "ring" party. (Forty-four is the most we've had aboard, and we couldn't allow them all aft or the cockpit scuppers would geyser!)

Usually the women filter down to help Carolyn with the soup and to organize the snacks, while I hang with the boys and get 'em laughing so hard they have to hold their stomachs. (This is easy. I just honestly tell 'em a few "how-I-fucked-up-royally" stories.)

Occasionally, I cup an ear down below and hear Carolyn asking, "Who brought the turnips? Oh, and the ham is delicious!"

Finally, she calls me below. With the tongs, I take back out the cherished stone for future use. I explain to everyone about Stone Soup—how we would never be able to survive without *A Little Help from our Friends*. They usually noisily protest that it should be *them* thanking *us* for the invite. There are smiles all around. We eat. We drink. I play guitar. Some dance. A few fall over. One drunk tumbles down the forehatch. The usual shenanigans.

Midway through the party, I cozy up to the smartest, most together sailor present (sometimes this ain't saying much!) and ask him, "Do you know where I could get a starter motor rewound—really cheap?"

This works. Not only do I usually get my problem solved in short order, I'm the most popular guy in town as well. Best of all: The stone doesn't show any sign of wear despite nearly 50 years of hard use.

Life always works out. What seems like a big deal today will be just a funny story tomorrow. There's no need to worry. Worrying is like paying taxes on money you might never earn. Worrying is silly.

Religious people say, "The Lord works in mysterious ways."

I'm cool with that.

Once upon a time in Chicago, a large vessel tied to the dock across from me, and offered to trade anchors. The only problem was that my just-salvaged anchor was worth ten times the tiny one he offered in trade, so I turned him down. The following morning the guy was gone, his boat was gone, and so was my anchor. No, he didn't leave the small one behind as a consolation prize.

I was so mad I could spit. This wasn't the Atlantic seaboard, for gosh sakes. This was the Chicago River. It was fall. I'd find the bastard and give him a taste of that anchor, alright. I searched and searched for three days. I got angrier by the second. But I never found the guy or his boat. For years.

About three years later, Carolyn and I were sailing along the coast of Florida. Actually, we were in Tampa Bay. Anyway, we had no engine at that time, and, even worse, were rather depressed. I needed a job immediately. We were out of water, food, and cigarettes—as broke as we'd ever been (and have ever been since).

But, despite my depression and my poverty, my eyes were still 20/20. And I've never forgotten a boat in my life. Suddenly I was screaming at Carolyn, "Take the helm, honey! Circle around. I've finally found that fucking bastard!"

I grabbed a bronze belaying pin from the starboard pinrail, dove over the side, and swam to the small marina where the offending boat bobbed with my anchor so prominently displayed. I was seeing red. I didn't knock on the boat, I pounded on it. My eyes were glowing. I was ready. I'd waited for this moment a long, long time.

It was the wrong guy but he had the right idea. "Oh, shit!" he said, and then sputtered. "Take it! Whatever it is, if it is yours—just take it!"

We got to talking. He'd purchased the boat innocently, not knowing half the stuff on it had been stolen during the previous owner's Mississippi trip. People kept coming up, yelping, and calling the police. His life was just miserable and there was nothing he could do about it.

I comforted him. He comforted me. He invited us to dinner. We became friends. He gave us some food, and some Bugler tobacco, too. Through him, we got jobs. We rafted alongside his boat. He became our local benefactor. I helped him on his boat. He lent us his car.

It all worked out. I even allowed him to keep the anchor—which had given far greater value than I'd ever thought possible.

Yeah, it will always all work out.

Sure, when we die our in-box will be full. So what?

It'll all work out in the end. And if it hasn't worked out yet, that's because it is not the end.

Always Have a "Go Home!" Bottle Ready

If you party as much as we do, especially with such a motley collection offriends and foe, there comes a time when you just want everyone to go home. We have a special bottle of Panamanian Port that is perfect for this purpose. It tastes like alcohol, is alcohol, and might not kill you. But it tastes like it will. One sip, and your armpits begin reeking. You fart. One eye rolls back in your head, while the other spins counter-clockwise. Drool runs *up* your nose! Lips twitch. Teeth chatter. Your ears pop as your bowels loosen.

This bottle is priceless.

Within minutes of being deployed, all the late-night drunks are in their dinghies and speeding off to the nearest AA meeting.

This bottle is worth its weight in gold. We purchased it in 1999 and it is still more than half full!

The Evils Of Flying Home

It would seem in this jet-age, that flying home often to "shake the money" tree might be a good idea.

It might. For some. If truly necessary. But migrating semi-annually like a jet-fuel-drunk bird has big disadvantages.

I once met a high-powered business exec who was doing a "speed circ" around the world. He had an experienced shore team who arrived at his destination a week in advance, made provision for him to immediately fly out, and took down a list of all the stuff that needed to be fixed/changed on the boat.

I only met him for a nano-second as he marched down the dock, surveyed his provisioned, refueled craft, and cast off the docklines.

You know what he said to me? He said, "Gee, Fatty, I thought cruising would be more relaxing."

Now, there's a dumb-cluck who just doesn't get it. Picture Josh Slocum returning to New Bedford after all those years, adventures, and sea miles. Now picture the "ho-hum" feeling Josh would have had if he'd flown back to the States every three months or so.

Cruising is an experience that requires time and choice and a million other indefinable things. It is not a carnival ride to be hopped-on or hopped-off of at whim.

"Wait, wait," you protest. "I'm talking about returning home strictly to earn enough money to continue on with my voyage. That's okay, right?"

Sure, if that's how you have to work it out. But I've seen this "six months on the boat, six months on the job" fizzle in dozens of cases.

It costs a lot to fly back and forth. Most people end up retaining their house and automobile. When you're away from the boat, you're paying for two residences. Suddenly you have a large number of non-boat-related bills.

Often, the boat isn't left in the best spot and something horrible happens to it. If this requires the owner to fly back to deal with something, then this negates the whole effort.

Occasionally, something goes wrong at the work end and the worker ends up staying Stateside for an additional year instead of six months. But this screws up the seasonal weather shift at the boat, so the worker stays 18 months instead of six.

By this point, the boat has been left alone for a long time. It is out of sight and out of mind and, often, out of luck. It might be damaged. The engine might freeze up. Or the bilge pumps stop. Or whatever! Thus, somebody takes the worker aside (the brother of the guy who was telling him not to shove off in the first place) and gives him a stern talking-to. The worker reluctantly agrees. He must get "back to reality." He puts the (non-functioning) boat up for sale in a foreign land, and gets pennies on his dollar.

My advice: stick with the boat and stick with the voyage. You don't answer your mobile phone when you're making love, do you?

Of course, there are family considerations as well. My mother is 91 years old, blind, and still partying her guts out on the streets of Santa Cruz. This won't go on forever. So once every five years or so, we blast back to the States and visit with "the mothers" as I call them.

Because I don't visit every year, I enjoy it that much more.

But this "when and how often to visit home" is a complicated subject. Even I am conflicted at times. For example, I just happened to be passing by the Danish skipper of *Sly Cat* when he got the word over the telephone that his mother had died. He was the oldest son. His younger brother was shattered and asked what he should do.

"What should you *do*? You should *bury* her!"

"But aren't you coming back?" inquired the younger brother.

"No," said the older brother, like the hardened seaman he was. "I've got a fair breeze."

"That's it?" said the younger.

"Oh, sure, okay," said the frazzled sailor who hated the many vexations of shore, "*Send me her coordinates!*"

Shit Happens

It's true. It does. Especially at sea. That's part of the charm of sailing, how it is always the same *and* always different.

But occasionally truly weird, unbelievable things take place.

I once noticed a skipper tacking back and forth in front of a windy harbor in French Polynesia. It looked as if he wanted to come in but... what?

I roared out in my dinghy. His engine wouldn't start. He'd just sailed from America and had been at sea over a month. He was extremely tired. Would I help him sail his vessel through the reef so he could drop his hook?

I agreed and hopped aboard. He told me he didn't know anything about engines and his diesel had failed to start about a week ago. Did I want to take a glance at it to see if maybe I could get it running so we wouldn't have to sail in?

I didn't, really. Sailing in seemed straight-forward enough, and I hadn't come out to act as a grease monkey at 45 degrees of tilt.

But to pacify him, I opened the compartment to the engine room, looked in, bulged my eyes a bit, smiled, slammed the door, and said, "No, I can't easily fix it."

Since I hadn't touched it or checked it or cranked it or anything, he hiked an eyebrow. How could I know I couldn't fix it?

"Because it isn't *there*," I said. "Your engine is gone clean off the beds. It has fallen into your bilge, held only by its twisted prop shaft. In my humble opinion, we should not attempt to start it in such a precarious position. Agreed?"

Melt Down Your Guns

I do not recommend you carry a gun aboard your boat because I believe it makes it much more likely you will be victimized *for* your gun. I believe the average boat gun exposes the owner to far more violence than it eliminates, that the gun is often, in-and-of-itself, the cause of violence and *very seldom* the solution to it.

If you are a gun owner who lives aboard your boat and wants to protect your wife from violence, deep six that gun right now.

Guns are expensive. Instead of buying a gun, buy another anchor. Or a large peace symbol to hit 'em over the head with.

The only thing worse than having a gun aboard—like many honest US sailors do—is to hide it and not declare it (as only a few risk-taking idiots do).

This makes you a criminal, often in a country that is much more likely to throw you in jail than your attacker.

One of the primary reasons not to carry a gun aboard is because where you really need it—they take it away from you. So you don't have it. And sometimes the officials sell this info to the drug dealers that they are in cahoots with. Then some really bad guys will know you own a gun and will have it aboard when you leave the country.

A legal gun makes you a target. An undeclared (illegal) gun makes you a criminal.

There is one thing even more dangerous than an undeclared gun aboard—buying one on the street.

I have a friend who, just before shoving off for the "Somali Shuffle" through the Gulf of Aden, purchased a gun from "a guy-who-knew-a-guy." It was in his possession about five minutes before a passing swat team "just happened to stumble upon it" by inspecting his (and only his) bus luggage. Oops.

His trip was delayed for many years as he languished in a Thai jail.

See how dangerous guns are?

However, just because you don't carry a gun doesn't mean that you can't be armed.

My friend Bob Griffith always smiled when he ticked off the "no guns aboard" box, knowing how much dynamite he was carrying. "Oh, those Red Sea pirates shear right off the moment they see those huge white geysers of water exploding in my wake," he told me with a smile.

I went through the Red Sea last year with a boat that had a milk crate of easily-grabbed grenades sitting in the cockpit.

Crossbows are popular and completely under the radar. They have many advantages—spearfishing and delivering fire (to ignite approaching pirate vessels) are two of them.

Pepper spray and tear gas aren't dependable, as the wind can play too capricious a part. But I know of boats carrying Tasers aboard, for use ashore and afloat.

Molotov cocktails are easily improvised from shipboard stores and can be deployed quickly, if prepared in advance.

I've mused about flame-throwers and imaginative shipboard uses for cutting torches.

Flare guns certainly look and sound effective at short range. Plus, they don't go out in wind nor water. Only when they've finished burning do they cease to be able to ignite those tossed Molotov cocktails.

I carry two 600-foot spools of floating polypro line to tow astern of me in pirate waters. Any vessel coming up astern gets caught as I wiggle my course upon his approach. This line can be a bitch to remove in the water, as it melts into the cutlass bearing, etc. I carry two, so if one works, I have another. If nothing else, this slows them down and allows me time to arrange other surprises for them.

If it is night, any camera strobe will momentarily blind them—but not you if you're ready. (While stunned, ram 'em as *Gandolf* did a few years back off Yemen.)

I carry (shhhh!) an extremely dangerous portable laser which can zap a hole in an attackers retina faster than they can blink. (This is especially effective if the eye is wide open on a dark night. The lens of the eye focuses the laser so much it audibly "pops" a hole in the retina.)

Acid can be nasty stuff, right? Yet it is easy and non-explosive to stow when not in use.

Fire, of course, is an age-old weapon. Just make sure the accelerant doesn't get on you, only your victim in the pirate boat next to you.

Spear guns. Slingshots. Fish gaffs. Darts. Death stars. Etc.

I know one fine yacht that has a specially-made, completely legal ceremonial bronze deck cannon—which has a removable pin if you care to fire real shotgun shells.

Sound cannons aren't cheap enough or small enough yet, but they show great promise for passive defense.

I repeat: Don't get killed by, and/or for, your own gun.

Smiling Through Customs

The amazing thing isn't that a dozen government officials have demanded bribes from me, but that 10,000 haven't.

Your average Third World official is at least as honest as your average Chicago cop. Most are as honest as the day is long, despite being, literally, hungry for food, water, and medicine.

If there is one thing I've learned in a lifetime of travel, it is that people are generally good the whole world over.

But, alas, I'd be lying if I didn't also admit there are a few bad apples in the Chicago Police Department and in the Third World.

Here are some tips.

Never, ever offer to pay a bribe. Always dress nice, as short pants (shorts) in many countries are considered insulting. Never lose your temper or "face." Never threaten—they can make it far worse for you in the short term (think, like, painful death) than you can make it for them in the long term. (If they kill you, they might be reprimanded. Maybe. Maybe not.)

Don't worry, if they're after money they'll bring it up early in the game. If, however, they are dragging you down into a dungeon to throw away the key and you'd like to talk a bit more before the key is tossed—ask if "an addition fee" can be paid or an "on-the-spot" fine, perhaps?

Never "stand on your rights" as you have none at times like these. (Any American can "throw their weight around" in the good ole US of A, as guaranteed by our glorious Constitution, which, alas, doesn't apply overseas.)

Each country will demand that you give them your "original ship's document." The way you comply with this is to never show them your original document and just give them a very good color copy without comment.

This works 98 percent of the time.

I've had them "lock up" my document in hopes for a bribe—that they never got. (I assume my US yacht documentation copy still resides in the locked drawer of that corrupt official in the Galapagos, patiently waiting for me to return from my vessel with the bribe money.)

If asked for a bribe, follow Nancy Reagan's advice and "just say no."

Don't argue or question, just smile and say, "No, I can't pay that. I don't have any money."

Carolyn came up with this trick. I thought it was totally stupid, but it works. More than half the time, they just shrug dejectedly and clear you in.

Strange, eh?

Sometimes, despite not wanting to pay a bribe, you have to. I stupidly got into a "nose-to-nose" in Venezuela during which, thank God, Carolyn managed to yell down the hall to me, "It's the equivalent of 47 cents, Fatty!"

Another favorite excuse of Carolyn's is saying, "I'm sorry, but my owner doesn't allow me to pay for anything I don't get a receipt for."

Carolyn does 99 percent of our clearing in and out for the simple reason she has never dragged an official across his desk by his tie. (I hang my head in shame. I totally have learned, the hard way, this is always the wrong thing to do. It *never* speeds things up!)

Strangely, in many Muslim countries, the preferred bribes are booze, cigarettes, and "gentlemen's magazines" such as Playboy.

Yes, our wakes matter. Please do not ever initiate a bribe. It is bad karma, to put it mildly.

Don't ever be like the jerk on *Miss DeMeaner*. He was a free-spending super-merger lawyer from NYC who pulled into the Galapagos aboard his mega yacht with ten guests to spend ten days, which at that time, wasn't possible, legally.

So he grandly offered to pay a suitable bribe.

The guy behind the desk, probably making $3,000 a year, said, "$10,000." He probably said it as a joke.

The lawyer blinked, sighed, shrugged, and paid it!!!

This screwed up clearing into the Galapagos for the rest of us for about a decade and half. Each of the 20 Customs guys were frantically rowing around the harbor, shouting, "Ten thousand to stay, and not a penny less."

Don't be that guy—not that you or I are in any danger of being such excessive spenders.

Moaning About Moorings

The latest scam in the Caribbean (especially, alas, my beloved Bequia) is to find a cinderblock, attach a frayed rope to it, toss it in the harbor, guide/force incoming vessels to use it—and charge them $30 per night.

I advise you to never allow yourself to be forced into such a situation—not only to save you money and to discourage such callous "entrepreneurs," but also to prevent your boat from being lost or damaged.

In Croatia, hard-muscled thugs just row out at dusk (sometimes wearing "harbormaster" t-shirts or carrying damp pieces of typed paper) and demand payment. Just yesterday, August 24th, 2011, a 50-foot boat was asked for $170 dollars for the evening!

If you capitulate to such blatant extortions, you have not only made yourself a mark (who knows what scam they'll have thought up by morning), but also done a grave disservice to the cruising community.

Sharing, Caring, and Making Forever Friends

We all live on a tiny fragile blue ball spinning in space. Earth is our life raft. We have to share our precious natural resources—or we will perish as a species. Nobody owns anything anyway, not really. We're just using it for a blink-of-an-eye while stupidly pretending that we're important. We're not. But we are all brothers and sisters. So sharing isn't an option—it's our future.

The best possible thing you as a sailor can share with both locals and cruisers alike is your time and food. If you want to have fun afloat, just row over to the boat next to yours, and invite 'em over for sundowners. If they turn out to be wonderful folks, (chances are they will be; you're wonderful, aren't you?) then invite them to stay for dinner.

You don't have to make a big deal with the food—just rice and beans and water is fine.

There is something about "breaking bread" together that is magic.

Example: Last week I observed a very funky 32-foot French vessel loaded with grubby-looking kids stern-to the town quay of Milos, Greece. The boat was there for about a week. It looked like the crew was dead broke. French kids don't have a good reputation in the cruising community, especially penniless ones. (Things sometimes go missing.)

I happened to be anchored all alone far away from the town—and thus was suddenly "on-guard" when that French vessel anchored right next to *Wild Card* while I was ashore. I immediately returned to my boat.

They didn't say anything, just stared.

There were four of them.

They were filthy.

I was nervous.

I considered moving.

Instead, I rowed over in my dinghy and said, "Can you guys come for dinner tonight?"

"But we are four," said the one with the best English.

"That's not a problem," I said. "It will be a bit cramped—but, hey, you're used to that, aren't you?"

"Can we bring anything?" asked another.

"Only your smiles," I said.

Carolyn didn't bat an eye when I told her we were having company. She only said, "Well, if they're French we can't feed them garbage, no matter how young they are."

That evening was one of the most pleasant we've ever had aboard *Wild Card*. Yes, they were dead-broke because they'd just recently purchased their lovely boat. "We anchor next to you and your boat because we hear you fabricated and install your staysail stay you-self. We want to ask you about it when you first come back aboard, but were debating whether our English was good enough to bother you. It is difficult, no, when you English no so good, eh?"

They ranged in age from 19 to 22 years old and were four of the nicest lads I've ever met. They were absolutely enthralled with the cruising lifestyle, and peppered us with a million questions. They couldn't believe I was friends with the famous Jean LeCam, had met Eric Taberly, and had just made a pilgrimage to Bernard Moitessier's grave in Brittany, France.

When they heard I was going aloft in the morning to replace our malfunctioning masthead VHF antenna, they insisted on returning to crank me up—"saving the cook's muscles" as they put it. In addition, they had some duplicate charts of the central Med, and...

We became almost instant friends. We're looking forward to hosting them when they pass through the Caribbean.

The food that we served them probably cost us five bucks—and we now have four new friends whom we'd love to see continue on to be circumnavigators. And they brought a good bottle of French wine over the following night—what a bargain, eh?

I've heard it said a hundred times in a dozen different ways. "I was first attracted by the sport of sailing and the traveling—but it is the people, the sailors themselves, who keep me hanging in after all these years. Every one of 'em has a story—and can spin a yarn as well."

It's true. Perhaps the most amazing thing about being a sea gypsy is the company you are allowed to keep on a daily basis. There are none finer on this planet. The true bounty of the sea is her people—crazy, fiercely independent, ruggedly individualistic, giving, careful, cautious, and fun.

I'm honored to be able to sing their praises.

Wrap Up

Buying, outfitting, and sailing a small boat around the world isn't rocket science. It's relatively easy if you just begin with baby steps.

The secret to success isn't a secret at all. It is hard work continuously applied. The life of a sea gypsy isn't an easy one—and I never said it would be. But the pay-off in freedom and fun is immense. And some of us just can't live among the bean-counters ashore. We dry up and die. We need a sea breeze in our hair and a rolling deck under our feet. And that deck doesn't have to cost a fortune—not if you follow the advice and spirit of this book.

One last point: I hope nothing that I've said in these pages makes you think you can go to sea unprepared. You can't—not if you want to live through it. The word "safely" is in the very title of this book, and, I hope, runs through the core of the manuscript. The sea is a harsh mistress. She simply smites those sailors who are foolhardy. But, that said, there is no price tag on Mother Ocean. Money means nothing to her. She'll overwhelm the rich and the poor alike—if they're unprepared.

Thus I recommend that, if you're a person of modest means, you carefully spend your pennies on "strength and safety issues" so that your shabby little vessel has a higher chance of survival offshore than that newfangled, expensive, computerized, rotating saildrive beast (with those amazingly shoddy U-bolts instead of chainplates for the backstays) which so desperately clings to its dock in South Florida.

Good luck.

Safe sailing.

The End

Cap'n Fatty Goodlander grew up aboard the 52-foot John G. Alden schooner *Elizabeth*, built in 1924. He salvaged, repaired, and skippered his first boat—a holed 16-foot rowing skiff he discovered awash in St. Petersburg, Florida—at eight years of age. At 15, he purchased the derelict 1932 Atkin-designed double-ender *Corina* in Chicago—aboard which he eloped with his wife Carolyn in 1970. At 19 years of age, he began building *Carlotta*, their 36-foot, 20,000 pound Endurance ketch in Boston. In 1989, at age 37, he salvaged his Hughes 38 *Wild Card* after Hurricane Hugo—a heavily-damaged vessel, which he and Carolyn then sailed twice around the world while raising their daughter Roma Orion.

Cap'n Fatty has written ten marine-related books (see www.fattygoodlander.com) and is now on his 51st year of living aboard. He is currently the editor-at-large of *"Cruising World"* magazine. He and Carolyn are, as this publication goes to press, leisurely cruising the Mediterranean Sea while continuing to trade words-for-money.

Acknowledgements

I'd like to thank my wife Carolyn, Gene Nelson, Gale Blacksnake Whitbeck, Richard West, David Jansen, Richard West, Dr. Selim Yalcin, Dr. Nadire Berker, and especially Sally Erdle. I am forever in their debt.

If You Liked This Book...

Most writers write for the approval of their editors. I do not. I write for the benefit of my reader. It is you, the reader, who ultimately signs my paycheck. I must never lose sight of that. It is your needs I must serve as an inkslinger if I'm to have continued success.

Most of my books are intended merely to entertain. This one is intended to also inform.

How did I do?

Your input is important. I can be reached via email at fatty@fattygoodlander.com. I personally reply to each message I receive but this often takes many months—because I'm on passage and/or snowed under with correspondence.

Our webpage is www.fattygoodlander.com. I don't update it as often as I'd like, but it is a good place to start if you need a Fat Fix or want to learn more about *Wild Card* and crew.

If you really want to help Carolyn and me continue our literary adventures on the printed page (and our sailing adventures upon Mother Ocean), you can write a review of this book (or, even better, all the books of mine you've read) on Amazon.com. This is very beneficial to us.

The simple truth will resonate best.

I currently write the On Watch column for *"Cruising World"* magazine. I'm extremely grateful for the amazing amount of "scope" this fine publication gives me. They allow me to write almost anything within the limits of good taste. This is highly unusual. I am, as I said, very appreciative. Please let them know when I write something you feel passionate about—regardless of the direction that passion takes. Their website is: www.cruisingworld.com.

You can join us on Facebook at www.facebook.com/capnfatty if you'd like to keep up with the daily madness of our bizarre, chaotic existence.

If you're in need of a chuckle, you can read the very wildest of my irreverent thoughts in All at Sea magazine (Caribbean-based and at www.allatsea.net). Please be forewarned—there is nothing "pc" about my scribbling here. It is Pure Fatty without any consideration to logic, rationality, or common sense.

Word of mouth is the very best, most effective medium for book promotion. Let's face it, we want to know what makes our friends laugh and cry. Cyberspace is, of course, an extension of this. So if you like one of our books, please tell people virally—especially around Christmas. Example: my favorite book is still *"Chasing the Horizon,"* which I published in 1990. It sold surprising well when released, and has sold a little bit better each-and-every year since. It is now selling more per month than it used to sell per year—all because of word-of-mouth!

Of course, the very best thing you can do to help us—from an entrepreneurial publishing perspective—is to buy some of our books, either in print or Kindle versions. It used to be, until recently, that an author received very little for his efforts per book, but that has evolved in our favor. We now get the majority of the money you pay for a book—which is a wonderful, dramatic change. This allows us, and others, to publish narrowly-focused specialty books aimed at miniscule niche markets that sell in the hundreds of copies rather than the millions of copies—and to get our message out.

Our message is simple: Live while you're alive.

We've chosen to do so on a small boat crossing big oceans—naked and giggling within our sun-kissed cockpit.

We hope you're broad-reaching towards Nirvana too.

In any event, we wish you fair winds, calm seas, and remember: Mind the rudder or meet the rock.

Major Skills Sets Required to Buy, Outfit, & Sail

The major skill set required to buy a boat is the ability to dream—to envision a better life. It is a leap of faith.

Sheep are land-bound.

Are you content with being a sheep—or do you think there might be more to life?

But, ultimately, mere dreaming isn't enough. You have to act. You have to say "yes" to the sailing life in all its watery uncertainties. This is scary. This requires courage. Faith. Hope. Bravery.

Most off all it requires self-belief. Are you willing to spend the rest of your life hearing about people who have lived their dreams—or being one?

The major skill sets needed to fix up a boat and outfit it for cruising offshore is tenacity. There are many aspects of fixing up a boat and outfitting it that are grim. You'll be surrounded by people who will not understand. Worse, as you approach your goal, they will want you to fail. Most of all, you'll be accused of being selfish—for wanting to live your life as you see fit. Weird, eh?

There is no way to win these people over. They are happy within their cultural blinders. They are recidivists. Fine.

All you have to do—is to keep on keeping on. That's it. If you don't give up, you will get to sea. Don't know how to figure out cabin top crown? That's fine—oil your tools instead. Move sideways, sure, but never give up. Because a door will open eventually and, if you're still in the game, you will be able to step through into the next phase.

"Don't give up the ship!" is, truly, the key to success.

The most important skill of a successful circumnavigator is the ability to laugh at himself. Mother Ocean is a classroom. We constantly have to learn as we go—to earn our sea miles by the sweat of our brow. The more we learn—the smarter we become—the more we realize how silly we are individually and collectively.

Laughter is, indeed, the only sane response to the world we live in.

Offshore Cruising Vessels and their Gear

I – Unacceptable

All legal safety gear (see USCG regs)
GPS
Manual bilge pump
Pocket compass
Chart of your area
Flashlight
Anchor and 200 feet of rode
Working jib and mainsail
Running lights and anchor light
Outboard
Bucket
Hat and sunblock for shade
Photocopies of Cap'n Fatty articles from *"Cruising World"*

II – Barely Acceptable

Level I equipment plus:
Fixed cockpit compass
2 anchors with rode
Inboard diesel engine
Racor filter system for diesel fuel
Manual fuel filter funnel
Solar panel
12-volt battery, secured in place
Boat hook
Stove for cooking
2 fixed bilge pumps (12-volt electric and manual)
Shade for cockpit
VHF radio
Large bright flashlight
Safety harness
2 fenders
Basic tool kit
Mask, snorkel, and swim fins
Rain poncho
Dinghy with oars
Dry bunk
5 gallon jerry jug for fuel
5 gallon jerry jug for water
At least one Cap'n Fatty book

III – Acceptable

Level I and II equipment plus:
Self-steering gear
Life raft
Depth sounder
Head with holding tank
Laptop computer
Binoculars
Sun shower
Sheet and halyard winches
Bimini top
Galley sink
2 solar panels with regulator
2 GPS (1 handheld)
2 deep-cycle 12-volt batteries
Dry comfortable bunk
Proper galley for good food
More than basic tool kit (more than hammer and screwdriver)
Jacklines on deck to attach safety harness when going forward at sea
Windex or wind direction indicator
Kitchen timer
Swim ladder
Water hose
Long extension cord
Grappling hook
Wind scoop
Three Cap'n Fatty books

IV—Good

Level I, II, and III equipment plus:
Single-sideband radio
Genoa
Whisker pole
Inflatable dinghy with small outboard
Barometer
Masthead tricolor
Laptop computer with digital charts and nav software (Linux freeware)
110-volt inverter to charge laptops, cell phones, etc. (220-volt if not in USA)
AIS receiver
Anchor windlass
Chain for one anchor
EPIRB

Life raft supplies and extra flares
Galley sink with fresh and salt water
Rainwater catchment system
Galley table
Jiffy reefing system both sides of main boom
Roller furling on jib
Cockpit dodger
Spreader light for night foredeck work
Way to lock floors, etc, in place in case of knock-down
Good tool kit with spare stainless steel screws and bolts
2 jerry jugs for diesel fuel
2 jerry jugs for fresh water
Bilge alarm
Good foul weather jacket and pants (PVC not Goretex)
Five Cap'n Fatty books

V -- Well-found

Level I, II, III, and VI equipment plus:
Anemometer
Paratech anchor or Series drogue and slowing drogue
Radar
Self-tailing winches
Storm trysail
Drifter sail or MPS
Stove with oven
Solenoid for propane system
Twin downwind poles
GPS with chartplotter
Cockpit switches and chain counter for anchor windlass
Staysail on roller furling
Watermaker
12-volt refrigerator
Masthead strobe light
Handheld VHF
Emergency VHF, GPS, AIS, and hand squeeze watermaker for life raft
Deck and anchor wash-down system
Bose speakers (inside boat)
Pactor Modem for email (to use with SSB)
Electric autopilot
Sewing machine
Extensive tools, some lumber, spares
220-volt inverter for non-American appliances (also used as back-up for computer, cell phone, etc charging)
Kindle book reader

Blender for smoothies, etc
Cockpit table
Cabin heater
12-volt cabin fans
Wind generator
Great foul weather gear
Sea boots
Six Cap'n Fatty books

VI – Plush

Level I, II, III, VI, and V equipment plus:
Bow thruster
Scuba gear
Kayak
Large inflatable dinghy with big outboard
Hot water heater
Gen-set
Electric winches
AIS transponder
Washing machine
Satphone
Ice Maker
Freezer
Code Zero downwind sail
Illumination for mast and underwater lights
Microwave oven
Electric bread maker
Heavy-duty sewing machine
Sailing dinghy
Wine refrigerator
Butter refrigerator
All of Cap'n Fatty's books autographed by Cap'n Fatty

A Wholly Unacceptable Craft

Do not buy an old, patched, fiberglass-over-plywood 22-foot trailerable centerboard daysailer to cruise the world aboard—especially if it has a bucket for a bailer, some waterproof cardboard for companionway slides, a dented mast with drooping spreaders, rusty rigging wire with expanded swages, a small Honda generator for 110 and 12-volt power for the trolling motor, and lots of food storage below the (only slightly cracked) cockpit floor via the sliding openings.

That boat is not remotely qualified to go offshore because it is probably rotten and lacks the ballast/beam to stay upright in a storm. Plus, she can't be bailed with a bucket unless a hatch is open, which compromises her water-tight integrity. The generator can't run outside in a storm and will kill the crew if used belowdecks. Mast dent? Rusty rigging? Corroded swages? Drooping spreaders? Why is the cockpit cracked? Is there a serious problem with the entire hull/rig structure? In any event, seawater splashed into the cockpit will leak into the hull via the sliding openings, and thus, she will sink if repeatedly pooped by following seas. There's no VHF, GPS, or life raft. She's a disaster waiting to happen.

Does this mean you can't sail offshore in a 22-footer? Of course not. Many have—and quite successfully (if not comfortably).

But the seaworthy 22-footer must be strong, watertight, and non-capsizable in all but ultimate storm conditions. It has to be a "wholesome" cruising design like the Nor'sea 27, a Westerly 22, or a Lyle Hess design such as the Pardey's 24-foot Seraffyn. It has to have at least two ways of removing water from the boat without having a hatch open, and a 12-volt power system (solar cells, batteries, and/or wind generator) to run the nav lights, GPS, VHF, etc. Its rig, hull, and deck must be strong. She has to be completely watertight—even in the event of a roll over or pitch-pole.

But the very first criteria are watertightness and structural integrity. If there's a hole in the boat, she can sink. If she cracks open like an egg, she will sink. If she sinks, you may die.

Thus, the bottom line: Every offshore vessel must be able to keep the water out during any conditions encountered at sea. There's no wiggle-room here. Your boat is both strong and airtight—or she is not.

If she is not, King Neptune will drown you before you can say "Oops!" or "Beam me up, Scotty," or "Mayday! Mayday! Mayday!"

Is the above statement a bit harsh—a tad too dramatic?

No, it is not. The sea doesn't suffer fools gladly nor for long.

If you don't want to abide by this "strong and watertight" rule—don't go to sea.

Where to Get What—Cheap

Panama
Beef (especially filet called "lomo")
Port wine
Dental care (excellent dentists, usually female)
Prescription drugs with no prescription
San Blas
Molas (San Blas Indians' unique fabric appliqué)

Galapagos
Restaurant meals
Mini-cruiseship "Last Minute" deals to islands off-limits to yachts

French Polynesia
Marquesas
Wood and bone carvings
Tattoos
Tuamotus
Black pearls
Pearl shells
Tahiti
Big discount supermarkets
Chinese supermarkets
Subsidized chicken, bread, and processed cheese
Pareos

Cook Islands
Black pearls
Fans made from black pearl shells

Tonga
Carved marlin and swordfish beaks
Wood carvings, especially war clubs
Hand-woven baskets

Fiji
Wood carvings, especially cannibal forks
Kava

New Zealand
Big discount supermarkets
Beer and beer making kits

Australia
Big discount supermarkets
Resale shops for good used clothes, bicycles, household items, etc.
Beer and beer making kits

Samoa
Canned Tuna

Philippines
Local fruit and veg markets everywhere
Big discount supermarket in cities

Hong Kong
Sails
Clothes
Fabric
Cell phones, new and used (most will not work in the Americas)

Malaysia
Big discount supermarkets
Clothes
Stainless steel fabrication (make sure you are getting 316SS)
Yacht-in-Transit Duty Free shipping into Langkawi
Prescription drugs with no prescription
Doctors (Medical Tourism is a booming industry in Georgetown)

Indonesia
Wood carvings
Sterling silver jewelry (be sure it is 925 solid sterling silver)
Sarongs
Printed batik clothes
Hand painted batik wall hangings

Thailand
Jasmine rice
Big discount supermarkets
Clothes, especially printed batik clothes
Fabric, especially in Muslim areas
Sarongs
Teak decks replaced (Phuket)
Stainless steel fabrication (make sure you are getting 316SS)
DVD movies and computer software
Computer technicians
Doctors (Medical Tourism is a booming industry in Bangkok and Phuket)

Plastic surgery (Sex change, anyone?)
  Dentists
  Massage
  Prescription drugs with no prescription

India
  Food (Fantastic fresh fruit and veg markets)
  Yoga classes
  Tailor made clothes
  Prescription drugs with no prescription (but beware of fakes)
  Rhum

Madagascar
  Wood carvings
  Rhum

South Africa
  Sails
  Game Park visits (rent a car to go on your own)
  Big discount supermarkets
  Beer
  Get taxes back on major purchases and last grocery provisioning before
    leaving the country, even by yacht (A check will be mailed to you.)

Yemen
Aden
  Khat (legal mild narcotic leaves)
  Big discount supermarkets
  Gasoline
  Diesel (if you can get it at the local's price)
  Fruit and veg market
  RPGs, AK-47s, and various other Mideast yachting equipment

Eritrea
  Coffee

Israel
  Big discount supermarkets
  Weekly fresh fruit and veg markets

Egypt
  Big discount supermarkets
  Gasoline
  Diesel (if you can get it at the local's price)

Sheesha (water pipes for smoking tobacco)
Cheeses in long-life packages that last months with no refrigeration
Dried fruits
Egyptian beer

Sudan

Swords and knives
Camel saddles

Turkey

Turkish wine and beer
Big discount supermarkets
Weekly fruit and veg markets
Weekly everything markets in most cities and towns
Doctors
Dentists
Turkish baklava
Turkish delight (candy)

EU

Wine
Big discount supermarkets
Many countries (like Italy and Germany) have weekly or daily
    "immigrant"   markets similar to Flea Markets in the US

USA

Canned fruits and vegetables
Electronics (computers, cameras, GPS, depth sounders, radios)
Boat equipment
Clothes
Shoes
Whiskey, scotch, rhum, tequila, beer
Flea Markets
Dollar Stores (Actually, there are types of "Dollar Stores" in most large
    cities all over the world, usually owned by Chinese.)

Additions from our Facebook Friends on "Fans of Cap'n Fatty"

Babes in Patong, Thailand (Chip Pough)
Haul-outs in Tasmania, Australia (Misa-le Fransen)
New head with all fittings $100 in Capetown, SA (Kris Steyn)
Food and services in Ecuador
Cheap haul-out in Green Cove Springs, Florida
Skilled labor in Columbia (Todd Duff)
Diesel and beer in Venezuela (Charlie Balch)
Parts machined Puerto Rico
Lobsters in Maine, US (Jenny Yasi)
Massage in Indonesia (Aleta Hansen)
Leather goods in Sitges, Spain (Bill Greene)
Wine in Soper's Hole, BVI (Denis Oudard)
Chocolate, alcohol, tobacco in Langkawi, Malaysia (Nicolette Leigh)
Solar shower at Walmart (Steve Young)
Travel deals from "Travel Zoo's Top 20" (Ben Gentile)
Boatwright artisans in Salt Creek, St. Pete, FL
Yard fees in Deltaville, VA
Slip rent in Solomons Is., MD (Jeff Hazzard)
Duty-free liquor in Chagaramas, Trinidad (Clark Beam)
Dockage in Curacao (Trip Lea)
Skilled woodworking
Dried seafood, especially squid
Handmade guitars in Philippines (James Almond)
Wine and free anchorages in Greece (Irene Legault)
Cruzan rhum in Virgin Islands (Cain Magras)
Caribbean rhum and mangos in Dominica (Frank Gazarek)
Vietnamese beer in Malaysia and VN (Erja Vasumaki)
Baguettes in Papeete, Tahiti
Spices in Grenada (Vikki Hoffman-O'Connor)
Nasi goreng and mie goreng in Indonesia (Gwen Hamlin)
Rice, tea, pepper in India
Electronics in Taiwan
Canned Tuna in Seychelles
Fresh Salmon in Alaska
Free access to museums in April in Italy
Chandlery items in USA (Jim Gracie)

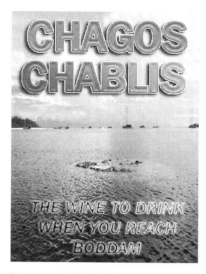

Chagos Chablis Rice Wine

2 ½ pounds sugar (about 4 ½ cups)
2 cups white rice
½ cup raisins
1 tablespoon powdered yeast
1 cup strong black tea (add 1 cup boiling water to 3 tea bags,
    let steep 3 minutes, then let cool)

1. Boil 2 quarts of water and slowly add sugar while stirring constantly until all sugar is dissolved and water is clear
2. Cool until lukewarm, not hot (If the water is too hot, it will kill the yeast.)
3. Pour cooled sugar water into a 2 gallon or larger container that can be stirred
4. Add 4 more quarts of room temperature water
5. Add yeast and stir until dissolved
6. Set aside in a place not too hot or cold (60-85 degrees) and stir twice every day until it stops bubbling (about 8-10 days)
7. After it stops bubbling, take out floating raisins (You can use them to make raisin bread or cake.) Then let rest one day without stirring.
8. Next day, siphon clear liquid into a clean container being careful not to get any of the rice sediment on the bottom. (Don't know what you can do with that. Any suggestions?)
9. Let rest for at least 7 days or until liquid looks clear like white wine. There will be more sediment in the bottom of this container.
10. Siphon from top, the clear rice wine into clean used wine bottles. The more "clear" the wine, the better it will taste. Your last bottle will probably have some sediment, so use it for cooking.

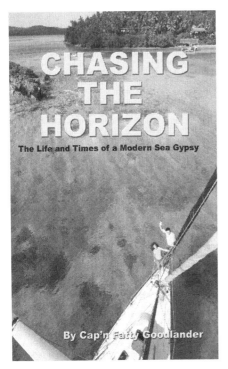

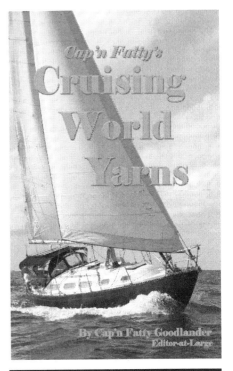

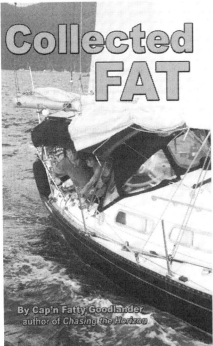

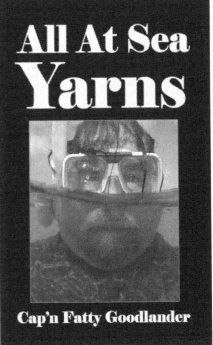

Also Available from
Cap'n Fatty Goodlander

Chasing the Horizon is a delightfully demented Celebration of a Way of Life. It is an outrageously funny, often touching, and continuously shocking tale of a modern sea gypsy.

Cap'n Fatty's story is too bizarre to be fiction. Father wears floral skirts; Mother is a tad vague. Sister Carole isn't interested in her millionaire suitor; she's too busy smooching with the kid in the cesspool truck.

All seem hell-bent on avoiding the cops, the creeps, and especially the Dreaded Dream Crushers. Dive in!

The Collected Fat represents the very best writing from one of the most outrageous writers in the Caribbean. Cap'n Fatty will enthrall you with his rollicking tales of Lush Tropical Vegetables, Wonderful Waterfront Wackos, and Colorful Caribbean Characters.

A number of these stories will make you laugh. A few will touch your heart. One might change you, ever-so-slightly, forever. All will entertain, enlighten, and amuse.

Cruising World Yarns is a collection of the best of Cap'n Fatty from more than a decade at *"Cruising World"* magazine.

Sea adventures don't get any funnier than this!

All At Sea Yarns is fifty of Cap'n Fatty's weirdest, most outrageous sea stories, culled from two decades of comic labor.

The story titles say it all: The Agony of Dried Snot, Insuring Yourself Against Idiocy, Getting Off on Shoving Off, The Appalling Apia Marina, Head Aches, and The Limitlessness of My Stupidity are just a few.

If you like silly and irreverent—this is the collection for you!

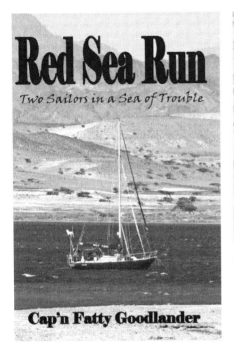

Red Sea Run – Two Sailors in a Sea of Trouble relates the 2010 journey of Cap'n Fatty and Carolyn on their sailing passage from Thailand to the Mediterranean - across the Indian Ocean, past the dangerous waters of the Somali pirates, up the beautiful but challenging Red Sea, and through the frustrating Suez Canal.

Somali Pirates and Cruising Sailors tells the true story of the 2,000 Somali pirates actively engaged in stealing, kidnapping, extorting, enslaving, imprisoning, torturing, terrorizing, and killing innocent sailors— seemingly, with impunity.

These pirates attack small yachts as well as large ships. This book chronicles each of these terrifying "pleasure boat" attacks on the Lynn Rival, Tanit, Rockall, and how and why the four American hostages aboard the Quest were executed in cold blood.

Order through our website: Fattygoodlander.com
All our books are available in print & Kindle editions.

37188172R00129

Made in the USA
San Bernardino, CA
11 August 2016